GW00336702

THE BRITISH

Classic

bike guide

THE BRITISH
Classic
bike guide

Choosing, riding and enjoying the machine of your dreams

Frank Westworth

Haynes Publishing

© Frank Westworth 1998

All rights reserved. No part of this publication may be reproduced or stored in a retrieval system or transmitted, in any form or by any means, electronic, mechanical, photocopying, recording or otherwise, without prior permission in writing from Haynes Publishing.

First published in April 1998
Reprinted 2002 (twice)
Reprinted 2004

British Library Cataloguing in Publication Data:
A catalogue record for this book is available from the British Library

ISBN 1 85960 426 9

Library of Congress catalog card no. 97-77757

Published by Haynes Publishing, Sparkford, Yeovil, Somerset BA22 7JJ, UK

Tel: 01963 442030 Fax: 01963 440001
Int. tel: +44 1963 442030 Fax: +44 1963 440001
E-mail: sales@haynes.co.uk
Web site: www.haynes.co.uk

Haynes North America, Inc.
861 Lawrence Drive, Newbury Park,
California 91320 USA

Typeset and printed by J. H. Haynes & Co. Ltd, Sparkford, Yeovil, Somerset BA22 7JJ, UK

While every effort is taken to ensure the accuracy of the information given in this book, no liability can be accepted by the author or publishers for any loss, damage or injury caused by errors in, or omissions from, the information given.

Contents

Acknowledgements

I would like to thank all those whose patience and encouragement made this book possible. You know who you are! Thanks also to my friends and colleagues on *The Classic Bike Guide* for their opinions and advice. Photographers who have generously allowed me to use their work include Simon Everett, Jim Reynolds, Jack Burnicle, Garry Stuart, Bob Clarke, Claire Leavey and many, many readers of *CBG*. Especial thanks must go to Rowena Hoseason, who read the various drafts so often that she can now recite large portions from memory.

Chapter 1

Why buy a Classic?

What better way to start a book than by asking the question that has to be one of the all-time motorcycling favourites: why should anyone buy a classic motorcycle? Neatly side-stepping the larger question of quite why that same anyone should take up any form of motorcycling, which shares its undoubted pleasures with decent doses of discomfort, risk and expense, why would any otherwise sane and normal adult choose to buy a motorcycle that probably costs as much to buy as a new or nearly new machine, but which is more likely to be worn out than willing. Quite so – why indeed?

If you sit yourself down in the company of a crowd of old bike enthusiasts, put up the price of a round, and ask this question, the answers are likely to be as various as the number of riders in the conversation, and the arguments can become really rather heated. I know this, because I have asked that question of my similarly afflicted riding buddies many times. Many, many times, in fact, have I asked *myself* that same question, most often while sat beside some remote back road, deep in the darkest night, contemplating the resolutely non-

functional electrics of some aged motorcycle; gazing through spectacles smeared with both oil and rain and promising some supposed deity that next time – next time! – I shall most certainly see sense and ride a nice new motorcycle. But we often don't, which is why we all delight in that question: why buy a classic? Quite so – why indeed?

If the question is an easy and an obvious one, the answer is, luckily for the art of conversation, less so.

It is commonly supposed by motorcycling scribblers like myself that otherwise relatively sensible riders lash out the family's fortunes upon some aged clunker because of some odd desire to recapture a lost youth. A variation

on this strange theme suggests that in this lost youth, the classic motorbicyclist was forced by both depth of circumstance and shallowness of pocket to ride around upon a wheezing two-stroke, when in fact he (or she – not all riders, classic or otherwise, are chaps, let us remember) really wanted to belt about the scenery aboard some fire-breathing monstercycle, tappets a-thrash, impressing the heck out of the local talent and generally becoming the envy of the rest of the noisy anti-socialites that we fondly recall ourselves as being.

This may well have a certain truthful element, but as I recall my own, fortunately long-lost, youth, things were a little different.

British classics are a fine way to get out and about.

For a start, there were a lot of cheap bikes about 20 years ago, and spares were fairly plentiful. Every town of more than a half-dozen inhabitants boasted at least three motorcycle dealers and at least a couple of breakers. This excellent supply of old bikes, combined with an equally excellent supply of almost correct spares, meant that it was easy enough and cheap enough to get some sort of two-wheeled conveyance on to the Queen's increasingly oily highway. In fact, I was given my first motorcycle, a 9E Villiers-engined Panther (which no amount of literary licence, strong drink or imagination could persuade me to describe as being a classic) by a schoolfriend whose mother refused to let the thing stay in the family shed for a single day longer. Giving the horrid thing to me was slightly preferable to scrapping it. And make no mistake, scrapping is what would have happened to the odious Cleckheaton clunker otherwise, because no bike-breaker would have given it either money or yard space. Times have changed.

When I learned to ride aboard that unlovely Panther, I knew full well that I could and would be able to give the thing away to some other apprentice unfortunate, who would wear it out a little further while passing his test. In fact, students of the minutiae of history may be relieved to learn that PTK 276 was eventually given to the dustbin man by a friend's mother, after the main frame broke and one of the gearbox castings cracked terminally. Not even the most enthusiastic application of black Hammerite and silver paint

Top: *The classic social world is large, and includes many road-riding events.*

Middle: *Some prefer to get out as a family, and enjoy their racing.*

Bottom: *Club runs can take you to the top of the world.*

respectively could have persuaded the MoT Man that the thing was even approximately legal, so its days were done. Interestingly, I recall that it was still rolling upon its original Dunlop tyres when it made that final undignified journey. Tyres quite plainly are not what they once were.

So, do I hanker after a classic bike to remind me of those glorious sun-drenched days aboard the Panther? No, dear reader, I assure you that I don't.

And as for hankering after something bigger, faster and more flash, well, OK, perhaps a bit, but I knew back then that I could always beg enough bits to construct some sort of 650 twin – and was not the fashion in the late '60s and early '70s for specials? It was indeed, and although a cunning combination of iron-head Triumph 6T engine and an Ariel Red Hunter rolling chassis might not shame the rider of that brand new Kennedy Triton into submission, neither would it embarrass me on those essential and briefly competitive blasts from one watering hole to another.

No, if there is a youth-recapturing exercise involved when considering the purchase of a classic Brit bike, then I would suggest that it is a desire to recapture the lost sense of fun. Although most of us remember some of the more entertaining motorcycles with something more than affection, maybe the rose-tints are best reserved for the memory of the days when the sun always shone (and if it didn't, who cared?), finances were simple, and relationships were true and relatively uncomplicated. Bikes helped a lot of this to happen – at least in my own life and in those of most of my friends of the time. Bikes provided the means of attaining the freedom from control that we all desired, and it is possibly the memory of that early freedom of movement and self-expression that could do with being recaptured by those reeling

from middle age and marital responsibility.

But before we start getting too serious, let me share with you another slightly self-indulgent reason for riding a classic bike. Classic bikes, especially the bigger, more sporty ones, look so good. They sound good too, so very different from many of today's supra-reliable modern motorcycles. They can mark out their rider as being someone who wishes to differ from the rest of the two-wheeled world – in short, they stand out, loud and proud, in any gathering, and they offend no one. More heads turn appreciatively when Mr Belstaff rumbles through the town centre on his 1978 Triumph T140 Bonneville than if he were mounted on anything less impressively modern than a Harley-Davidson or a Honda Gold Wing. Non-motorcyclists do not notice much about that passing FireBlade or Thundercat, but they will all turn to look at the old Beesa chuntering by.

There are, naturally enough, loads more reasons why the purchase of a classic bike may appeal. The machinery itself is generally simple enough for the halfway competent home spannerjack to pull to bits and play with over a winter, while still having a good chance of getting it all back together again come the spring. The engineering is usually robust, too, and well capable of withstanding the inexpertly wielded wrench. There is a tremendously active and rewarding social scene based around the ownership, appreciation – and sometimes even the riding – of classic bikes. The historical side can easily become fascinating, even obsessive, and a little nostalgia for the days when British bikes and British industry at least *appeared* to lead the world is not uncommon among gatherings of old bike-riders. There is a very keen and thriving world of classic bike competition, too, where those old enough to know better pit themselves and their

supposedly venerable machines against each other and either the time clock or the scenery.

Best of all the reasons, in my opinion, is that a decent old bike is just classic to ride. In the affordable automotive experience, the simple joys of trundling through the back lanes or pounding across country on the old A-roads aboard a throaty old warhorse, a beast that its rider knows intimately, take some beating. No matter what the name on the tank, or the number of cylinders, or the exact vintage of the bike, the joy is the same. Old bikes are very involving; their genteel eccentricity makes every trip a slight challenge, and every completed journey a minor achievement. The best part of owning any motor vehicle must surely be in the using of it, and this book aims to guide its reader towards selecting a machine that will enable its rider to share in the pleasure of riding that open road.

Why buy a British classic?

The very word 'classic' has become seriously devalued over the last two decades. Time was that in the four-wheeled world, marques such as Bentley, Jaguar, Aston Martin and Alvis were the names the very mention of which stirred deep emotions in the breasts of enthusiasts everywhere. These days, we are expected to believe that even the Austin Cambridge is some sort of hand-crafted design icon, fit to be revered by all. Things are becoming depressingly similar in the two-wheeled world.

Way back in the years immediately following the Second World War, a fine chap by the name of Titch Allen dreamed up and founded the Vintage Motorcycle Club – the VMCC for short. Mr Allen (or Founder Allen, as he is reverently known within the VMCC) had the unutterably splendid idea that old bikes (and he was thinking of bikes dating from the pioneering days of motorcycling, not just of last year's model) were well worth preserving. And not only that – he also considered that these old warriors deserved to be campaigned on both road and track. What had been an excellent machine in its day was surely still able to exhibit this excellence to a later generation of rider and enthusiast, or so he reasoned. Titch Allen was completely correct, and we should all take our hats off to him.

In the early years of the vintage movement there were strong feelings and heated debate over what exactly constituted a 'vintage' machine, as opposed to just an old one, and guidelines, lists and definitions were eventually accepted. So – defining a vintage bike is not too difficult, then? Well, no, not in theory, at least.

Sadly, the situation regarding a sensible definition of the term 'classic' has never really been thrashed out. Oh, there has been seemingly endless wordy – and occasionally worthy – debate in the pages of the specialist press, all too often when authors of stories have sought to justify the inclusion of some dismally developed and desperately deficient device from the sad world of 1950s ride-to-work two-strokes in a 'classic' feature, but no particularly firm definition of the term has been set into stone. So far as this volume is concerned, the reader is going to be asked to accept that the author is horribly biased in what he considers to be a classic bike. Basically – and fantastically modestly – I shall define a classic as being an old bike that is capable of providing its owner with pleasure and involvement on the roadways of the 1990s. I almost wrote '. . . providing its rider . . .', but to be truthful the simple fact of ownership can be a pleasure in itself.

I do happily accept that this definition cannot be all things to all classic bike buffs, and that some may delight in the possession of such a ghastly contrivance as the two-stroke Panther I have already mentioned; but you may look long and diligently through these pages only to observe that the truly bad gain only passing mention. For the fact is that, as in the four-wheeled world, anything that is both old and two-wheeled is in danger of being touted around as a classic bike. This is sad. Almost all old motorcycles can offer some sort of charm, and it must be admitted that not everyone can afford the bike of their dreams, but do riders really aspire to the ownership of an Excelsior Consort, James Scooter or Raleigh Wisp? Perhaps they do, but I would be at a loss to offer any convincing reasons for buying one, whereas there would be no such trouble should the bike under discussion be a Triumph Tina, for instance (the generally style- and performance-free Tina is at least of some mechanical interest by virtue of its transmission design). Should you wish to disagree with the machines that I suggest make for good classic rides, then feel free – good-tempered argument has filled many a wintry club night.

So, having neatly side-stepped a proper definition of the term 'classic', I am about to suggest that the classic motorcycle you should consider first should be a British classic motorcycle. This isn't just a little gratuitous jingoism; I would suggest that buying British is eminently sensible. For a start, there are more British classic bikes about than there are those from any other country – although this could well be changing – and the range of choice is very wide. There is a large number of specialised classic bike dealers scattered about the UK, and there is a wealth of knowledge about the history, facts and faults, good points and bad, of all of the major British marques. And quite apart from that, this book is entitled the *British Classic Bike Guide*, so it would be odd if we were to devote its pages to learned discussions of the merits of ancient Russian designs, for example.

No, for anyone contemplating the purchase of an older motorcycle, buying British makes a lot of sense. Let's take a brief look at some of the reasons for this. Ignoring the emotional 'I had one of those/always wanted one of those when I was but a youth . . .' nostalgia attacks, the prospective classic purchaser will note that there is a positive wealth of models to choose from. I shall be launching into reams of more model-specific details later on, but for tasters, British builders offered two-stroke singles and twins, along with four-stroke singles, twins, triples and fours in a variety of formats, and of course they even offered a rotary engine or two. Available capacities range from next to nothing (if you can cope with the singular pleasures of a 32cc cyclemotor), through all of the traditional 250, 350, 500, 650 and 750cc, up to the full litre, encompassing sundry odd sizes on the way. And that – surely – offers enough choice for anyone?

There are few problems when it comes to finding spares for the more commonplace of marques and models, either. Indeed, there are those who would suggest that the supply of those essential consumables and those vital shiny bits is rather better now than it was when some of the bikes were still in production. I can recall a rich buddy, back in 1972, who had bought himself the brand new Norton Commando Roadster of his dreams and who suffered the great misfortune of dropping the three-month-old machine on a patch of spilt diesel. He was off the road for so long, waiting for the local Norton agent to supply parts, that he bought himself a Reliant plastic tricycle to keep both his job and his sanity. When I put a re-imported 1975 Norton Commando back on to the road for a magazine feature in 1992, I bought all of the necessary spares off the shelf. The only delay was caused by the shallowness of my wallet, not by the unavailability of essential parts.

When I was a student, back in the early 1970s, I ran a 650cc Matchless G12 of 1961 vintage, and buying spares for it was always a nightmare outside London. Indeed, when it ran its big ends (my fault – I broke a piston ring during a decoke and thought that as it still ran OK it should manage a hundred-mile ride on a single tank of oil. It didn't . . .) I scrapped the bike because I could not get hold of a set of new shells anywhere. I currently have a 1966 AJS 650cc twin (which is nearly identical to that '61 Matchless), and almost everything apart from some of the tinware (mudguards, toolboxes, etc) is available new.

British bikes of the classic era (which for the sake of argument we'll call 1950–1980) are also blessed with a fair range of style. I should mention that I am trying hard to ignore most of the ride-to-work two-stroke smokers here, by the way. Students of motorcycle design and styling will already be aware of the gradual evolution of the Universal British Motorcycle from 350 or 500cc single-cylinder engine, via 500 and 650cc twin, to 750cc twin or triple cylinder layouts; it is also interesting to observe how their styling changed from the sombre shades of the 1950s, when motorcycles were seen primarily as everyday transport and sported voluminous mudguarding to protect the everyday all-weather rider, to the full chrome and bright metallic paint finishes of the 1970s. By that time, motorcycles were recognised as

Top: *Classics are also a great way of getting away from it all on your own.*

Middle: *You rarely need to pamper your old bike, provided that you buy carefully.*

Bottom: *Almost everyone is prone to nostalgia when it comes to choosing an old bike, but bear in mind that some are less suited to modern traffic conditions than others.*

Exercise is good for body and soul, but careful machine choice can save tears.

being primarily a form of leisure pastime, and a fine-weather one at that, the mudguarding reflected this in its high-shine slimline brevity.

Another good reason for choosing to buy a British classic is that there is a vast store of knowledge about the bikes available to any enthusiast, from individuals, from the pages of books and magazines, and from owners' clubs. Whatever, and no matter how obscure your problem may be, it will already have happened to someone else. This may serve to discourage those who really do enjoy solving arcane puzzles without help, but for anyone who actually wishes to ride an old bike on or off the road this fund of knowledge can only be a bonus.

The classic social scene is also biased heavily towards the British machine. Although the car park outside the meeting places of many a British single marque club can often resemble an advertisement for either the BMW or modern Triumph concerns, the riders of these modern machines are there because of their shared enthusiasm for their preferred classic machine.

And finally, the majority of older British bikes are still perfectly useable on the roads of today. True, it would be asking a lot of a 250cc BSA C15 to undertake a lot of long motorway journeys, but any bike of 500cc or over should provide perfectly adequate transport over any A-road expedition. I ran my 1966 AJS 650cc twin for many years in the late 1980s as my preferred two-wheeled transport. In that time we covered many tens of thousands of miles together, and the Ajay shared its shed with a 750cc Honda and a 1000cc BMW; both were sold because I preferred riding the AJS. That's a possibly eccentric, but certainly true story. The AJS – which I refer to in the past tense because I crashed it, not because I sold it in favour of another machine (although a rather different Norton had by that time taken over much of the riding duties, to be fair) – was happy to cruise at the legal A-road limit, steered very well and was simple, reliable and frugal to run and maintain. Buying British certainly makes sense.

Which classic?

Two questions need to be answered, and they can only be answered by the bod doing the buying: what is the old bike for, and how much are you prepared to pay out for it? The second question is a bit of a trick one, because you should always bear in mind that the expenditure does not cease when the new prized possession rolls its wheels across the threshold of your shed. Oh no, quite the contrary . . .

Exactly which of the wide range of available British classic bikes is the one for you is down entirely to your understanding of what you want it for. If money is no object and your main desire is to wow

There is an almost endless debate over exactly which bikes are classics, but really the choice is yours.

your fellow enthusiast and collect prizes at shows, then your choice is likely to be different from that of someone who wants only to have a bike to restore in the shed of his (or her, maybe) retirement. Likewise, if you fancy getting seriously filthy, frozen and far too tired by riding in trials, then you would be unlikely to be looking for the same machine as someone who wishes to don once more the white silk scarf and black leather of his youth and go out to burn up the bypasses of his memory.

Choice of machine is very important. OK, so the Cosmic Motorcycle Supply Company may limit your options by introducing you to that chap down in the Bull & Dog who has owned his Vincent Black Shadow from new, who has preserved it perfectly for the last 40 years and who now wishes only to give it away to a good home, but for the rest of us making the correct choice can mean the difference between years of fun on the road or years of futile effort and expenditure in the shed.

Your first consideration should be to examine realistically the depth of your pocket. At this often sobering moment, you should remind yourself that the expenditure does not cease with the initial purchase of the bike of your

dreams. Every single motorcycle that it has been my undoubted delight to buy second-hand – and I must have owned well over a hundred bikes by now – has required that I spend money on it after purchase.

It is perhaps well worth considering that for you to be buying a bike, someone else has decided to sell it. There are no doubt many perfectly valid 'genuine reasons for sale', to quote the famous line from the small ads, but you should always try to ascertain that the 'genuine reason' has more to do with either a desire to acquire a certain sum of money or another, better bike than with the fact that the beast in question is such a total lemon that the hapless owner is cutting his losses before insanity and bankruptcy set in.

Having decided upon how much loot you have available to spend, and having set aside a sensible sum for those essential jobs that you will somehow fail to discover until after your new bike is paid for and in your possession, you can now set yourself to specify exactly what it is that you require from your new purchase. Only once you have worked out what you want the thing for should you start looking for it. And if that sounds reasonable, indeed like simple common sense, then perhaps it would be an education for you to take yourself off to a classic bike dealer's premises and spend some time observing your fellow would-be buyers, as they browse undecided through the shiny (or not) offerings. A lengthy chat with the proprietor of

Top: *If you're intending to ride your oldster, choose a style of machine that is comfortable for you.*

Middle: *Not everyone is comfortable cruising aboard a 750cc roadburner.*

Bottom: *It is for you to decide whether an oldster or a more modern classic is best suited to your riding needs.*

such an establishment can be an education – in so many ways.

Should you fancy a simple restoration project, and don't really want to ride the finished article too much (there's no need to be shy – lots of folk do this), then a good bike for a first restoration could be one of Triumph's or BSA's finest learner bikes, or maybe one of the better of the Villiers-engined products from Greeves, say, or James or Francis-Barnett. These bikes will be cheap to buy and should be reasonably easy to restore, but don't expect mounting excitement on the highways when the job's done or a profit should you decide to sell it.

If you are healthily put off by the idea of restoring a two-stroke, take a peek at the smaller four-strokes, again from BSA, from Triumph, Royal Enfield, Norton and AMC (AJS and Matchless). If asked, I would suggest that a classic 250cc four-stroke would just about provide performance that should not be too embarrassing in modern traffic. But be warned – most lightweight commuter bikes from the '40s, '50s and early '60s were supplied with brakes that were barely up to the traffic of the time. I once rolled the infamous Panther slowly into the back of a VW Beetle at a red light; the brakes were full on and my speed was low, but the bike was just too heavy and the anchors just too feeble to haul up in time. I also once had the dubious delight of calling out to my pillion that she had better put her boot soles to the

Top: *Don't be put off if you're not a strapping bloke – lots of women ride classics!*

Middle: *A lot of classic riding is about 'remembering a lost age of fun . . .' as this rider of a 1971 BSA Thunderbolt will know.*

Bottom: *There is no need to confine classic riding to the public road!*

tarmac, as we appeared to be speeding up while descending a steep Cheshire hill – this with the brakes fully applied on a '53 AJS 500!

Many will not thank me for pointing out the deficiencies in the older, smaller-capacity bikes, but that's just tough, I'm afraid; this book will always try to be both honest and opinionated. For example, many of the smaller machines from the '50s had lighting to match their braking, so as machines for regular road use they come hard to recommend. They are interesting (some of them are very interesting indeed, and sometimes for the right reasons!) and they are steeped in the charm and history, which is so essential a part of the classic scene, but valid transport for today they ain't.

Moving rapidly on, should you actually wish to acquire a bike for one solo or two slight riders to use in classic events, then anything in the capacity range 350cc and upward should be equal to the job. I would always suggest that a bigger banger makes for easier riding, so my own preferences are for big twins from the mid-'60s onward when most manufacturers had acknowledged the highway advantages offered by decent stoppers and 12-volt lighting. Having said that, many marques listed 500cc twins that were basically that company's 650 twin with smaller bores and pistons. These

Top: *Choice of machine is crucial if you are to enjoy your classic. Older bikes, like this 1926 Scott Squirrel, require a degree of mechanical expertise . . .*

Middle: *Likewise, anyone attempting a daily commuting run aboard this 1951 98cc Sun Delux would need to count optimism and perseverance among their attributes.*

Bottom: *Similarly, although a 1978 Silk 700S is a most fine machine, and well up to today's roads, it can be a touch temperamental.*

Many riders have fond memories of machines like the BSA Bantam (this one's a 1968 D14), and a Bantam can be a very sound first classic.

bikes – and BSA's Royal Star, Norton's Dominator 88, AJS's Model 20 and the Matchless G9 spring easily to mind – are usually cheaper to buy than their bigger brothers and are often less vibratory, easier to start and just as handsome.

If you want a bike that has decent middleweight performance but is dimensionally suited to someone whose physique is of less than international wrestler stature, then BSA's late range of singles, from 250 through to 500cc, are good sensible options. And if you are weak of leg as well as slight of build, the similarly sized Triumph middleweight twins, in 350 or 500cc capacities, take some beating. From about 1968 onward, middleweights from both BSA and Triumph are good practical options, particularly for the vertically challenged.

Spares availability for all of the popular marques is at its best in the most common capacities, so you will have little trouble in finding engine or cycle parts for any of the machines mentioned above. Equally satisfying, and almost equally well serviced by the spare parts industry, are the middleweight and heavyweight singles from the likes of Royal

Enfield, AMC and BSA; once again, wherever possible I would recommend the larger-capacity bikes, simply because they are better performers and are thus easier to ride on modern roads.

On another tack, you may fancy riding more than restoring, and you may also fancy a decent turn of safe speed on the road. All the classic British bikes that survived the marketplace shake-ups of the late '60s found themselves

equipped with decent handling, bright lights, sensible brakes and adequate reliability by the early '70s, and these machines are the ones that provide fast, affordable fun for any modern non-motorway road. Sadly, by the early '70s the choice had shrunk more than a little, and it was to all but vanish completely as that decade drew to a close. Bikes like the T140 Triumph Bonneville 750, BSA's last A65 650 twins and Norton's Commando are the models most likely to offer performance and classic styling in a characterful package, and there are loads of them about. Indeed, following the repatriation of a very large number of machines from the old manufacturers' export markets, and primarily from the US, there are possibly more roadworthy bikes from the '70s about today than there were a decade ago. And once again, the spares supply for these bikes is at least as good as it was when they were in production.

Casting my mind back more than 20 years, I recall that in 1976 I was running a 1975 Triumph 750 Bonneville as my everyday transport. While I liked the bike, and only rarely actually failed to com-

Riding a small-capacity oldster is a challenge. This 250cc BSA C12 completed the National Rally a few years ago – and its rider was still smiling after 20 hours in the saddle!

plete a journey on it, the spares availability for it was truly appalling. An example: on one memorably saturated but rapid night-time ride to Somerset from Clwyd, the Bonnie lost all of its lights bar the front right-hand indicator, which would not turn off. It didn't flash, it just remained steadfastly illuminated. Both front exhaust brackets snapped, one silencer split and both speedo and tacho ceased to function. In a weekend of frantic searching, I managed to replace the light bulbs and the speedo cable. I could pick up the telephone today and replace the lot within the hour. Bear in mind, if you will, that the Triumph was then a current model.

Finally, we should mention the bikes that are hard to categorise – those machines that are capable of providing huge doses of the classic experience, plenty of performance, great style and lots of what I will politely refer to as involvement. These are the bikes that should really only be tackled by someone with a little previous experience of the quirky behaviour that ensured the Japanese take-over – the bikes which when they are good are very very good, but which when they are bad, are horrid. Bikes like the Norton Combat or Norvil Commando. Bikes like Triumph's T160 Trident. Bikes like the Ariel 4, and the Velocette Venom Thruxton. Bikes like the AJS,

Other riders – the majority – prefer to ride faster bikes, like this 650cc BSA Spitfire (but they're more expensive).

Matchless and Norton 750cc hybrids. These bikes, and several others like them, offer rewards at least equal to the effort that needs to go into their ownership. Worryingly, that effort is often very great. But we will talk about these, and loads of others, in a later chapter.

Chapter 2

General Precautions When Buying a Classic Bike

Wear and tear

The first, and arguably the most important, thing to remember when you decide to take the plunge into the classic bike marketplace is that the old bikes to be found in that marketplace are all – by definition – old. Surprisingly, a lot of folk forget this, often to their cost and regret. Even if a bike has been restored to that most elusive of states known confusingly as 'original and concours', the major components will usually all be as old as the original date in the registration document. This is a bit of a sweeping generalisation, as new and improved major components are becoming available for some more popular old bikes – Norton Commando crankcases, for example, spring to mind – but the consideration behind the generalisation remains perfectly valid.

Many and depressing are the letters that land on the doormats of the classic two-wheeler publications from over-optimistic born-again classic bikers who have shelled out substantial quantities of that which folds in return for a shiny replica of a motorcycle. A motorcycle, as every prospective purchaser needs to remind himself every hour and on the hour, is a piece of machinery originally intended to be a means of transport. It was not generally designed to be either an ornament or an objet d'art, to be kept on display for the purely visual delectation of its owner. All right, so in these slightly strange days a restored classic may well be acquired by an affluent enthusiast to provide an interesting talking point while it is parked up on a plinth in the withdrawing room, but when bikes of the classic period were originally sold it was with the idea that they would be ridden, either on the road or off it.

When any machine is used, it is a fair bet that it will wear. Eventually, and with enough use, it will wear right out. Things will become damaged, either by simple wear and tear or by being bounced off the scenery. Things will fall off – many of the later high-performance British big twins had reputations for self-disassembly that were only slightly exaggerated by the Press of the time. The well-worn road-testers' cliché that 'some vibration was apparent . . .' often meant that the bike under discussion would shake both its own innards and those of its rider to jelly when periods of sustained high-speed use were endured. Vibration damages machinery as much, if not more, than it damages a rider.

Finding a machine like this Norton Model 50, in original, unrestored – and running! – condition is rare these days.

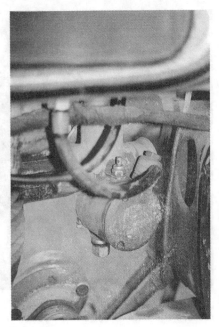

Above, left: *Original machines are particularly interesting, as they show exactly where and how the factories fitted their components.*

Centre: *Beware – carbs that haven't been touched for a couple of decades will inevitably leak . . .*

Right: *. . . all over the similarly elderly electrics. Sparks and petrol should only mix inside the engine.*

Prospective buyers should remember this when they go to look at a bike, especially if it is an expensive bike that had sporting pretensions in its day. Whereas anyone with a little sense and experience should expect a high-mileage middleweight commuterbike from, say, the mid-1950s, which has been languishing neglected in the back of the traditional barn, to be comprehensibly time-expired – from its hard life and many miles, if not from decades of neglect – that same person should also accept that the low-mileage, one-careful-owner road rocket from the late-'60s is likely to be just as tired. It is always worth remembering that a long succession of high-speed, high-acceleration, cold-engine, short-duration sprints,

from caff to caff for example, will wear out an engine rather more rapidly than will a 10-mile daily commute at gentle traffic speeds.

It is also worth remembering that although a lot of standard touring bikes were not over-blessed in the performance and glamour departments, their sport-ing siblings only rarely boasted beefed-up power train compo-nents to accompany the tuning that provided the extra perfor-mance. Thus, for example, the sporting CSR versions of AJS and Matchless 650cc twins featured a higher capacity lubrication system than the less flashy standard

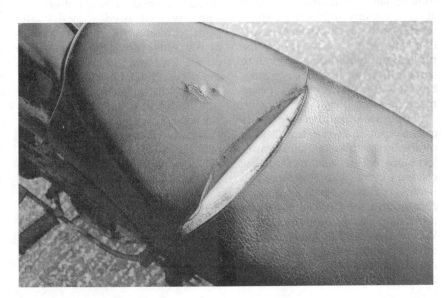

Superficial damage like this is easily repaired at home, and should not detract much from the value of the bike.

Left: *Surface rust is no problem. The hard part is deciding whether to restore the bike . . . or simply touch it up and ride it!*

Above: *This particular machine had been offered at auction, but was sold privately afterwards.*

twins, but apart from that the power train and non-cosmetic cycle parts were almost identical. Indeed, in one particularly baffling year (1963, for the benefit of pedants everywhere) the CSR brakes were of an earlier, lower specification than those of the standard twins, which had been up-rated for that year.

There are many, many things to watch out for when buying a classic – as opposed to just old – motorcycle. I shall attempt to chat about as many of them as space permits, but no list can be exhaustive, and there must be some pitfalls that would be new even to someone who has been riding, buying and selling this type of machine since 1969.

Simple wear and tear is usually easy to spot. In their enthusiasm to re-acquire the bike of their dreams, too many enthusiasts overlook the obvious items, like stretched and useless primary and secondary chains, and the hooked sprockets that usually accompany them. When the hooked sprocket in question is an integral part of the clutch drum, and said clutch drums are unobtainable, this sim-

ple and overlooked wear can be the difference between a purchase that is sensible and one that is not.

Here's a nice example for you of an easy mistake born of simple wear and tear. Many classic riders like Triumph 750 twins, and many riders who might buy a version fitted with an electric starter (starting big twins with a kickstart is something of an acquired taste, after all) may not be too put off by the 'it doesn't work at the moment because it needs a new battery, or something; it used to work all right . . .' conversation at the point of sale, especially if the bike is otherwise OK, and runs well. When the new battery fails to ignite the engine's fires, further investigation may well reveal that the starter's sprag clutch is an ex-sprag clutch and that the starter will not start the engine until a new one is fitted. New ones are currently unobtainable . . .

Use and abuse

Every single moving part on a motorcycle can, and will, wear out. How long it takes to do so depends upon the level of use, or

abuse, and how well the bike has been maintained. Over the many years of a bike's life on and off the road, it will most probably have endured the attentions of many and various owners and riders. I was once offered an AJS heavy-weight single of venerable years that had in its time been a standard roadster 350 (when it was new, fairly obviously), then it had been converted into a sort of ponderous trials replica (when the huge heavy mudguards were binned, along with the sensibly proportioned petrol tank and comfortable seat). It was then transformed into some highway hooligan's heavy metal nightmare (by throwing away the toolbox, handlebars and fork shrouds, engine plate and primary drive covers, then fitting a leaky fibre-glass tank and a seat of such excruciating discomfort that no averagely proportioned male could perch thereon for more than a couple of minutes).

Following this slightly unlikely incarnation, the poor thing was 'chopped', by removing all useful lugs and brackets from the frame, moving the footrests a couple of

Many original machines find their way on to the market via registration number dealers – the Norton was one of these.

feet forward and fitting another bizarre tank and matching ape-hanger handlebars. After this, the plucky beast had been consigned to a dark shed, in all likelihood happily for all concerned. Some years later, it had been unearthed and cosmetically 'restored to original' by the chap who offered it to me. He had learned of its sundry personality changes by contacting the previous owners, many of whom still possessed photos of their strange mechanical manipulations (but none of the original parts). Dear reader, I did not buy this bike, and in any similar situation I recommend that you do likewise.

Generally – and personally – speaking, if you require an old bike to ride, then look first at bikes that show signs of recent use. If a machine has been ridden on the roads a fair bit by the guy selling it, the chances are that he will be pretty familiar with its little quirks and oddities; if he is half-way honest (and the great majority of old bike-riders are), he will share these minor idiosyncrasies with you. There's nothing sale-threatening here, by the way, so if you are selling rather than buying, be straight about it. I would always rather buy a bike from an enthusiastic rider than from some sullen bloke who won't discuss anything about it. There's nothing to be gained by refusing to talk about its last breakdown, for example ('It's never let me down . . .' is just occasionally not entirely the case).

A rarely acknowledged indication that the bike under scrutiny was recently mobile is that it has been crashed. It is extremely difficult to crash a motorcycle if it is incapable of self-propulsion. And a perfectly genuine reason for sale is that the vendor has hit the tarmac and decided to take time out

from motorcycling. We will all hope and trust that the preferably lightly damaged individual will soon feel up to more miles in the saddle, but in the meantime a slightly abraded machine should always be considered. And no, I am not suggesting that the heavily shunted bike with its front wheel charmingly tucked up under the crankcases is necessarily a good buy. A prang of my own a few years ago revealed that planting an AJS twin into the front of a coach can be almost terminal for both parties. It also revealed that when an insurance company writes off a machine, that machine may well be genuinely beyond repair. That 20mph shunt so damaged the 650cc AJS that only the gearbox, engine internals, rear mudguard, chainguard and seat were easily recoverable.

Take a look around the shed, too, for evidence that the seller knows what he's about on the maintenance front. If his entire visible toolkit consists of two lump hammers, a pipe-wrench and a couple of push-bike spanners, then the announcement that he has just completely rebuilt the engine may not offer quite the encouragement needed to fill you with confidence and close the sale. If, on the other hand, the shed features a stout workbench, general cleanliness, a current owners' club

calendar and a stack of high-quality tools, things are looking better already. The obvious caveat for this, naturally, is that the vendor is indeed a wonderfully skilled spannerjack who has wrestled for months with the hateful unreliability and abysmally poor performance of the bike you are looking at, and has decided to sell it rather than become completely insane. Minor signs of personal desperation on the part of the vendor are always useful negotiation topics at this point.

An aside. Way back in the 1960s, when old bikes were just old bikes, a good friend of mine (who went off to design jet engines, alarmingly) was offered an Ariel Huntmaster by its owner. This 1958 650cc twin featured an engine that was closely based upon BSA's 650 of the day, the A10, and indeed an almost complete BSA was included in the deal. The Ariel had been completely rebuilt, and looked delicious in shiny red and gleaming chrome. The many departures from standard trim were, in 1969, viewed as improvements . . . Anyway, the bike's entire power train had been overhauled, and the engine was completely new inside. The carburetter was new, the magneto was new, and the whole thing shone in the Somerset evening sunshine like the jewel in its owner's crown it should have been. But it would not run.

Oil it had, fuel it had, sparks it had. Its owner, a police constable, had given up on the shiny but static Ariel and had bought a self-starting Honda for his daily commute. My friend kicked the Ariel over a few times, eliciting nothing more encouraging than a flatulent cough from the silencer. He knocked the price sharply down to about half the cost of a gearbox rebuild, and we wheeled the Ariel and the spare BSA back to my parents' home. Upon arrival my friend swapped over the two spark plug leads, kicked the starter just the once, and rode off home for his tea. It ran well, too. YTT 293, where are you now?

If you are looking for a bike to restore, your major considerations will be that it is what it claims to be, and that nothing entirely unobtainable is missing. Only you will know what constitutes an acceptable condition to your own eyes, and only you will know which bike you fancy. Only you will know how much the bike is worth to you, and you will accept that there can never be a meaningful price guide to motorcycles of which only a handful were ever constructed. Only you will know whether you have the physical and financial resources to com-plete an ambitious project. And only you know that you are most likely already a skilled restorer, in which case this section of the book is only offering you some entertainment and hopefully a shared wry smile or two. The really serious restoration game, in which a valiant soul sets out upon an enterprise to raise the one and only 123cc Prestatyn Prowler from a handful of rusty castings, broken bolts and out-of-focus photographs into the world-beating sportster that its long-departed maker once intended, is a mystery to many, including me to be truly honest. Almost all of the bikes that I have resurrected have been offered a new lease of life for the sole purpose of being ridden on the road. Or, to be fair, to be sold to finance the next slightly mad and always optimistic project.

If – as I hope – you are choosing a classic motorcycle to ride, it is important that it runs, or at least that it has recently run, and run under its own steam. To this end, a squint at a stack of recent MoT test certificates, noting the changes in the mileage figures, is a helpful indicator of the recent life that the bike has led. Then again, the fact that the mileage shown on the form has not altered in five years does not necessarily mean that the bike has never travelled anywhere – speedometers wear out too, you know.

Checking the bike's identity

Talking of MoT certificates, you should also remember that every production motorcycle frame is stamped with an identifying number. And don't forget that this number is quoted on both the V5 registration document and on the VT20 MoT certificate. If you change the frame, the law tells you that you are changing the identity of the vehicle, and your Local Vehicle Licensing Office (LVLO) may decide that you cannot use the original registration number. You are then faced with two choices: risk losing what could be a valuable or personally important registration mark or break a law by re-stamping your original number. Before you decide upon the latter, it is worth reflecting upon the fact that this particular piece of legislation was intended to make life harder for thieves. It is also worth remembering that every time some well-meaning and otherwise scrupulously honest soul re-stamps a frame or engine number, a little piece of history, and a rather bigger piece of the bike's identity, is lost.

Before you buy any bike – or any other motor vehicle, come to that – you should always check that the numbers stamped on the engine and the frame are the same as those writ in the log book (OK – the V5 registration document, for the modernists among us). If for any reason the numbers on the motorcycle are at variance with those quoted in the sundry docs, talk sternly to the vendor, and think deeply before parting with the money. If originality is important to you (and why not?), check with the relevant owners' club that the engine and frame were origi-

Talk to your local bike shop – it may be that they're quite happy to work on your classic.

nally partners; most clubs offer an inexpensive service whereby this engine/frame relationship can be verified, and it is well worth using it – if only because an original machine will be easier to sell, and indeed will be worth a bit more when you decide to sell it. Which you almost inevitably will.

Some clubs have copies of the original factory records, and can tell you the exact date upon which your Pride & Joy was first released into this cold world, and indeed who the original customer was. Along with a fair proportion of fellow enthusiasts, I love detail like this, and consider that every little extra item of info adds to the pleasures of ownership. Is my anorak showing?

While on the subject of engine and frame identifying numbers, a couple of thoughts spring to mind. First, make sure that you are checking the right number on the frame. Most manufacturers bought frame lugs from outside foundries, and many of those lugs have numbers on them. Many indeed are the log books that quote a foundry casting number rather than an actual frame number. Second, don't get carried away by the idea that all bikes have matching engine and frame numbers, ie that the numbers stamped on engine and frame are identical. They often aren't. Once again, owners' clubs are a vital source of information for the prospective purchaser. Third, by the end of the 1960s the major manufacturers were making some sort of feeble efforts towards making the bike thief's lot a less easy one, and would stamp the engine number on a boss that was already imprinted with the marque logo. Most notably BSA and Triumph did this, and it makes subsequent re-stamping of the number more easily detectable. On later Commandos, Norton would stamp

the number between two large asterisks, which might help a little.

A piece of advice: if you are looking at a bike to ride, you would be a little batty not to carry out the numbers checks listed above before presenting the vendor with a wad of Her Majesty's finest currency notes. You would, at least in my less than humble opinion, be quite utterly deranged to hand over money for a motorcycle that does not have the documentation necessary for getting it licensed for road use. But we all make mistakes.

Getting re-registered

Should you find yourself so blinded by the enthusiasm of purchase fever that you have acquired a bike without papers, you will need to correct the situation as rapidly as possible. The Law will not let you ride a bike on the road without its being inspected, registered and taxed for that purpose, and if you have a bike – or the remains of a bike – that is without any related paperwork, you are going to have a lot of fun and games before you can hack down the highway upon it.

There are several ways in which this lamentable situation can arise, possibly the most common being when a bike has been found in a

barn or shed, where it may have lain, decaying gently, for half a century. This really is not too unusual an occurrence, as a bike languishing in the corner of an old farm building is not much of an impediment to the normal use of the barn, unlike a car, for example, so there is little incentive to remove it if the owner of the barn doesn't realise that old broken motorbikes have a value.

Other routes to the paperless motorcycle include the common scenario of an enthusiast building a bike up from all the bits he's had laying around the place for years. Time was, you could do exactly that and just register the bike by using an old log book for an approximately similar model from approximately the same year. So long as the bike passed its MoT, no one seemed to care whether the BSA 500 referred to in the log book was a DBD34 Gold Star or an M20 side-valve sidecar tug. Do not ask me how I know this. Sadly – or not, depending upon your viewpoint – the law has been tightened considerably over the years.

The late 1980s and early '90s also witnessed a great deal of re-importing of classic British motorcycles from all over the world, as their values in GB rose rapidly to far exceed the prices being asked for them in their orig-

A few years ago, many ancient Brits were repatriated from their original export markets.

inal export markets. Every vehicle that is re-imported is liable for import duty and VAT, and if you are buying such a bike, you absolutely must ensure that it comes with a certificate showing that all the taxes are paid – the 'pink slip'. Without this, not only may you find yourself liable for any outstanding taxes (and Her Majesty's Customs & Excise, who administer Value Added Tax, are not at all sympathetic to excuses and pleas of ignorance), but you will also not be able to register the motorcycle for road use. See what I mean about only buying bikes with all of their documents intact?

But OK, for some no doubt valid reason ('It seemed like a good idea at the time, officer . . .') you find yourself with a bike that is complete and that you wish to put on to the road, but which has no paperwork at all. What do you do? The first thing you do is join the relevant owners' club and approach their Machine Dating Officer or similar official, begging this worthy to supply you with a letter or certificate stating when the machine with your bike's engine and frame numbers was first manufactured. It is essential that you do this, as you will not get an 'age-related' registration number without such a letter.

A word of explanation, perhaps. Old bikes can be eligible for perhaps three categories of

Top: *The re-imports included many models that were rare on the UK market, and although they were often tatty, they were also often original and complete.*

Middle: *This 1967 Norton N15CS was re-imported privately by the author, and was almost complete, almost original, and ran again with little effort.*

Bottom: *Not all of the re-imports were from dry climates, requiring only a little work to put back on to the road. This 1979 Triumph Tiger 750 was one of a batch that returned from Nigeria.*

If you are buying a bike that has only been registered overseas, make sure that you receive a proof of ownership.

registration number. The first is the bike's original number, which can have been separated from the machine for a number of reasons, such as its owner's failure to register it with the Swansea DVLA computer, or a previous owner selling off the number to one of the cherished number merchants. To retain an original number without it already appearing on the bike's V5, you will need some considerable proof that the particular number goes with the machine in question. The sort of things that the LVLO will want will be the original green or buff-coloured log book, maybe a pile of old MoT certificates or tax discs, and possibly some photos of the bike in olden days proudly displaying its number. Only your own LVLO will be able to tell you whether the docs you offer in support of your claim are sufficient for them to re-allocate the number.

Second, your bike will be eligible for a 'Q' plate. This is a modern number that has the letter 'Q' as its prefix instead of the current annual registration letter. These are generally considered to be undesirable on an old vehicle, so you can apply for an age-related number, which will be a registration mark from an appropriate year that was never issued. These are less undesirable than Q-plates on old bikes, but are usually easily recognised, so they are less desirable to some than the machine's original number. If your documetation and the bike's engine and frame numbers are acceptable to your LVLO, they will offer you a Q-plate. If you ask, and if you have proof – in the form of a dating letter from an owners' club, for example – that your bike really is a treasured relic from golden days gone by, rather than a pile of worn-out bits you've bolted together to turn a quick quid, they should

supply you with an age-related number. It's quite simple really.

The next thing to do is to book the bike in with your nearest MoT station for the roadworthiness inspection, which will confirm that your Pride & Joy is as well-built as you thought, and will also provide you with the Vehicle Test Certificate, or form VT20. You can ride your bike to the test, provided that you are insured to do so and that the test is booked.

When your bike has been admired by the helpful souls in the test station and has been duly awarded its test certificate, you will notice that the examiner has entered the frame number in the little box on the form where the registration number usually goes. If you cannot show him a frame number, or if he is concerned about the likelihood of its being tampered

with, he is unlikely to do this, and you are in something of a mess.

You now need another form, this one imaginatively called the V55/5, which applies for a registration number and road tax disc for your bike. You will need to send, or take, the completed form, along with the supporting paperwork it requires (MoT certificate, insurance, cheque for the road tax, some convincing and hopefully accurate and true reasons why the bike needs a new number when it is plainly already very old, and a dating letter confirming the date of manufacture of the machine) to your LVLO. You will find their address in your local *Yellow Pages*.

The folk at the LVLO will arrange to inspect your bike, and, assuming that they are happy with both the vehicle and its supporting documentation, they will issue

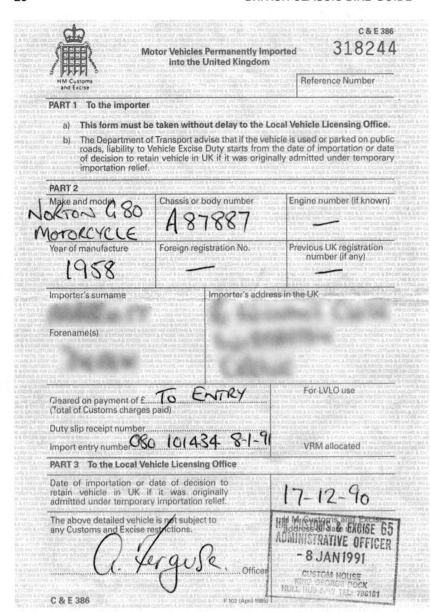

When a machine is brought back into this country, VAT is usually liable. Obtain a certificate showing that it has been paid – or you will be liable.

you with both a tax disc (oh, all right, a Road Fund Licence) and a registration number. If they are unhappy, they will tell you why, and you will have to produce whatever they require. If you get frustrated, just be thankful that you are registering a motorcycle. I once imported a Trabant, a small East German two-stroke cardboard car, and was unable to register it without a certificate of Type Approval, which of course it had not got. No Trabant has ever won a Type Approval certificate. That was a truly depressing experience, and illustrates exactly how good an idea it is to carry out your research before you buy the bike.

Anyway, when you come to consider a bike seriously for potential purchase, the areas for physical examination can be broken down into two main ones: the cycle parts and the power train. So in the next two chapters let us look at each of these in a little more detail, remembering all the time that the bike is not brand new and that many faults are likely to be present to a greater or lesser degree. Your task is to determine whether the bike is in a condition to suit yourself and your pocket, and I shall try to help a little.

Chapter 3

Checking the Cycle Parts

Back to the plot. After checking the obvious items mentioned in the previous chapter (which should always be checked when buying any motorcycle, whatever its age), move on to the other wearing bits that enthusiastic buyers too often overlook. The brakes are an obvious example.

Brakes

It is not enough that the brakes simply work. They should work well enough to stop the bike should a small child run out in front of it. That is the test I recommend – do not simply lock on the front anchor while the machine is stationary, bounce the forks up and down and pronounce that all is well in the stoppage dept. Ride the thing and try out the brakes on the road. If you want a static exhibit, it is acceptable to buy a bike with sad stoppers – in any other case it is neither acceptable nor sensible. And no amount of bleating that your dismal stoppers were great when new is going to help should that child run out.

If the bike in question has a pair of drum brakes, check that both operating arms are angled away from the cable or rod that operates

them, not towards it. This simple observation is a fairly reliable indicator of how worn and/or well adjusted the shoes are. Unusually weak or juddery braking on a bike with drum brakes can have many causes, from contamination of the brake linings with oil (often from the fork seals, running down the slider on to the brake plate, then into the drum itself when the bike is parked on its side stand), by grease (melted from the wheel bearings by the heat generated by a binding brake), to deep scoring of the surface of the drum caused by the invasion of gritty things over many years and many thousands of miles.

If the brakes are in any way

hydraulic in their operation, always open the reservoirs and take a peep at the level of the fluid – you do not want to pump air instead of brake fluid when that child runs out in front of you. Always check that hoses are not split, and that the pads are endowed with some meat; this is especially important in the case of early Norton Commandos, which have been known to spit their pads out of the calliper when the lining has been worn down to the backing plate. Not too uplifting an experience, that one. The discs themselves can suffer from buckling, scoring and from the gradual disappearance of any chrome plating that may have been applied. In

Check the front discs for scoring, and all hydraulics for leaks or damage.

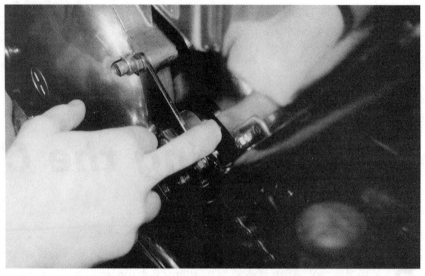

Left: *Check for play in the swinging arm bearings and the rear wheel bearings by trying to move the wheel.*

Above: *Swinging arm movement shows up at its pivot.*

bad cases, slivers of chrome can become embedded in the pad material, so make it a ritual to replace the pads of any new purchase as soon as possible. They're cheap enough, after all, and cautionary replacement is rather preferable to discovering suddenly that your brakes don't work. It is of course a famous truism that you only discover that the brakes don't work when you need to apply them, hard . . .

Look out as always for rounded nuts and bolt heads; these are always indicators that someone doing the spannering is not very good at it, and they are always most worrying when found in the stopping department.

Swinging arm pivot

After the anchors, the wise buyer can turn the glinting eye of his or her attention upon the bicycle's two big hinges: the swinging arm pivot and the steering head. Should your intended purchase feature a rigid frame, this bit is half as hard.

Far too many purchasers, blinded no doubt by the discovery of their dream machine, ignore the condition of the swinging arm

pivot. This is done at your peril. It is a far far better thing that you find out about the worn-out bushes in the rear fork before you buy the bike rather than at a subsequent MoT test. Swinging arm bush replacement is often unpleasant, and usually expensive if a shop does it because of the dismantling involved. If you really do fancy the bike and the bearing is shot, ask the vendor to get it replaced; if he won't, get a quote from a bike shop you know and trust before signing that cheque.

An easy hint: look for signs of lubrication. If the bike is an AJS or Matchless heavyweight or a Norton Commando, for example, the swinging arm pivot is lubed by oil, despite the fitment of either a grease nipple or the provision for one. Lubricating these bushes with grease will wear them out quickly. Triumph and BSA twins are good at wearing out these big hinges too, in my experience.

There can be no excuse for failing to check the swinging arm as well. Simply put the bike on to its centre stand, take hold of the wheel spindle end of the swinging arm and attempt to waggle it sideways. If you can waggle it easily and can feel a marked clonk, it's

worn out. If you can waggle it just a bit and the pivot looks like it has just been pumped full of grease, it's probably still worn out. By the way, this method can be unreliable if the bike is a Norton Commando, as maladjusted rear Isolastic mountings can offer similar symptoms.

Steering head

Moving briskly forward, also check the condition of the steering head. This is done in much the same way, by lifting the front wheel off the ground (it usually takes operation of the centre stand and a third party to achieve this, unless you are spectacularly strong yourself), grasping the wheel spindle at both ends with both hands and attempting to rock the wheel backward and forward. If you can't do this, then all is usually well. If you can, either the wheel bearings, the fork bushes or the steering head bearings (or all of them) are worn out.

Having found wear by this simple, fun-for-all-the-family method, locate its source by observing which parts of the front end assembly move relative to each other. Start at the top: does the top

Grasp the forks and try to move them; play here will require work to fix.

yoke move relative to the frame's steering head? If it does, there's wear in the steering head bearing – this is not always a tragedy, for replacement is usually cheap and often easy, and sometimes the bearings are adjustable, too. If the fork sliders (the bottom metal tube things to which the wheel spindle is fixed) move relative to the stanchion or shroud above them, there's wear present. Fork re-bushing is a tedious job and is also therefore expensive if you choose to operate the wallet rather than dirty the hands. As in the case of the swinging arm bearings, get them fixed or get a quote before purchase.

Wheels and tyres

Right, that covers the frame's pair of big hinges. Another often neglected, but extremely important, wearing area of the bicycle are the wheels themselves. Think about this for a moment. All of the weight of both the motorcycle and its rider(s) is borne by the wheels, and all of the powering and braking forces are transmitted through

them; it is therefore essential for the sake of the rider that both wheels are in good condition and are capable of travelling in approximately the same direction. It is not sufficient that the tyre has plenty of tread and that the chrome on the rim is in good and sparkly order.

If a bike is to steer properly, it is a good idea to have the wheels in decent alignment. Simply put, that means that the back wheel follows exactly in the path of the front one when the bike is travelling in a straight line. Assuming that the frame, swinging arm and front forks are straight, if the back wheel does not follow the front, the wheels have been badly rebuilt. I possess an elderly AJS with a half-width front brake. For the sake of this discussion, this means that half of the spokes are fixed to the outside of the brake drum, the other half to the hub itself – thus the brake is half the width of the hub. When I bought the bike, it showed a great enthusiasm for left-hand bends, and at the same time a reluctance to negotiate right-handers. Much head-scratching, standing back and observing the front end revealed that when the wheel had been rebuilt the rim had been positioned equidistantly between the two spoke flanges on the hub, when it should have been offset towards the brake to position the rim centrally between the fork legs. Re-lacing the rim solved the steering problem.

When spokes rust – as they are prone to do over the years – they weaken. Weak spokes can result in the collapse of the wheel. If spokes are not correctly tensioned, they will wear unevenly and the wheel may run out of true. Damaged or missing spokes will seriously impair the safety of the wheel, and in really bad cases this can also result in the collapse of the wheel. Broken spokes can flail about as the wheel revolves, and the end inside the rim can chafe away on the inner tube, causing a puncture. Collapsing wheels and front tyre punctures can mean a little more

than just a minor inconvenience for the rider – please remember this whatever sort of bike you are contemplating. If spokes are rusty, damaged or just loose, replace them; spokes are cheap enough and a properly rebuilt wheel will provide many years and many thousands of miles of worry-free riding. Stainless steel spokes will last a very long time, too.

The tyres themselves are often overlooked in the enthusiasm of making a new purchase, and it is especially important to peer at the things closely if you have any intention whatsoever of actually entrusting your life to them. In the final analysis, the only point of contact between motorcycle and road surface is the pair of tyre contact patches. Everything else separates rider from the road; the tyres actually roll over it. If it has never occurred to you before, spare a moment to consider just how tiny is the actual footprint of rubber on tarmac that is expected to provide sufficient grip for all of that wild power, those savage brakes and the crazy cornering angles we all know and love so well, in both wet and dry weather. Then, having passed but a moment in silent contemplation, bully yourself into committing to the expenditure of the cost of a pair of the very highest quality replacement tyres. Always buy new tyres, too; surely your wellbeing and that of any pillion you may be fond of is worth the cost of a pair of new tyres?

There are those who prefer to fit a tyre that matches the original appearance of their aged motorcycle rather than a tyre of the latest super-sticky rubberish compound. This is fine if the bike is intended either exclusively for exhibition or for the most gentle of demonstration runs around, say, a pub car park. Do you not owe yourself and that favourite pillion the best possible chance of survival come an emergency? I think you do, and where modern tyre compounds are available in the correct size for your chosen steed I will always recommend that you fit them. Luckily for those who ride classic Brits with 18- or 19-inch wheels, there are several modern compound tyres that look much as they did in the days when their predecessors were fitted as original equipment by BSA, Triumph, Norton, etc. And you can rest assured that your BSA B33, or whatever, will steer far better on a pair of Avon Roadrunners, for instance, than upon the original Avon SM tyres it wore from new. I have ridden several older motorcycles fitted with 'vintage-pattern' tyres from some more obscure manufactory in the Far East, and I'm afraid that given the choice I would bin them in favour of the most modern rubber from a manufacturer whose name is familiar.

Should you be contemplating buying a bike that has been re-imported to the UK from its original export market, and which has covered but a nominal recorded mileage, pay special attention to those tyres. Many bikes that have returned home from hotter overseas climes feature, as well as their most welcome low mileage and good overall condition, a pair of low mileage and original tyres. Throw them away before riding the bike, no matter how good the tread appears to be. Tyre rubber hardens and cracks with age, and its gripping characteristics also deteriorate to the point at which the first greasy road will find you exploring that body-tarmac interface that is always so unwelcome.

When you replace the tyre *always* replace the rim tape (insulating tape will work as a last resort), inner tube and valve as well. Never run a bike without tyre valve caps fitted, either; a valve cap will not prevent a valve leaking, but it should slow it down, and a gentle deflation is always preferable to a sudden one. And as an aside, if you have cause to utilise one of the proprietary puncture replacement aerosols because you've suffered a flat,

always replace the tube and clean out the inside of the cover thoroughly. New inner tubes are admittedly more expensive than a puncture repair kit, but a new tube is less likely to deflate than a repaired one. And always buy the best inner tube available – any economies made where your life is at stake are false ones.

Front suspension

So, you have now determined the condition of the bicycle's brakes, wheels, tyres and its pair of big hinges while the machine sits immobile on its stand. It is now time to take a peep at the suspension itself, and the best time to do this is after the test ride. I shall repeat this simple phrase many times in this book: *never buy a bike without riding it first*. Test rides should bring to light many faults, if you know what to look for; and if you don't know what you're looking at yourself, try to take someone along with you who does.

During the course of the test ride (I always feel that it should be written The Test Ride, because many a fine story can be told about test rides!) – which will be covered in greater detail in the next chapter – try to throw the bike around a bit. OK, this can be a little difficult if the rain is heaving down or if the tyres are seriously past their best, or even if the beast is physically a lot bigger than you are used to, but always try to actually *test* the bike a little. This is, after all, the test ride. Try to make the suspension work a little bit, at least; braking hard a couple of times is a little more use than just bouncing up and down on the seat (although this is perhaps best done out of the worried owner's anxious gaze).

When you have returned from the test ride, and after you have reassured the owner that his P&J is in as good a condition as it was before you set out to test it, peer closely at the suspension units for signs of leakage. Hydraulic sus-

pension units – and this includes most common types of telescopic front forks – should not leak their damping fluid at all. In fact, visibly leaking dampers should result in an MoT test failure.

If the front forks are leaking oil – and in serious cases duff fork seals can result in what appears to be a most mysterious engine oil leak, as the oil gets deposited by the rushing wind over both the engine and the rider's boots – the seals will need to be replaced before the bike covers any meaningful mileage. Fork seals in themselves are not usually expensive, but if the forks are being stripped to replace them, and you are buying a specialist's time to strip them, you should at least consider having all the wearing parts of the whole fork replaced at the same time. It does make sense, you know, and it's always a good bargaining issue to point this out to the vendor. I am not saying that if the seals are goosed then the bushes are worn out; some early (and some not so early) teleforks used rather primitive sealing materials, and the designers appeared to compensate by using substantial bushes.

If the forks have not leaked any oil, ask the vendor if you can remove the oil drain plug, which you will find at the bottom of each fork leg. It is, after all, entirely possible that the reason why the forks have not leaked is that there is no oil inside them to leak. And if there is no oil in the forks, the bushes will have been running on the stanchions without lubrication. Metal to metal contact is not famous for being kind to the components concerned.

The action of the forks, ie the up and down sliding bit, should be both smooth and well damped. In other words, there should be no graunching or grittiness as the forks extend and compress, and the whole assembly should not bounce around as though suspended by an old bed-spring. Most forks provide suspension by extending and compressing a coil spring, and most forks control the spring's tendency to bounce by using oil to damp it.

Another wearing area of a telescopic fork that is all too often neglected in the white heat of purchase fever is the stanchion itself. The stanchion is the long tube that is clamped at the top by the yokes and upon which the sliders slide, appropriately enough. The fork movement is generally quite short (4 inches or so being pretty good) and the bushes wear away at the stanchion a little bit every time the fork compresses and rebounds. Sometimes this wear is apparent – on the forks of most 1970s' machines, for example, where the chrome on the exposed stanchion can wear away very obviously – and sometimes it is invisible, as when hidden behind the shrouds or rubber gaiters fitted before the adoption of the 'Italian look' in those early '70s. A bike should fail its MoT test if the stanchions are worn, too.

An interesting aside. You may come across a bike whose fork legs are straight and true, but which has handlebars that do not point in the right direction. I have owned two Triumph Tridents like this. The cause is simple, and simple to fix, but could be used in bargaining if you are unscrupulous and the vendor innocent. It is quite possible for the fork legs to twist in their yokes in a minor third party contact scenario, and although wheel alignment will be fine, and the individual legs will be straight, the steering will still feel odd. To correct this, simply loosen every fitting you can lay spanner to and bounce vigorously up and down. Then re-tighten everything. Everything!

The cost of the parts required to totally refurbish a set of front forks on most classic motorcycles is not high, but the labour cost of paying someone to do the work will be. On the other hand, dismantling most common forks should not be beyond the abilities of even an average home mechanic, provid-

ing he or she is armed with the right tools (many forks require the use of a special tool or two) and a decent set of instructions.

One or two of the classic British bike builders used forks that were of less conventional design. Ariel two-strokes, for example, use a neat leading link design, while Douglas – and the unlovely two-stroke Panther referred to in Chapter 1 – preferred the fitment of an Earles type of front suspension, where the wheel is held at the end of a swinging fork. Both of those systems still use springs as the suspension and oil as the damping medium; real oddities like the Douglas 'Radiadraulic' and Greeves 'banana' fork used more subtle methods, like rubber in torsion, to the same end. Whatever the method used to hold the front wheel of your dream bike to the tarmac, you can safely bet that it will have become worn over the years, so do your best to assess exactly how far gone it is. If you fancy a machine with an unconventional suspension, read up as much as possible before you sign the cheque, and check that wearing spares are both affordable and available.

Rear suspension

Almost all motorcycles from our self-defined 'classic' period will feature rear suspension as well, and this also deserves a little inspection. When the first primitive forms of rear wheel springing were unleashed upon the great British bike-buying public, more than a couple of manufacturers did their best to avoid major chassis revisions by removing the rear end of their existing rigid frames and substituting what was, rather strangely, referred to as 'plunger' suspension. I can think of many verbs to describe the operation of these half-hearted twitches in the direction of progress, but 'plunging' is not one of them.

Most forms of plunger consist of a pair of springs sandwiching the

rear wheel spindle, allowing it some vertical movement. That is a pretty sweeping simplification, but it's fairly accurate. Some – but not all – plunger back ends also featured some form of damping arrangement, whereby the rider was saved from the indignity of bounding up and down alarmingly for several hundred yards after every bump had been successfully negotiated. The spring units were themselves clamped into strong lugs, which were in turn attached to the bike's frame.

The biggest drawback of most of these plunger frames was that the movement they offered was very limited. They could also wear unevenly, especially when the bike was being used as a sidecar tug and when essential maintenance had been lacking. The resulting solo handling – after the almost inevitable removal of the sidecar – could be a trifle entertaining, to observers at least. Add to this the fact that the rear chain was prone to rapid wear because the wheel moved up and down in a straight line (thus moving the centre of the wheel and the sprocket attached to it away from the fixed gearbox sprocket, so tending to stretch the chain), and it could be suggested that unless you particularly and desperately fancy a plunger model – and the plunger BSA Golden Flash is a particularly handsome and pleasant motorcycle for which I could happily find room in my shed – then perhaps a rigid or swinging arm model would be a better bet.

A few manufacturers avoided the plunger blind alley, going their own sweet ways towards the common goals of sweet handling, better road-holding and greater rider comfort. Triumph invented a unique 'sprung hub' arrangement, whereby the hub of the rear wheel was rather larger than average, because it contained an arrangement of springs that enabled the wheel rim to move relative to the spindle, thus affording a form of suspension. Sprung hubs have a dreadful reputation for being

Try to pull the back chain off its sprocket. It shouldn't move (much).

both evil-handling and evil to rebuild; the former reputation is a little ill-deserved when the hub is in good condition, but the latter is entirely accurate.

Ariel went down another blind alley of their own, and offered their otherwise discerning customers the opportunity to sample the suspensory delights of the 'Anstey Link'. This was a slightly sophisticated version of the plunger that went some way towards addressing the rapid chain wear feature of other plunger suspensions by clamping the wheel spindle in a pivoted

Rear suspension units have a hard life, especially if you ride hard. Check their condition, and check also that they're not bent . . .

shackle. The over-complicated construction of the link, and its wondrous ability to wear with almost magical rapidity, ensured that Ariel developed their fully sprung frame fairly promptly.

Another aside. Probably the worst-handling bike I have ever ridden was a 350cc Ariel Red Hunter fitted with an Anstey Link. The poor thing had once hauled a sidecar – the performance must have been very much less than electrifying – and the links had worn very badly and very unevenly. When I tell you that the bike's steering was worse than that of the awful two-stroke Panther upon whose grimy saddle I started my riding career, you can judge for yourself how dire indeed was the Ariel. Did I mention that the Panther's frame had snapped just above the swinging arm pivot? No? Well it had, and the Ariel's handling was worse than that . . .

Luckily for us all, by the mid-1950s most manufacturers were offering their bikes with pivoted fork (or swinging arm, as it is more usually known) rear suspension. This is the superficially sensible system where the rear wheel

spindle is clamped at the end of a fork, which pivots about a bearing behind the gearbox. We have already discussed wear at that pivot itself; now I can reveal that the suspension units themselves can also wear out with alacrity.

The pre-purchase tests applied to the front fork should also be applied to the rear. After a test ride, ask yourself these few simple questions: do the suspension units leak, do they operate smoothly, and is there play in their mountings? Happily, if the units are worn out the most sensible method of repair is replacement. Some early units, like the AMC 'jampot', can and should be rebuilt, because only the originals will fit properly, and only the originals look right. Although a few concerns offer a rear shock reconditioning service, there are at least a couple of modern units that not only replace the originals without altering the appearance of the bike too much, but also offer improved performance.

Frame damage

In these strange days, when every old bike seems to be revered for being in some way wonderful, too many bike buyers content themselves with a most cursory squint at whether the paint finish on their prospective purchase is up to scratch. Everyone – OK, almost everyone – understands that if a frame is seriously rusty, rusty to the point where it needs a complete repaint, then the whole bike has to come to pieces to allow a decent job to be done. Any total dismantling exercise is going to be expensive, either in terms of hours spent spannering or in the quantities of notes changing hands. What a lot of folk forget, as their enthusiasm for a bike casts that rose-tinted glaze over the proceedings, is that frames can get damaged, too.

Buying 'specials' can be a path fraught with dangers. Somewhere under here there was once a 1955 G9 Matchless. It would be a challenge – but very uneconomical – to restore a bike like this to anything like original condition.

Frame damage comes in a number of forms, all of them easy to ignore in that flush of pre-purchase excitement. The most obvious damage results from riding the motorcycle into something hard. I can reveal with some embarrassment that I once bought a 350 AJS (it turned out to be mostly a Matchless, but that's another story) that featured the quickest steering known to any fan of Plumstead. This bike was truly eager to change direction, and the slightest twitch upon the handlebars was sufficient to send bike and hapless pilot heading for the hedgerows. It was more exciting to ride than are most 350 heavyweights, and that's for sure.

The cause of this navigational nervousness was the fork geometry, with the angle of the front forks being rather steeper than is usual. But the forks themselves were straight enough, so . . . so it was the frame that was bent. The big, sturdy front downtube was bent into a gentle S-shape when viewed from the side. Viewed from the front it was perfectly straight, and the wheels were in line (I'd checked that, of course, before parting with my money).

Finding a replacement frame is easy enough, but finding the correct replacement frame proved to be a real headache. OK, everyone knows that the ancient Brit bike builders didn't change their frame designs for years. True? False. Most of them changed their frames rather more than they made announcements advertising the fact; for example, the 1957 350 single AJS frame is different from

Much of the running gear for this chopper came from another mid-'50s Matchless, this time a G80.

both the 1957 500 single and the 1958 350 single. Did you know that? The only way to uncover all of this most arcane lore is to join the appropriate owners' club, and I shall repeat this advice frequently through these pages.

Another form of the bodging (I cannot bring myself to describe demented and irreversible hacksaw work as 'customising') that too often gets neglected at the moment of potential purchase – and most especially when the bike is being bought as a box of bits for restoration – is when a machine has been converted into some sort of special during its life. This is not a dig at anyone who has carried out such improvements to their

bike over the years; a bike is the property of its owner, and anyone owning any bike has every right to do with it what they will! No, this is a cautionary note for inexperienced bike buyers.

If you are buying a bike that has at some stage of its life been converted into a replica road racer, trials tool or back-street chopper, it is entirely possible that the frame will be missing some essential bracketry or other. It will be pretty hard work, for example, to fit the correct petrol tank to a T140 Triumph if some ardent customiser has cut off the fitting on the frame's top rail that takes the central bolt. That's a bit of a radical example, but many are the frames

Some specials, however, are very
desirable. This neat machine
started life as a police Norton . . .

I've seen with oil tank and tool box brackets removed in some misguided but earnest quest for trail bike or street racer lightness. As I said earlier, it can sometimes prove a little difficult to locate that unexpectedly essential fresh frame.

One minor concern – or maybe not, depending upon your viewpoint – is when you view a bike that has had its frame powder-coated, painted with epoxy-based coatings or daubed with some of the other modern chemical concoctions that are commonly used nowadays instead of the original finish. That original finish was most likely to have been stove enamelling, a paint process prized by the ancients because of its lustrous finish and resistance to wear. I always view resin and powder coatings with the deepest suspicion, largely because of the number of poorly prepared repainted frames I've come across over the years. Indeed, one repainted Triumph swinging arm that I was contemplating was wearing a coating of something that the owner assured me was high-quality powder coating. High-quality it may have been, but I was still able to peel it off with my thumbnail, revealing a fine coating of rust upon the surface of the steel beneath.

Don't ever forget that repainting a frame properly takes an awful lot of time and effort, and as ever, if you are paying for someone else's time and effort, it will prove rather costly.

Ancillaries – tinware and such

After checking that the bike's frame is straight, that it belongs to the bike you're looking at, that the wheels are round and go round, that the suspension systems are doing their best in the circumstances, and that the brakes are worthy of their name, it is time to take a long, hard look at the rest of the bicycle. In short, it is time to look at all of those many bits and pieces that supply the engine with its vital fluids, that determine the comfort of the rider, that control the sundry functions and that lighten the darkness. And so we will do just that.

The engine is fed its vital fluids from two tanks, you will not be surprised to learn. Petrol comes from the petrol tank – that big shiny thing above the engine – and oil comes from an oil tank traditionally mounted below and behind the rider's right knee. Usually. There are of course many and varied deviations from this generalisation, but we'll think about those a little later on, in the appropriate part of the book.

If you add together the two tanks, the mudguards, the toolbox and headlamp, and stir in any other sundry bits of stylish or otherwise pieces of bodywork that the manufacturer may have seen fit to inflict upon the model of your choice, you will find that you are talking about the bike's tinware. Tinware is as important as the frame and the powertrain in some folks' eyes because, unlike most wearing mechanical parts, a lot of tinware is no longer available. Before the invention of the 'classic' motorcycle, non-standard tinware, tinware of the wrong model or year or tinware that was simply absent, detracted hardly at all from the value placed upon a particular breed of bike. Indeed, some of the most valuable British bikes at the dawning of the classic age were the most non-standard: Egli Vincents, Dow Gold Stars and sundry mix'n'match supposedly sporting specials spring easily to mind.

These machines were often viewed as being at the very pinnacle of desirability because they represented developments of favourite models long past the point where the original manufacturers had called it quits. And because these after-market pinnacles were so often supposedly competition-developed, with that extra lightness and starkness that is assumed to provide the competitive edge, just about every quick kid on the block felt the need to turn his cooking Crusader or pedestrian Panther into something that looked like some kind of paddock refugee. The easiest way of doing this – as I seem to have mentioned earlier – was to ditch all that heavy steel mudguarding, those comfy upright handlebars, those well-padded seats and anything else that made the motorcycle into a sensible means of transport.

(Whether a motorcycle was ever a sensible means of transport is a moot point, which we will ignore completely.)

What this means today is that there is a small but lively industry that caters for those who wish to return their cherished, but slightly stripped, relics of the coffee shop racedays into a replica of a factory stock machine of the appropriate year. Non-standard tinware only rarely prevented a machine from functioning, and it often did in fact improve things, but the prices asked for a given model will suffer if the currently essential standard cladding isn't all present and correct. When you come to view a bike as a prospective purchaser, you must bear this in mind, because when you try to sell it on yourself at a later date, you can bet that all of your prospective customers will savage your asking price if the bike lacks its original tin. So if, for example, you are toddling off to take a peek at a late non-unit Triumph Tiger 110, which was originally swaddled in a bizarre and unattractive inverted coal scuttle sort of thing around its rump (the odd tinny arrangement known at the time as a 'bath tub'), and you find that some proud owner way back in the mists of history has sensibly consigned said bath tub to the nearest midden, and has instead fitted later stainless steel sports-type mudguards, it may not be wise to heave a huge sigh of relief at the vast visual improvement. Although the old Tiger's dignity may have been much enhanced by the removal of its skirts, its value on the open market is as much diminished as its appearance is improved. Oh, go away – surely no one actually likes the bath tub? Do they?

Another way of viewing non-originality is to tell yourself that it is unimportant to you. This is a particularly handy stance should you really intend to use your oldster for riding delight rather than for impressing the heck out of your mates by winning useless but shiny trophies (for owning a useless but shiny bike perhaps? Surely not!). If you adopt this viewpoint, one strongly favoured – if not always practised – by myself, you can save a positive fortune when you buy a bike.

Example time again. Back in the 1950s BSA invented the Gold Star (and yes, I know they did that a while before, but I'm thinking here of the swinging arm models), a bike that was based – as inconspicuously as possible – on the very dull-cooking singles of the day. Now, while there may be absolutely no comparison between the riding delights offered by a DBD34 Gold Star and its B33 cousin, it is quite possible to add and subtract bits and pieces to make the latter resemble the former. Disposing of the vast and cumbersome mudguards and enveloping rear chaincase, ditching the cast iron cylinder head and barrel, replacing the lot with Gold Star replica parts in shiny alloy and chrome, is going to improve the old plodder no end. The bike, assuming that the conversion work has been carried out by someone with more mechanical sympathy than a substandard gorilla, will be nicer to ride and nicer to look at than before. It is always a surprise, therefore, to see that in many cases the original B33 would be commanding a higher price than the non-original one.

It is of course well worth recalling at this point that for every well-executed customisation of a motorcycle, there are probably a hundred artless bodge-jobs. Please remember this when you go to view anything described as 'special'.

Anyway, the tinware. Back in the olden days, when these bikes were being hand-assembled by loving craftsmen (or not, as may be the case), most manufacturers changed their models on an annual basis. Every year the major makers would attempt to convince potential purchasers that the 1956 model was a great improvement over the 1955 model, for example, and in any case their product was far better than similar bikes (of pretty well identical specification and performance) offered by their rivals. They transformed their bikes in many ways.

The easy changes to spot are when major alterations to the basics of the bike were introduced: new frame designs are pretty obvious, as are fundamental changes to the engine's design, or to its major castings. The main problems for identification arise when just the details have been changed, and you are unfamiliar with what you are looking at. It is simple enough to equip yourself with as much as possible of the literature covering your chosen machine and compare the physical reality with the manufacturer's original product when you are wondering whether the petrol tank was the right one, but only someone with The Knowledge and their eyes open might notice, for example, that the bike under view has the wrong type of gearbox for its claimed year.

A note: several companies, AMC prominent among them, would employ the skills of an air-brush artist to convert a photograph of, say, a 1960 650 model into the new 1961 version. This was done with sensible motives (like getting the catalogues printed up in time for the big shows before the new models had actually been built), but it poses problems for someone considering the purchase of an 'original' bike 40 years later. It is a really good idea to locate both an expert (that owners' club again) and an original road test containing photos of the model in question before you part with your pennies.

It is always possible that you are unconcerned with this sort of thing, and don't care that the 1962 BSA Star twin under view has been fitted with a tank, cylinder head and side panels from a 1968 Lightning – you may even think that those parts are a great improvement – but if originality is important to you, choose your bike with care, and with help.

Most tinware for most popular models is available in some form or another these days, and although a purist will be offended by a bike wearing fibreglass replica mudguards instead of its original steel ones, they will not make the machine any less pleasant to ride.

So, to conclude, let us wander around a hypothetical old bike to see some common faults. First, are the mudguards rotted? Does the fuel tank leak? Does petrol drip from the carburetter? Is the seat badly re-covered or rotten? Do all the sundry parts fit securely and do they look as though they belong together? That last question is most important; stepping back and scratching my head once revealed to me that a Matchless I was intent upon buying was fitted with a completely incorrect rear sub-frame. I bought the bike anyway, but at a much reduced price.

A damaged petrol tank can be a most expensive item to restore, too, especially if it is heavily chromed and has a metalflake paint finish. Expensive like several hundred pounds. Damaged steel-work – like mudguards and rear enclosures – can also prove to be expensive to repair; bodges using car body filler and fibreglass matting can look good, but vertical twin vibration ensures that filler falls out – fast!

Missing badges, missing transfers, missing brightwork, missing covers and the presence of ill-fitting parts suggests that the bike may be a lash-up, and I suggest that you should proceed only with care. The condition of the non-essential parts of a motorcycle can often provide good clues to its internal condition – and no owner is going to let Joe Buyer dismantle his engine to see whether there are the remains of a previous catastrophe lurking within.

Finally, remember that if the bike you are bent upon is in any way rare or obscure, a lot of the bicycle ancillaries will not be available. This applies as much to mundane ride-to-work bikes as to purebred competition tackle.

Chapter 4

Checking the Power Train

At last, we come to consider the heart of any motorcycle, be it classic or not – the engine, that hopefully impressive shiny lump in the middle of the bicycle that carries out the job of propelling motorcycle and passengers along the highways and byways of our green and pleasant land. The engine is probably that part of the machine that most of us consider when deciding upon our own personal choice of conveyance. I must of course tip my cap in the direction of all of the myriad other factors that may lead an enthusiast to choose the mechanised companion for his or her travels – like styling, handling and perceived pose value – but for me it is most often the engine that is the deciding factor. I like four-strokes myself, and oddities, which is why my two rotary-engined Nortons currently share their shed space with a Sanglas 500cc single. Variety of engine type is one of the most appealing parts of the classic scene for this writer, which is why the bikes mentioned above also share their shed with a Matchless G15 and a Triumph Trident.

If a bike has a useless engine, an engine that completely fails to inspire its rider, whether through general awfulness or great sloth or an unreliable nature – or all three! – no matter how astounding may be the other features of the machine, it will never achieve greatness. And if an owner doesn't think his classic bike is great, then why own it at all? Answers should be written on £20 notes in invisible ink and sent to me c/o the publisher.

A good example of a fine motorcycle with a fairly useless, albeit fairly charming, engine is the Norton Model 50 in either of its featherbed incarnations. I ask you – why lumber the best-handling chassis of the whole classic era with a wheezing and pedestrian 350cc power plant? Power plant, I say. Hah!

The engine, of course, does not exist in isolation, but shares its propulsive duties with the rest of the power train. This comprises the primary drive (from engine to clutch), the clutch itself, the gearbox and the final drive (from gearbox to back wheel). For the sake of a little logic, we will commence our journey around this fictional bike that we are considering by looking at the engine.

The engine

If you are even a little new to the old game of buying old bikes, please don't be fooled into thinking that just because the bike you are contemplating is fitted with an engine, and that engine runs well enough to move the thing along without your having to sprint alongside it ... don't be fooled into thinking that all is just great in the propulsion department. It may well be – we don't want to breed a generation of paranoid bike-buyers here – but equally it may not.

Once again, you need to ask yourself (and answer truthfully, please) exactly what it is that you want from your classic motorcycle. If you truly require merely an alternative form of two-wheeled transport, then it doesn't matter a jot if the bike's engine has not spent the whole of its automotive existence being carried about in the particular set of cycle parts that it now occupies. You can, therefore, concern yourself solely with the condition of the power train, deciding along the way whether its performance meets your own individual criteria.

Should you prefer your classic as any form of investment or piece of rolling history, however, and should you wish to sell it easily at some stage in the dim and maybe not-so-distant future, it becomes more essential that engine and frame started out down their road together. And if this is the case, you will need to check this out by unravelling the sometimes strange numbering systems adopted by manufacturers of old. Once again, I would always recommend first of all that you join the appropriate owners' club, and that you overload your bedside table with every

Check the bike's numbers; this Triumph's engine number confirms its age and model.

reference book available that covers your chosen marque.

The engine number is always stamped on some fairly prominent part of one of the crankcases –

usually at the front left corner, which, incidentally, is also where we are supposed to hang the tax disc. These numbers can take several forms, often listing the engine's year of build and original model. Thus if you're looking at a 1964 AJS 500cc scrambles single with an engine number beginning 57/G3LS, beware, because those crankcases started their life as the power plant of a 1957 Matchless 350 cooking roadster. On the other hand, if you're contemplating any sort of late Triumph and the numbers (not the letters, the numbers) of the engine and frame are identical, then engine and frame started out together. They could have been re-stamped along the way, of course, but you must decide where common sense expires and paranoia takes over!

If you value originality and dislike difficult conversations with either the constabulary or your local MoT man, avoid bikes where either engine or frame number has been obviously tampered with in any way. Likewise remember that no bike left its factory without both engine and frame numbers. And yes, of course I accept that replacement crankcases were available for those that suffered the unwelcome attention of an escaping con-rod or two, but any sensible owner back then would have re-stamped the number when fitting the new cases.

By far and away your best bet to find these numbering sequences will be to join the owners' club

Does the crankcase joint leak (a bad sign)? Is the frame repaired? Check for out-of-view damage.

and consult all the reference works on your chosen bikes. Repetition gets tedious, I know, but that is probably the best piece of advice offered in this book. Personally, for this sort of reference I use the excellent marque reference books written by Roy Bacon, and would recommend that you do the same.

Visual examination

First, then, take a good long *look* at the power plant of any machine you are considering for purchase. An awful lot of information about the state of an engine can be gained by looking at it with a knowing eye, so ensure that you take a knowing eye along with you, preferably four of them, as a second set is likely to spot things that your rose-tinted and optimistic ones may have missed.

Like missing fasteners, for example. If an engine is missing simple and non-debilitating items such as the screws that retain the timing cover (the big and probably shiny cover on the right of the bike), it immediately indicates one of two things. First, the owner is not particularly fastidious and hasn't noticed, or that he knows perfectly well that the screw is missing, it's just that . . . It's just that, second, the thread in the crankcase that is normally engaged by this screw is stripped. Unless you don't care about such things, re-tapping threads into blind holes in the crankcases is a rather less than joyful pastime.

Missing fasteners elsewhere can have a far more deleterious effect upon the wellbeing of the engine, and the wise person checks that all visible nuts and bolts are present and correct, both on the engine itself and upon its ancillaries, like the electrical gubbins and oil and fuel lines. If a Triumph twin – especially a pre-unit one – has a particularly oily top end, it is a fair bet that one or more of the plethora of fiddly fasteners that retain the rocker boxes is either missing or is wearing a worn thread. Likewise, if the head joint of a Norton twin looks weepy to front or rear, check that the inaccessible nuts beneath the exhaust ports are both present and tight. There's another madly sited stud at the back of the block, and I have come across more than one Norton twin where some leaf-brained rebuilder has not bothered to tighten these fasteners simply because it's difficult to get at them properly. So, please cast a sceptical eye across the fasteners.

Look next for signs of damage to the engine's major castings, particularly the crankcases themselves. Broken lugs in aluminium castings are not the simplest things in the world to repair accurately, and bodged repairs are common. Once

Head gaskets blow – check the joint.

Carburettors wear out, leak and radically affect the running of any engine. Check for leaks, missing filters, bowed joints and signs of Mr Bodger.

upon a time it was not too uncommon to discover AMC twin crankcases that had been welded to repair the damage occasioned by an emergent con-rod. Unless expertly carried out, alloy repairs can be famously porous, so check for oil smears in strange places.

Next look for evidence of recent unskilled surgery. Most usually this will take the form of squeezings of gasket cement from visible joints. If the vendor claims to have rebuilt the engine recently, and you can see beads of silicone RTV jointing compound dribbling from external joint faces, remind yourself at once that while this may be merely unsightly, that same orange (or blue, or whatever) gook can do a lot of damage if it strays into internal – and invisible – oilways deep within the engine. Again, make a cautionary mental note.

Other signs of oaf-handed spannering include the tell-tale marks at joint faces where a screwdriver has been inserted to separate them, witness marks from the brutal application of a pipe-wrench, and rounded nut and bolt heads. Take special notice of the all-too-common appearance of one fastener in a set that is plainly of a different type to its fellows; unless there is a reason for this, it suggests that some clown may have compensated for a weary female thread by winding in an oversize bolt. Not recommended, that one! Similarly, broken or badly bent cylinder and cylinder head cooling fins suggest that the approach to the engine's maintenance routines has not always been of a deeply sympathetic nature. Realistically, you should always also remember that the bike is an old one, and its current owner may well not be responsible for mechanical mishaps earlier in its career.

The other side of the eyeball examination coin is that a neat, clean and smart – not necessarily over-polished – external appearance leads us toward a trust that the internal assemblies will be equally sound. Although others may disagree with me, I would never mark a machine down at a concours – never mind for regular use – for wearing a decent set of modern electrical connectors or stainless cap-head fasteners instead of the feeble bullet connectors and cheese-head screw efforts so often used back in the 1950s. Likewise, an engine's cleanliness is always a good sign, although I would suggest that you don't even start looking for oil leaks until after the test ride; modern degreasers are very good indeed.

Starting up

Only after the eyeball test should you start the engine. Allow the owner to do this, after noting whether the engine is warm already. If the engine is warm when you arrive, it may merely suggest that the owner is a little nervous and hoped for a dependable start with the engine already run up to operating temperature. It may also indicate that the thing will not start from cold without a run-and-bump and an extra bowl

Check the engine for leaks – Triumph pushrod tubes are notorious.

that he can be forgiven for being unfamiliar with every single starting routine. Unless you are personally familiar with the starting routines of big Velocette singles, to quote a cliché, watching a long-term owner start his can be fascinating. Any machine that is claimed to be in regular use – and which you may be considering for that purpose – should start easily and with no hesitation. Modern spark plugs are better than those of old, and if you are contemplating one of the more common models from major recent manufacturers, you may find that modern ignition systems are greatly improved over some of those used in the past – both of which ease starting.

A tip: you should never buy a bike until you know that you can start it. So try it before you buy it. Preferably at the vendor's base, rather than half-way around your 20-mile test ride . . . There is very little to be gained from the ownership of a bike that you cannot start, unless you are building up a collection for its own sake. Once the owner has fired the beast up, it would be sensible to have him

or two of powerful breakfast cereal. If you are that concerned, consider turning up to look at the machine either much earlier or much later than arranged. And be prepared for the owner to be either out or eating his tea . . .

I generally find that it is both an education and an entertainment to watch a vendor start his motorcycle. I exclude all traders here, because a trader will see so many bikes passing through his stock

Is an oil filter fitted? It's a good sign if it is, but check that it's not loose or leaky.

switch it off and attempt to repeat this simple – but essential – feat yourself.

There is quite a lot of information to be gained from the way a bike fires up. Does it emit dense and fuming clouds like an enthusiastic convention of old pipe-smokers? Does the owner rev the poor thing half-way around the tachometer dial from cold? Does it fire up on all of its cylinders? Does it settle quickly to an even tickover?

Once the engine is running, you can make a few checks. First of all listen carefully to it, and ask the pal you have brought along (either as an expert or as moral support) to listen too. Even a well-worn engine should not sound particularly rattly at first; thick, cold oil can mask a multitude of ailments, and a steady tickover does not exactly test the engine's appetite for work. From cold you should be listening for even running. You should check that all of the cylinders are firing (if in doubt, poke a tentative digit in the direction of each exhaust pipe – gentle warmth suggests a lack of serious combustion, while sudden excitement and reflexive removal of the smouldering digit confirms its presence). I have heard claims that Experts can hold a hand near the outlets of a twin's separate silencers (assuming that it features such things) when the engine is running, and can instantly determine a lack of compression on one cylinder. Personally I don't believe this, but if you have a friend who is such an Expert, I may be wrong.

If the bike carries its engine lube in a separate oil tank, check that the oiling system is operative, and after a couple of seconds check that the oil returning to the tank is doing so in an appropriate man-

ner. A what? What is an appropriate manner? Engine oil pumps are designed so that the scavenge side of the pump (which returns the oil from the engine to the tank) has a greater capacity than the feed side (which pumps oil from tank to engine, naturally enough), and when the engine is running the oil should return in the company of a lot of bubbles, or in a discernible series of pulses, rather than in a continuous flow. If the oil is squirting in a continuous stream from the scavenge pipe, something is not right.

It is commonplace for bikes that have a worn oil pump to allow their lube to seep, under gravity's constant tug, from oil tank to crankcase. When the engine is started, especially after a lengthy period of inactivity, there will be a continuous stream of oil returning to the tank until the crankcases are drained once more. This should not take a very long time. When the crankcases are emptied, the returning oil feed should be seen to pulse, as mentioned earlier. Failure to do so can suggest several things, not least among them the terrifying possibility that Proud But Hopeless Rebuilder has connected up the oil pipes the wrong way round. Don't laugh – I have seen this on several AMC twins, and on more than one Triumph . . .

The other major failing that strange behaviour in the oil tank suggests is that the oil pump itself is very worn. Some bikes are more prone to this than others, and an AJS 650 twin of my acquaintance, if left standing for more than a week, can drain all of its oil into the crankcases. Upon eventual re-start, the exhaust smokes like a Second World War destroyer confusing the submarines, treacle-like oil squirts into the oil tank with all the energy of a maverick fire hose, and black lube oozes menacingly from every engine orifice it can find. Not pretty.

There are sundry cures offered in the specialist press for this common affliction. Some folk suggest inserting a non-return valve into the oil feed pipe, while others suggest fitting a tap. If you buy a bike fitted with anything like this, my suggestion is that you remove it at once, possibly for use as an ornament, as you only need to forget to turn on an oil tap once. If you are not keen on unexpected engine rebuilds, this would be regrettable, as engines are reluctant to run for long without oil. Far more sensible is to either recondition the oil pump or to simply accept that if it's been stood for a while then it's going to leak, and simply fool the thing by draining out the oil from

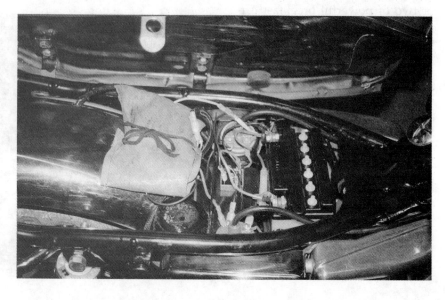

Look around the bike's battery, as leaky batteries corrode the metal around them. Corrosion is messy, occasionally painful, and can be costly to remedy.

the sump before you start it up. Oh, and do remember to refill the tank with clean, fresh oil of the correct grade.

Another thing to observe before actually setting the machine in motion is whether the charging circuit shows any significant signs of life.

Electrics

If the bike is fitted with an ammeter, it should register a healthy charge when just starting up. If it is fitted with but a warning light, that light should glow when the engine is not running, but not when it is – just like an oil warning light (and remember that some T160 Tridents have their warning lights incorrectly labelled . . .). Whenever I come across an electrical indicator light or dial that informs me that the system is not charging, I believe it.

Call me a cynic if you wish, but I am firmly of the opinion that anyone selling a bike would replace a blown bulb or a dead ammeter – but maybe not a weary dynamo or incapacitated voltage control box. If you are in any doubt, switch on the headlight – main beam will do nicely – and observe the ammeter; it should discharge frantically (applying the rear brake to activate the brake light will send the ammeter into even further paroxysms of panic, should you feel vindictive). If the bike's charging circuitry is working, the ammeter should balance by about 40mph in top, and show a charge by around 50mph. Please remember that wildly revving the engine of a stationary motorcycle to the point at which its system will charge against a full load of lights may induce apoplexy in both the vendor and his neighbours.

If the bike is unendowed with the luxury of an ammeter, or even a warning light (which only indicates that the dynamo or alternator is sufficiently energetic to dowse the warning light, incidentally), then repeat the above test, but observe the headlight itself rather than the absent ammeter. Crudely put, the lights should brighten when you rev the engine, and dim when you don't. If the lights don't brighten with a brisk assault upon the twistgrip, something is not right. Always.

As we have already mentioned, most early British classic bikes supplied energy to their spark plugs (cheap, easy to both clean and to replace) from a device known as a magneto. All too often the word 'magneto' was preceded by a (deleted) expletive. Mags usually provide their electrical energy by spinning a lot of copper windings inside a magnet, and over the years the insulation between the individual copper wires can break down, reducing their effectiveness, and the magnetism can fade, reducing their effectiveness, and everything can get cooked and shaken to bits by heat and vibration, reducing their effectiveness.

If you have a faulty mag (lousy starting, dreadful hot starting, a tendency to cut out after, say, 10 miles, then restart when things have cooled down), you have two courses available. Neither is cheap. First, you can have the dead mag replaced with a better one or rebuilt by a specialist. Second, you can replace the whole tired gubbins with a more modern solid state ignition system – some of these are even available disguised as (or fitted inside) magnetos! Personal choice? I like (good) mags, because unless they actually die on you (and they usually give you lots of notice of this) you are going to get home under your own steam. This is not the case with anything requiring a battery to provide sparks.

Bikes with magnetos usually – but not always – charge their batteries from a direct current dynamo. I have upset fans of these lugubrious instruments before by saying this, but I have never had an entire dynamo charging system work for more than a few miles in a riding career spanning dozens of bikes and maybe a quarter of a million miles.

Dynamos follow the same general electrical principles as do magnetos, but their voltages are much (much!) lower. As is probably obvious, the faster a dynamo is spun by the engine, the higher its output, and the resulting potential difference (or voltage) is regulated by . . . an electro-mechanical regulator. The regulator is usually a box hidden away under the seat or inside a toolbox, which contains a pair of coils and a pair of contacts. This is the weak link in a dynamo charging circuit. Regulators really do not like being cooked, frozen, shaken to pieces or soaked, and my night-time riding career has been blighted by their failure.

Once again, help is at hand in the shape of modern solid state voltage regulators, which will often fit inside the old casing, thus convincing everyone that you are an electrical genius and not to be tangled with. I prefer alternators and, when I used to ride AMC 650 twins all the time, I usually bought alternator models and replaced the coil and contact breaker ignition assembly with a mag.

Progress being what it was, and faced with the constant demand for electrical components that were cheaper, Lucas (who supplied most of the electrical systems of the classic period – notable exceptions being the Miller systems used by Velocette and Vincent) replaced the magneto (lots of parts, expensive to fix, robust) with a system depending upon an ignition coil (few parts, cheap to fix, robust) and a contact breaker assembly (few parts, cheap to fix, delicate). This was disguised as progress and many of the major engine redesigns of the 1950s and '60s were intended to accommodate the changeover from one system to another. Thus, for example, the BSA A10 is an interesting-looking engine, with drives to both dynamo and magneto built into its timing side, while the BSA A65 engine looks like a big alloy blob, with no drives to anything.

The test ride

Right! So the engine's running, you are certified capable of being able to restart it yourself, there are no truly horrible noises (and it is not true that all Panther singles sound like the hammers of Hell on party night!), and Proud But Desperate To Sell Owner has consented to a test trip. It is time to go for a ride. A test ride will reveal to you the condition not only of the engine and the bicycle, which we have already discussed at some length, but also of the gearbox, clutch and final drive.

The test ride is the most crucial part of the bike-buying process. Some sage souls instruct vendors never to let anyone ride the bike before they have parted with the cash. I insist that you buy nothing you haven't ridden. If the vendor won't let you ride it, don't buy it. A pillion ride is not acceptable. I once bought a BSA A65 and sidecar (I was very young at the time) after a pillion ride with the owner, and my terror was such that I failed to notice that it had several teeth missing from the transmission, it only had three gears and the front brake didn't work at all. The bike was sold to then 18-year-old me by a large London dealer. They are now out of business. I am glad.

The test ride is going to show you all of the non-cosmetic failings of the bike that your examination has so far failed to uncover. It is also going to let you decide whether the bike is the right bike for you, so carry out your test ride

Instruments are not cheap. They should work, match, be the right ones for the model – and preferably show a low mileage.

carefully. Leave something valuable with the vendor, or invite him to ride along with you on your own bike, or something like that, for mutual peace of mind – but you *must* ride before you buy.

Clutch, gears and gearbox

Check the operation of the clutch before you engage a gear. Is it smooth, and does it feel to be in good adjustment? Lousy adjustment can mean that the clutch and/or its operating mechanism are seriously worn, as well as that Proud Owner is hopeless with the spanners. There should be about one-eighth of an inch (less than half a centimetre) free play at the lever. Much less than this means that there is tension in the withdrawal mechanism, which wears things rapidly and may make the clutch slip; more play than this is shoddy maintenance. The clutch action should also be fairly light; well-adjusted clutches and cables in good condition do not require Herculean efforts to operate them. If the thing feels gritty, notchy, jerky or like it was set up to provide forearm development exercises for a keen body-builder, there's something wrong with it.

Engage first gear. It should go

in easily and without too much of a crash. If there's a crash the first time, but not subsequently, don't worry too much, because it is probably caused by the clutch plates being stuck together by a film of the oil in the primary chaincase. If there's a crash every time, there's something wrong with the gearbox (or, less dramatically, it could simply be that both drive chains and their sprockets are well past retirement age). If the gear shows a reluctance to engage, and the bike tries to creep forward, the clutch is dragging (in its worst forms, clutch drag will stall the engine or cause you to leap forward rather sooner than intended). This can be caused by both wear and poor adjustment.

And while I think about it, remember that different British bikes require different vertical movements of the gear lever to engage their gears. AMC boxes, for instance, are up for first, then down for the rest, while Triumphs are the opposite. Do not get this wrong while Proud Owner is in earshot; an unexpected full-bore change from third to second gear instead of fourth may well entertain any onlookers, but will not amuse the vendor. Remember also that some late

British bikes have their gear levers on the left . . .

On the move

The way a bike pulls away can impart a lot of information about it to anyone who is observant. This information can often help you decide how honest the vendor has been in his description of the bike he is selling. For instance, if a bike is described as being freshly rebuilt, it would not be unreasonable for its engine to feel a little tight, for its gears to be slightly reluctant to engage, and for all the controls to be in less than perfect adjustment. It may also run a little warm, if the running-in is yet to be completed. All of these things improve with use and implementation of the ongoing adjustment scenario so beloved of some of us. So . . . so it would be more than reasonable to expect a bike described as being in regular use to have controls that work with smooth ease, to have very functional and well-adjusted brakes, an engine that starts up readily, and a completely functional lighting system. A bike that is described as being 'sold as seen' merely requires that you look at it with your eyes wide open, and not shrouded by the hazy glaze of rose-tinting.

On the move, does the machine accelerate smoothly, without hesitation? Does the engine feel 'happy'? Do all of the gears engage cleanly and with whatever precision the type of gearbox is noted for? Gearbox precision? Yes – generally speaking, the later the bike, the quicker and cleaner its gearchange, and because the trend was for ever shorter gear levers, the length of foot travel required to effect a change became gradually less as time rolled by. This is a generalisation, as a well-adjusted early box may change with unusual ease, while a well-worn-out shift in the most noble of marques may be horribly sloppy – be observant is the message.

To generalise further: pre-war-type gearboxes, and the products of the Burman and Albion concerns, usually have rather ponderous gearchange actions (in other words, if you try to boot the pedal through a fast change, the box may emit a loud graunch of protest, and may well miss the gear entirely – this gets worse with age, mileage and inadequate attention to the service routines). When Associated Motorcycles introduced their own gearbox across the AJS, Matchless and Norton heavyweight ranges for the 1957 season, a new era of quick, clean shifting was ushered in (and lasted until the demise of the Norton Commando in 1978!). Royal Enfield kept their Albion gearboxes to the end, and that change is an acquired art, as is the shift on Velocette singles, although this is an observation, not a criticism. Unit construction BSA and Triumph machines usually feature better shifts than their predecessors, and by the time the end of British mass-production arrived in the early 1980s things were generally slick in the gearbox. With the exception of Heskeths, which change gears with most of the finesse of a food processor chewing up bolts.

Before you condemn a gearbox as needing a complete overhaul, it would only be fair to remind you that worn-out drive chains can make a gearshift less than pleasant, and they are a lot cheaper (and a lot simpler) to replace than a whole gearbox. Beware also of the vendor who is well aware that his chains are past the point of no return and who has over-tightened them in the forlorn hope that you will think that they are OK. A bike that has too tight a primary chain will almost always emit a whine of protest from the primary chaincase, and a bike that has suffered chronic over-tightening of the final drive chain will feel generally odd (when the suspension moves through its arc, assuming that the bike has rear wheel springing, the tension of the main chain will be increased still further, and can even result in failure, so be warned and be careful!).

You should always attempt a test ride of several miles, over as many types of roads as may be found locally. After a couple of miles you should be coming to terms with the general feel of the bike; you should also be becoming aware of any deficiencies in the steering and stop departments.

Try out the brakes – both singly and in unison – as early in your test ride as you like. Try them for effectiveness and progression. Hard braking should highlight any serious failings in the front forks, although you will of course already know about this from your visual inspection. Strange things can happen to the brakes of an old motorcycle, and the time to discover whether your intended has bizarre behaviour in the braking system is while the bike still belongs to someone else – not when you have bought it, have decided that you can put up with its braking idiosyncrasies, and have just observed that, yes, that van has indeed pulled out in front of you. Lousy brakes require fixing, and fixing at once. Preferably before you part with money.

Odd braking things that can happen? A 650 AJS of my acquaintance suffered from the repeated contamination of its front brake shoes with oil. I thought that some clown had filled the hub with grease, so I cleaned and dried the brake shoes (soak them overnight in a strong chemical solvent, then set them on fire with a blowlamp) several times – only for it to happen again. Stripping the hub revealed that the hub was filled with the correct grease, not oil. Baffled. Then I realised that a fork seal had failed completely, I had optimistically topped up the fork oil for the bike's MoT, and it was pumping out of the fork sliders, then dripping into the brake drum whenever the bike was parked on its sidestand. Simple.

A friend had an Ariel that would haul down from 65mph to 5mph in fine style, but the best way of shedding the last few mph was to drag your boots along the roadway. The reason? An enthusiastic previous owner had fitted racing brake linings. Beware cheap-pattern brake linings and cheap, badly made brake cables. Your life depends upon your brakes. Remember this.

So – you are becoming familiar with the bike, and the braking is up to scratch, or not. Does the machine run straight and true when you lift your hands from the bars? It should, although a wobble as you decelerate is no great worry. What is important is that the bike tracks in a straight line, and does not attempt to pull either to left or right of its own accord. Is one hand further away from your body when the front wheel is pointing straight ahead? If so, something is out of kilter somewhere, and if the wheels are in line (when you checked while the bike was stationary), either the bars are bent or the forks are twisted. I would suspect the latter, entirely because I am a cynic and a pessimist.

Riding positions are adjustable – more so on older machines than on younger – and whether or not you are comfortable is a matter only for you to decide. I cannot ever get comfy aboard anything fitted with rearset footrests and dropped handlebars, but you may be of a more slender construction, and may enjoy having your nose an inch from the speedo.

As you become more confident of the bike, attempt to push it a

little into the corners – is it as easy to steer left as right? If not, again something is wrong. The frame may be out of true, the wheels may be out of line and the suspension may be extinct on one side. That last can be a baffler; I once test rode a bike for a friend and its steering was deeply dreadful. Only one rear suspension unit was working, and under hard cornering loads the swinging arm could be seen to twist. The swinging arm bushes, not surprisingly, were also well past it. The bike was a 1959 Tiger 100; my friend did not buy it.

Riding along will also reveal whether or not the clock(s) work. Proud Owner may suggest that a drive cable must have snapped the moment your bottom hit the saddle. Believe him without question, insisting only that he replace the cable before you part with your money. Speedo and tacho repair is not cheap, and it may not be possible to repair the late magnetic Smiths types.

When you have completed your ride, ask yourself first of all whether you enjoyed the experience. If you did not, then why not? If you did not, then why are you still interested in buying the bike? Only you can answer these questions.

A couple of things for the après-ride moment. Is the engine covered

with oil? Is the ground below the engine covered with oil? Has anything dropped off? If everything is satisfactory, you have enjoyed your ride (often evidenced by a silly uncontrollable grin), then it is time to buy the bike.

Making a purchase

I am not a good negotiator. If I am buying a classic bike, the questions I ask myself are of the 'Do I want it and can I afford it?' variety. Only you can determine how much the bike is worth to you. The best price guides in the world are only guides and can only offer an average view; if the bike you are looking at is of special importance to you, for whatever reason, then the price is between you and the vendor. If you are just after an old bike to do up, or to ride until it needs doing up, enter into as tough a bargaining session as you like; only the vendor knows how much the bike is worth to him, and how much money he needs from it.

There are a couple of thoughts I would like you to consider before you part with your money. First: if you want a particular machine and are not short of money, no price is too high. Second: if you don't want a particular machine, no price is low enough, so save your money and search elsewhere.

Buying a bike for restoration poses several entertaining challenges of its own. This 1966 Matchless G15CS is a returnee from the US. It is almost complete, very standard, and is missing only seat, wiring harness, exhausts and rear mudguard. A sound basis for an interesting restoration project.

There may be a quantity of spares to go with the bike itself. Only you know whether you wish to house them. You may be able to sell them, especially if they are valuable and useful, but remember that it seems to be a universal truth that the same parts always wear out on a particular model of motorcycle, and that none of the spares offered with it will be the parts that wear out.

It is also often good to bear in mind that the person selling the bike could well be a source of spares, enthusiasm and helpful contacts for the new owner, so it may not be a sound policy to make endless insulting offers . . .

If you are buying a machine from a dealer, it would be sensible to ask for a warranty. You may not be offered one, and whether this is acceptable to you only you can tell. I would always ask that the dealer service the bike before I collect it, as part of the purchase price, and that he correct any deficiencies that your examination and test ride have highlighted. If he refuses, well . . . there is always another day, another bike.

If you are buying a bike from a private individual, always check that he is indeed the owner of the bike, ie that his name and address appear on the V5 registration document. Buying a bike from someone who claims to be selling it for a friend may not be sensible, for obvious reasons.

If you are buying a motorcycle

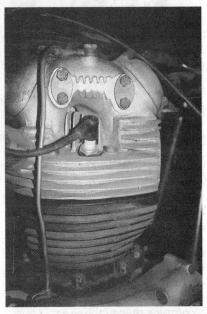

Top: *The engine number has not been messed with, and matches . . .*

Middle, left: *. . . the frame number.*

Middle, right: *The engine's fastening shows no 'witness marks'. In other words, they have never been undone.*

Bottom: *Even the exhaust port threads – always a problem area on Norton twin engines – are perfect.*

What it is all about – fine bikes, a fine sunny afternoon and a friend to ride with. Classic motorcycling indeed.

for a restoration project, a lot of the foregoing may not apply to you. Only you will be aware of the levels of your own competence in the various skills required to refurbish a complex machine like a motorcycle, and only you will know just how big a wreck you can realistically hope to restore. Please remember that the pages of the old bike press are packed with failed projects, and that the reason for the failure of that project is all too often a terminal attack of over-optimism at the point of purchase.

Restoring an old motorcycle can be a serious financial and emotional drain – although the rewards can be very high. If you are contemplating the purchase of someone else's failed project, find out why they failed. It may simply be that they have run out of funds and/or enthusiasm. It may be that a particularly vital spare is utterly unobtainable and they lack the skills or contacts to make the parts themselves. It may be that they have only realised post-purchase that the whole thing is a pile of scrap that they are anxious to unload upon some other sad soul before they bankrupt themselves. Do not become the latter person. Please remember, it always pays to buy carefully.

Chapter 5

Ariel

The famous name of Ariel was out there in the marketplace right from the very beginning. In fact, the name appeared on several examples of the wide range of push-bikes that predated the motorcycle industry in their home town of Birmingham, and the original Ariel Cycle Company, which was formed in 1897, was owned by Dunlop, who used the Ariel name in an attempt to distinguish between their tyre and cycle interests. That concern was bought in 1897 by another, Cycle Components (and you get no prizes for identifying their products), who used the Ariel label on one of their first powered vehicles, a tricycle, in 1898. There is a certain sad irony here, for the very last vehicle to bear the illustrious and fairly ancient name of Ariel was also a tricycle. That was in 1970, and the Ariel label had appeared on a uniquely varied range of powered two-wheelers in the intervening decades.

By the end of the Second World War, and the arrival of the 'classic' period so far as we are concerned here, the Ariel company found itself part of the giant BSA Group, having been sold to that vast and impressive conglomerate during 1944. Ariel continued to operate from its home base at Selly Oak in Birmingham – and in fact there had been a rare strike of the Ariel workforce when the

This section of the book is devoted to a highly opinionated (but hopefully fairly accurate from historical and technical aspects) overview of the major players on the British motorcycle scene during the 'classic' period. For the sake of simplicity I shall regard the classic period as being post-war, and for the sake of space the major players are limited to AJS and Matchless, Ariel, BSA, Norton and Triumph. Towards the end you will find a consideration of some of the other marques: Vincent, Velocette, Royal Enfield, Panther and Sunbeam.

I have attempted to provide a brief history of each marque as it struggled towards oblivion after the Second World War, and have mentioned a couple of personal favourite motorcycles from each of the manufacturers' ranges. Several years spent working as a scribbler in the classic bike magazine world has provided me with the opportunity for gaining the acquaintance of large numbers of motorcycles – motorcy-

cles fairly ancient and fairly modern, and motorcycles variously good, bad and indifferent – and it is from this range of riding experience that I have selected the bikes included on these pages.

Naturally, being a democratic sort of soul I have discussed my choices with friends and fellow writers, and several original selections have been changed as a result. I should express my gratitude to Jim Reynolds, Dave Minton, Steve Wilson, Rowena Hoseason, Claire Leavey and Julian Ryder at this point for their occasionally constructive remarks.

For anyone interested in the reasoning behind my decision to omit some manufacturers, such as Hesketh, entirely, I can only claim a completely personal bias. I have attempted to devote space in these pages to those machines that are the most popular on the roads in the closing years of the 20th century. The way I have done this is by reading through all the ads in all of the classic press – all the private ads, that is.

BSA takeover was announced, a strike that was lifted only when it was confirmed by the new owners that production would remain for the foreseeable future at Ariel's long-time Selly Oak factory. This was surely only common sense, as the Ariel range was a strong one and the product identity (if you like modern

marketing-speak) was very well defined.

Once the upheavals of wartime production requirements had settled down into the supposedly less chaotic ways of the new peace, the range of machines offered for sale became truly impressive. Although considered by many in the modern-day classic scene to be one of the less imposing of the major marques – for no apparent reason beyond the fact that their range of sturdy four-strokes went out of production in 1959 – Ariel featured a wider range of models in their post-war catalogue than almost anyone else.

The Four-stroke Heavyweights

Ariel's four-stroke models were almost always intended to be good, sound machines, ruggedly constructed and capable of high mileages without requiring too much in the way of unplanned attention. Their traditional post-war finish was generally in either a most attractive shade of deep red or in black, and they were not given over to flashy paint schemes or to an excess of chrome plating and exaggerated claims of high performance. Ariels were entered for competition while the company was under BSA ownership, but that competition was largely based around the off-road rather than the road-race arena. In short, Ariel motorcycles projected a 'working' rather than a glamour image, and their advertising was based around some mysterious horsy concept, featuring lots of equine imagery and a very stylised logo in which the 'A' of Ariel was worked rather unconvincingly into a contrived rendition of a horse's head.

If one of the strengths of the Ariel marque was the sturdiness of their machines, another lay in the range of machinery they offered. I shall make only a passing mention of the 200cc Colt lightweight, largely because it is too feeble to be of much practical use on the modern-day road, and also because it is

a pretty rare bird these days. The heavyweight range encompassed not only the industry standard four-stroke singles (both side- and overhead-valve) and twins, but it also contained the unique 1000cc Square Four figurehead, a splendid machine with its four cylinders arranged – not entirely surprisingly, given the model name – in a square. A wide range indeed.

The bicycle

The company followed the conventional chassis progression in moving away from the rigid frame and girder fork arrangements of pre-war days, but developed their very own version of the plunger rear suspension that so often fitted uncomfortably between the rigid and swinging arm frames. The unique Ariel way of grafting some sort of limited rear wheel movement on to what was basically still a rigid frame design was the invention and use of a device known as the 'Anstey Link' (after its inventor Frank Anstey), a device that was recognised as being an attempt at something a little more elegant than simply stitching a set of springs between the rear wheel spindle and the main frame, which is what several other companies, including Ariel's

BSA parent, did, but which was too easily let down by inadequate maintenance.

In brief, the increased performance of motorcycles brought with it a need for improved roadholding, and improved suspension of both wheels was identified as being highly desirable. As well as providing race-proven enhancements of a bike's roadholding, improved suspension brought other benefits, not least that the ride for the pilot was much enhanced, and the battering endured by the bike's more delicate components, such as the electrics, could be considerably reduced. The snag was that many companies had stocks of the older rigid frames and wished to use them up before retooling and offering the buyer a full swinging arm frame.

Ariel had introduced their first sprung rear end on the Square Four machine in 1939, and it spread across the rest of the range until the appearance of the swinging arm frame in 1954. Unlike other manufacturers, however, Ariel had decided to tackle the problem of varying rear drive chain tension that accompanies the fitting of plunger-type rear springing, but unlike some German companies they did not manage terribly effectively.

Chain tension is a problem when the rear wheel moves up and down

Post-war, the Ariel's frame (seen here on a 1952 VH 500cc single) implemented an unusual form of rear springing. The Anstey Link was crude and largely ineffective.

vertically in a straight line. If you think for a second, you will see that the tension of the chain is increased by moving the rear wheel away from the gearbox (this is what you do when you adjust the final drive chain, after all), and to keep the distances between the rear wheel and the gearbox constant while allowing the wheel some vertical movement requires that the wheel moves not in a straight line but in an arc. Ariel's complex rear link allowed this to a limited extent, and chain stretching was kept to a minimum. Sadly, the link depended upon three pivots on each side of the wheel, and all of these pivots could wear rapidly and at different rates, allowing a certain amount of apparently random movement of the wheel to take place, depending upon just how worn were the sundry pivots at any one time. A badly worn rear link is not a delight to experience, especially when attempting to ride hard around a bumpy road, when the rear wheel can behave in a truly unsettling manner. If you are buying a machine that features this springing, it would be a good idea to check both sides for slop – unless you enjoy low-speed excitement, of course.

At the other end of the bicycle, the approach adopted by Ariel's gifted designer, Val Page, set the standard for the rest of the BSA group. The Ariel telescopic front fork was announced in 1946 and was used not only across the Ariel range, but also on most BSA models and the Sunbeam stablemate's in-line twins.

As an aside, the Ariel company were never afraid to experiment, and in 1953 they showed several of their models equipped with Earles-type leading link front suspension. They never put this alternative form of fork into production (although it was actually catalogued), but at least it showed that creative thinking was alive and well at Selly Oak.

Should you be seeking out an early post-war Ariel, I would sug-

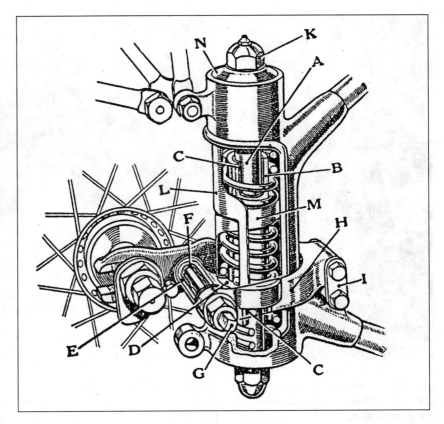

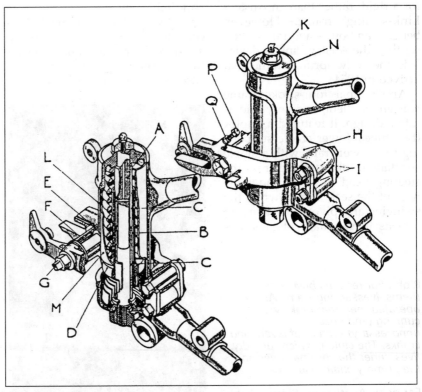

The Anstey Link itself. The shackle (H) held the wheel spindle and allowed it to move against the springs that were fixed to the main frame. When wear occurred the handling could become lively . . .

Left: *Ariel brakes were competent rather than good. This single-sided device struggled to cope with the power and the weight of the 650 Huntmaster.*

Above: *The later full-width drum, here fitted to a 1959 VH 500cc single, was a great improvement over earlier devices.*

gest that if you enjoy riding your chosen machine up to the limits of its performance you should look for a rigid, rather than an Anstey-Link-sprung frame. However, better than both – and far, far better than the Anstey-Linked device – is the fully sprung frame that arrived in 1954.

Ariel's final four-stroke frame was an excellent, and very under-rated, design. It featured a duplex (two tubes) lower cradle support-ing the power train, with a single substantial tube running from the steering head to a lug under the nose of the seat, then down to the swinging arm pivot. The swinging arm itself was made of pressings

welded into a box-section, rather than from tubes as was more often the case, and the whole thing handled very well indeed. It even featured one of the better-considered and stable (if easily grounded) centre stands of the time. This frame provided the basic bicycle for all of the roadster

singles and twins until the demise of the four-stroke range in 1959. It comes recommended.

Ariel brakes, however, come with less of an unreserved state-ment of approval. The single-sided front stopper that was fitted up until the arrival of the full-width hubs in 1956 was adequate – but

Right: *For reasons best known to themselves, spring-frame Ariels operated their rear brake via a cunning (and possibly unnecessary) system of levers and cranks. The clutch, which runs dry, lives under the chrome cover on the primary chaincase.*

Far right: *Another neat touch is the full enclosure of the rear chain. Restorers' note: these are now available only in fibreglass.*

The spring-frame singles, like this 1956 VH 500, were a great improvement over the Anstey Link models.

only just – for the weight and performance offered by the twins, and although the full-width alloy item offered thereafter was better, and was also used on several BSA models, it is only just about up to coping with modern traffic conditions.

Throughout their post-war production life, Ariel motorcycles used a four-speed gearbox supplied to their specification by the Burman company. They were not alone in this, and spares for these boxes, while not exactly available from your friendly local bike dealer, are not entirely impossible to find. The Burman box is very reliable in normal use, is very robust and has a slightly slow but dependable change.

The primary drive to the gearbox is by a single-row chain to a dry multi-plate clutch, which lives under a chromed steel cover in its very own oil-free compartment in Ariel's most handsome primary chaincase. Like the gearbox, the clutch is a fairly strong device and should give little trouble over many, many miles with little maintenance. Lousy clutch action can usually be traced either to seriously worn-out clutch plates or to wear and damage to the tongues on the plates that engage with either the clutch hub or the basket. New-pattern plates for these clutches should not pose too much of a sourcing problem for the committed Arielist, and sticklers for originality should be able to find corks to re-line the original plates if they so desire.

The single-cylinder models

After the war Ariel offered their customers a traditional British choice of singles: the 350cc NH, the 500cc VH and the 600cc side-valve VB. They also initially offered de-luxe versions of the ohv models, coded NG and VG, but dropped that idea in 1950, prior to a fairly radical redesign of the engines' camshafts. In the new design, the original pair of cam lobes was replaced by a single very wide cam, in an elegant piece of work intended to cut both wear and cost.

Apart from this unusual feature, the design of the Ariel single engine was conventional for the time, and remains easy to ride and easy to repair should the need arise. There is simple pushrod operation of the two valves, carburation is provided by Amal, and electrical functions are shared between the two halves of the Lucas Magdyno, drive to which is by a single-strand chain powered off the camshaft. The oil pump is a fairly dependable twin-plunger design that will be familiar to all fans of the Triumph twin, and which is also driven by the camshaft.

Nice rider touches include an access hole for the valve clearances built into the rocker boxes from 1955 onward, and the leak-free cast-in pushrod tunnels in the 500 from 1955 and the 350 from a year later. An unusual and slightly interesting variant that lasted for just the one full year was the VHA, which was essentially the normal VH but with a competition-type alloy barrel, with integral pushrod tubes. Probably in a successful attempt to confuse Ariel historians of the future, Ariel named this alloy oddity the Hunt Marshall, as opposed to the more commonly accepted title of Red Hunter for the run-of-the-mill roadster singles.

On the road

Performance of the roadster singles was about par for their time too; the 350s accelerate as well as you would expect with around 15–18bhp to propel around 350lb plus rider, and they cruise comfortably at 60mph or thereabouts. The 500 single pushes out perhaps 5bhp more, so is a little brisker off the mark and should cruise realistically in the high 60s. As discussed earlier, the steering of the duplex swinging arm frame models is exemplary, the bikes are comfortable for both rider and

Photo: *Bob Clarke*

Above and opposite: *The final form of the single was the 1958/59 VH 500, and by the time this bike appeared the Ariel was a pretty viceless motorcycle. Its engine was perfectly complemented by one of the better bicycles of the period, and in handsome maroon paint contrasted with a tan saddle it remains distinctive to this day.*

pillion, and are reliable with it. Lovely details abound on Ariels, and they come recommended.

In my view, the best Ariel single to own would be the last of the 500cc VH line, the final version built from 1957 until the end of the four-strokes in 1959.

But what of the side-valver – the VB? The VB was intended entirely for the sidecar pilot, a breed of rider who apparently preferred to sit out in the elements away from – but close to – the rest of his chair-bound family rather than enduring the many supposed delights of the increasingly popular small car. The VB was not a bad example of the side-valve single, and in its later alloy-headed form it produced around 17bhp at 4,000rpm, making it capable of

Middle: *People still do remarkable things with the robust Ariel single engine. These bikes are sprinters, in an ancient tradition.*

Bottom: *A 1951 350 Red Hunter; at this time the Ariel was still available with a rigid frame. But only just.*

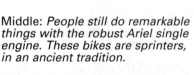

powering an outfit along at a happy 45mph. If this suits you, consider one, although you should remember that the Ariel design shared the common side-valve failing of over-heating when worked hard, and that spares for the Ariel, like its Norton equivalent, are not as common as they are for BSA's M20. It would be hard to recommend that anyone should buy a side-valve for use in modern traffic, but there is little wrong with this one if the fancy takes you.

The twin-cylinder models

The first twin to appear in the post-war Ariel range was their own Val Page-designed 500cc KH (Fieldmaster or Red Hunter, depending upon which trim option the buyer chose). As with the alloy-engined single, the VHA, there was a similar single-season oddity with a similar twin-bored alloy block typed as the KHA (which could be bought unusually finished in a fetching shade of Wedgwood Blue).

Page's twin had a pair of camshafts (inlet behind the block, exhaust in front of it) with the pushrods situated at the four corners of the block. Otherwise the design was conventional, with both pistons rising and falling together, drive to the camshafts by duplex chain, an oil pump at home in the sump, and with sparks from a magneto (either Lucas or BTH) situated behind the block with DC

Top: *By the end of the four-stroke line in 1959, Ariel's working single was looking dated but was still handsome enough.*

Middle: *Ariel's side-valve single, the VB, was a worthy but rather dull machine.*

Bottom: *Ariel's first twin, known variously as the 'Twin', 'Ariel Twin', 'KH' and 'Fieldmaster', was a slightly unusual interpretation of the standard British twin layout.*

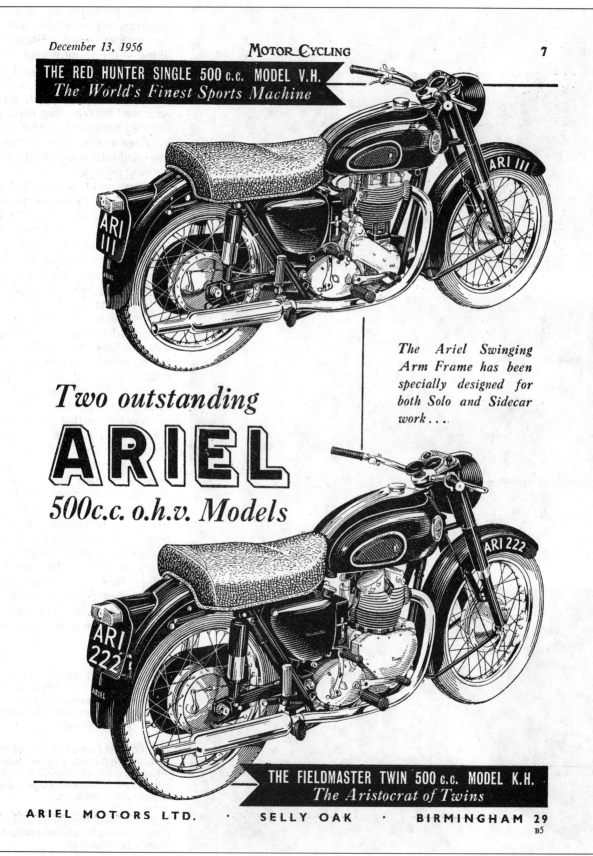

December 13, 1956   MOTOR CYCLING   7

THE RED HUNTER SINGLE 500 c.c. MODEL V.H.
The World's Finest Sports Machine

The Ariel Swinging Arm Frame has been specially designed for both Solo and Sidecar work . . .

Two outstanding

ARIEL

500 c.c. o.h.v. Models

THE FIELDMASTER TWIN 500 c.c. MODEL K.H.
The Aristocrat of Twins

ARIEL MOTORS LTD.   ·   **SELLY OAK**   ·   **BIRMINGHAM 29**
B5

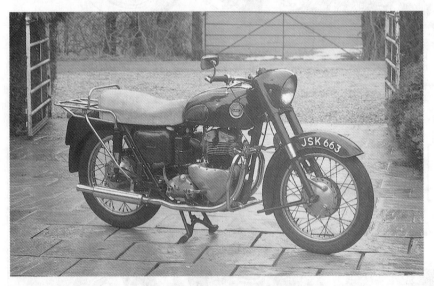

current provided by a dynamo mounted in front of the block. One feature that I must confess to disliking is the slightly mad method of fixing the cylinder head to the block by using short, downward-pointing studs that locate and are anchored by nuts that need to be inserted between the cylinder fins. Val Page was not alone in choosing this method, so my dislike of it is nothing personal.

Apart from this small quirk, the KH engine is pleasant from the rider's point of view, if notably vibratory when stretched. There was little development, apart from detailing, and it gained the swinging arm frame with the other roadsters in 1954, along with an alloy cylinder head. The 500 twin met its demise in 1957, and is a little hard to judge as a modern-day working mount. It has few faults, apart from vibration and a tendency to leak oil, which is a result of the curious head fixing arrangement already mentioned, but few virtues that are not present to a greater degree in its bigger brother, the 650cc FH Huntmaster.

The Huntmaster was the last new four-stroke Ariel to be introduced (apart from the odious Pixie, and we will ignore that), and was actually powered by a cunningly disguised BSA A10 engine mated to Ariel's transmission. Many are those who would consider that the marriage of BSA-designed engine with Ariel bicycle was made in heaven, and I am one of them, having covered

Top: *This is a 1955 version of Ariel's homegrown 500 twin. By this time it boasted the fine swinging arm bicycle and a smart alloy cylinder head.*

Middle: *1957 saw the end of Ariel's homegrown twin, and although all Ariels are worth consideration, this one has a recommendation and a charm all of its own.*

Bottom: *View from the saddle. Ariel's neat and stylish cockpit – the rider's perspective.*

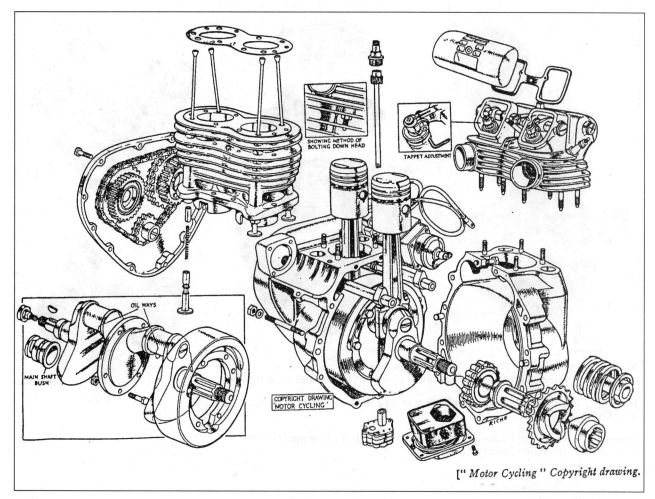

Exploded diagram of 500 twin engine. (Copyright Motor Cycling *1955)*

very many miles on just such a machine in the early 1970s.

The disguise of BSA's Hopwood-designed twin engine was neat. It comprised a re-styled timing chest, with the legend 'Six Twin Fifty' emblazoned on its cover, and a much more sensible set of rocker boxes than BSA ever fitted. This engine differed from Ariel's own design in having just a single camshaft mounted behind the block, and a complex timing chest arrangement, where the chain drive to the dynamo lived in its own grease-filled compartment outside the one where the oil-lubed timing gears were to be found. Its oil pump was of a gear type and was to be found at the base of the timing chest. Unlike the

500 twin, the 650 never gained an alloy cylinder head (although you may find one that has later BSA components, including an alloy head, grafted on by a previous proud owner).

Thus, although almost all of the internal components of the Huntmaster are interchangeable with the BSA A10, all of the major castings (head, barrel, crankcases) are different.

The 650 twin – the FH Huntmaster. Although the engine was a disguised version of BSA's A10, its character was, strangely, wholly Ariel. It also suited the Ariel bicycle very well.

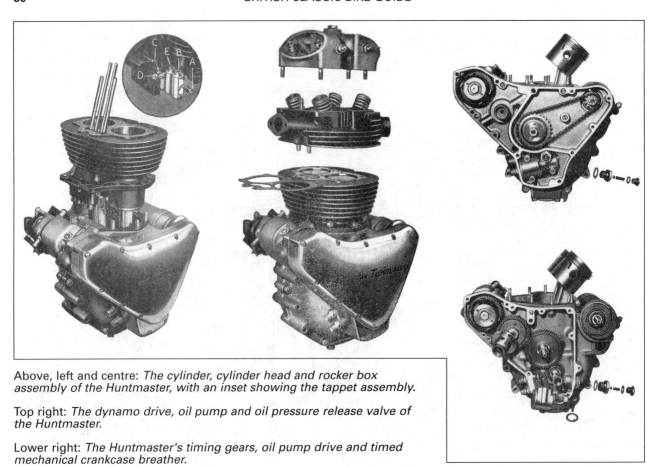

Above, left and centre: *The cylinder, cylinder head and rocker box assembly of the Huntmaster, with an inset showing the tappet assembly.*

Top right: *The dynamo drive, oil pump and oil pressure release valve of the Huntmaster.*

Lower right: *The Huntmaster's timing gears, oil pump drive and timed mechanical crankcase breather.*

Left: *Although the engine was based on a BSA design, surprisingly few parts are interchangeable. Ariel's 650 twin utilised the Ariel primary drive, drive clutch and Burman gearbox.*

Below: *Although one classic publication once claimed that there were only 20 Huntmasters left in the world, there are rather more than that. This 1959 model was in regular use when photographed at Oulton Park.*

The Square Four: four cylinders, two crankshafts. Is this really the ultimate British twin?

The 650 engine suited the Ariel bicycle very well indeed, and complemented the range perfectly, with a power output of around 35bhp permitting a top speed of (just) over the magic 100 mark when new, and a cruise in the region of 70mph. Vibration could be a concern, but the iron-head engine was tractable and reliable, and shared the good handling and comfort of the rest of the range. Like the rest of the four-stroke range, its production finished in 1959, and again like the others a good example is a good buy indeed, and one that is eminently suited to real riding by a modern-day classic rider.

The Square Four

Most folk are at least slightly logical. In other words, their thought processes tend to move in straight lines: if this happens, then this will follow, and so forth. It would perhaps be logical, therefore, to think that the designer of the world's most popular parallel twin motorcycle engine, flushed with the success of his creation, would consider doubling the thing up, so producing what is in effect two parallel twin engines, one behind the other, and able to use the rest of the power train and bicycle. A little judicious strengthening and lengthening might be necessary perhaps, but you get the idea.

Oddly, it all happened the other way around. Ariel employed a gifted designer back in the late 1920s, by the name of Edward Turner, and Edward Turner sketched out the idea of an engine

Early versions like this 1950 Mk 1 had a reputation for overheating the rear cylinders. Treated gently, however, they make fine riding machines to this day.

with its four cylinders arranged in a square, rather than in a vee or in a line, as would be more conventional. The story goes that his sketch was done on the back of a cigarette packet in the very best *Boys' Own* tradition, but who knows . . .

Turner's original engine displaced 497cc and opened its valves via an overhead camshaft. The version of the machine that concerns us here, however, in our sampling of post-war machinery, had grown to a full litre (well, all right, 997cc) and the valves were prodded by pushrods, but the

principle of the beast remained the same: four cylinders arranged in a square, twin crankshafts, great torque and considerable smoothness.

The post-war Square Four, or Squariel, to give it its common name, did not share the otherwise common bicycle of the other Ariel heavyweights. However, in common with other models, the Squariel recommended peacetime production with a rigid rear frame and girder front forks. By 1949 the four had gained civilised suspension at both ends, and although the engine was developed further,

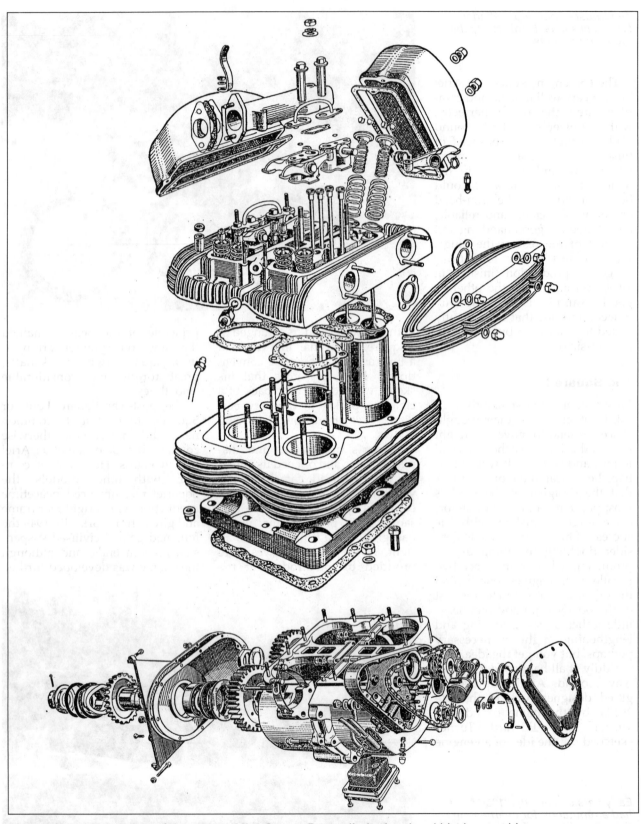

Above: *An exploded view of the 1,000cc Mk 2 Square Four cylinder head and block assembly.*

Below: *The bottom half of the Mk 2's engine.*

The end of an era. Ariel's big Four left the shops in 1959, and there was no new British 'four' for over 30 years.

as we shall see, the bicycle remained much the same until production of the only British post-war four-cylinder four-stroke before the modern Hinckley Triumphs ceased in 1959.

Rear suspension remained in the unique Anstey Link form, sadly, and although a prototype was built Ariel never produced a swinging arm version of their flagship. The arguments at the time concerned its perceived role as a sidecar tug extraordinary, but that sounds like a poor excuse. Several enthusiasts have built their own versions of the 'Four that never was', and all appear to be delighted with the result.

On the road

The Square Four is one of the most charismatic British bikes built after the great leveller that was the Second World War. A good ride on a good example reveals the gentle and forgiving nature of the big engine. The litre motor pulls very well from almost any speed, and in fact it is perfectly possible to pull away fairly smoothly in top gear alone. The top speed was never as high as might have been expected from an engine of this capacity, and indeed Ariel did not advertise the bike with the sporting pretensions of the other litre bike from Vincent. They instead depicted tweedy and immaculate young things piloting their Squariel through a field of bemused lambs, in one particularly mystifying advert; the sad fact is that the lambs would have run a mile at the sound of an approaching Four. Not that the exhaust was particularly noisy by the standards of the time – it wasn't – but the clattering of even a low-mileage engine was enough to give ample warning of your approach.

The big Four's steering was a source of involvement, too. No effortless featherbed this one, but a steady bike all the same. The machine's lengthy wheelbase and low-slung weight helped it negotiate long, fast sweeping curves with some aplomb, but at the same time those same features stopped it being the most flickable of models through tight corners. And as with the rest of the range, the experience of a well-worn rear suspension could be a speech-loosening one.

The best version of the Squariel is, I would argue again, the very last. In 1953 a 'Mk 2' version was offered, with the big engine's inherent cooling problems finally addressed by the inclusion of not only an alloy head and barrel, but by a redesign of the cylinder head to incorporate two exhausts on each side. One of the reasons for the Square Four's relatively low power output was the difficulty of effectively cooling the block, and overheating traditionally went hand in glove with oil leaks, flange distortion and blowing head gaskets.

The final version also featured a full-width alloy front brake, an oil tank of giant but distinctive dimensions, which contained a full gallon of lubricant (to aid that cooling again), and one of the most handsome styling jobs carried out on a British motorcycle.

Its braking could still be a little marginal, its handling was never the very best, and the chorus from the engine would awaken the most deaf of heavy sleepers, but the Ariel Square Four is still one of the greatest British Motorcycles. Ride one and see what I mean.

If you try to live with one, and decide to use it long and often, you will find that you have a rather special motorcycle, and one for which spares are less than easy to obtain. Join the excellent Ariel Owners Motorcycle Club before you buy, speak to lots of owners, and contemplate your finances. Then buy one anyway!

The Two-strokes

When Ariel – by that time part of the BSA Group – decided to launch a whole new range of motorcycles based around a two-stroke engine, they were being rather more brave than is probably apparent to the modern-day reader. In the mid-1950s two-stroke meant BSA Bantam, James and Francis-Barnett – in short, it meant the sort of machines used by tens of thousands of workaday commuters to get to and from factory life. The Ariel vision was finer than that.

The company had a vision of a more or less single-model range, and proposed to close down production of their entire established

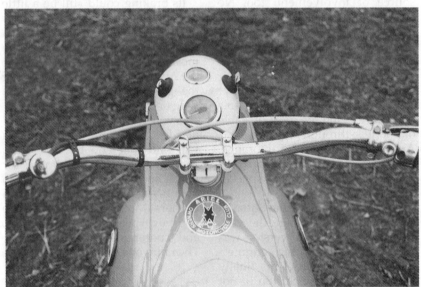

range of four-stroke singles, twins and fours, to concentrate instead upon a whole new generation of machines, based around a common chassis and engine. Brave stuff indeed!

The story goes that Ariel conducted market research (which was presumably less reliable then than now) and canvassed public opinion regarding the sort of motorcycle they wanted to ride in the future. The answer, apparently, was that Everyman wished to ride a two-stroke 250 twin. Armed with this information, Ariel set about developing the bikes that were to become their swan-song (discounting BSA Group nomenclature follies in their later years, of course): the Ariel Leader and Arrow.

The bicycle

The use of a two-stroke engine to power the new range was not the only brave decision taken by Ariel when considering their new model. They also decided that they would do away with conventional cycle parts as they were known and loved in this country, replacing the sundry lugs and tubes with pressed steel box sections from which the power train and suspension systems would be hung. There were several reasons for this, notably those of cost, and, less obviously, convention – but not convention from within the British motorcycle industry. The car world had been building vehicles from assemblies of pressed steel components for some time, and the engineering advantages were obvious, so why should

Top: *Ariel's new look for the New Era of the 1960s was the 250cc Leader.*

Middle: *Pilot's view, Ariel Leader.*

Bottom: *Although dilapidated now, this weary Leader is almost all there and should make a challenging restoration.*

bikes not be built in the same way? There is no reason, of course, as Honda have shown us with every step-thru they have built.

The bicycle itself is an assembly of pressings, eight main ones and sundry smaller ones, making up the chassis, the legshields, the dummy petrol tank (the real fuel tank is the box section below the seat), the rear chain enclosure, the mudguards and even the fork legs, because even the front suspension was unconventional by British standards, using a trailing link format instead of the more usual telescopic effort. Trailing link suspension is no great mystery, and is exactly what its name suggests: the wheel spindle is carried at the end of a link that pivots from its mounting at the front end of the 'fork leg' assembly. Damping was controlled by using Armstrong telescopic dampers, and – joy of joys – the device worked well, blessing the Leader with excellent handling and fine steering.

Improved technology was also evident in the use of die-castings in the engine, at a time when most of the rest of the industry used sand castings. There is no space here for a discussion of the relative merits of the different casting techniques; suffice it to say that the advantages of die casting over sand casting are many, although the initial tooling cost is a lot higher. The same argument holds for the use of pressed steel for the bicycle; individual pressings are cheap once they are being produced by the thousand, but the initial tooling cost is high.

All of this fine and forward-looking engineering was recognised by the enthusiast public, and the Leader won the *Motor Cycle News* 'Machine Of The Year' competition in its first year, 1959. As ever, a rapturous response from newspaper-reading enthusiasts does not guarantee sales, and the adventurous two-stroke range only lasted until 1964, by the end of which year it had faded away. That was a shame, because given the profits that follow a decent level of sales, it is likely that Ariel would have been able to avoid complete absorbtion by their masters at BSA, and may have been able to further develop the 700cc four-stroke four-cylinder prototype based around the Leader's design that they had been working on.

The Leader

The Ariel Leader was announced in July 1958, and was a major sensation. For a start, there was no other British-built motorcycle that was as up-to-the-minute as the new Ariel, and since the demise of the Vincent Black Prince there had been no machine designed to be sold with complete rider weather protection and engine enclosure as standard. The Leader was a radical piece of concept and design from an industry that was all too often locked in tradition, and because of this deserves a special place in the history of the British motorcycle industry.

Viewed from the point of view of the modern rider, the Ariel is in many ways an attractive proposition – especially for someone who has no wish to ride very fast. The reason for this is simple; the Leader is pretty slow for today's road conditions. The 247cc two-stroke twin engine with its 16bhp may have been OK for the roads of the late 1950s, but on the congested main roads of the '90s it struggles a little to keep up with the flow. Having said that, the engine is willing enough, and is pleasant to use at its comfortable cruising speeds (45–55mph). The brakes and lighting are also adequate for the engine's performance, but again, judged by modern standards, both are less than wonderful, and indeed on my last night ride on a Leader I rode for over an hour on country A roads, along with a fair amount of traffic, and discovered only at the end of my journey that I had left the headlight set on main beam for the whole ride. No one coming the other way had flashed at me in irritation, probably because they had not realised that I was using main beam!

Having said that, the Leader is very pleasant, and boasts a host of extras, from wind-up clock, via styled panniers, indicators and mirrors, to bumper bars, thus offering a whole world of happy autojumble scouring for the committed Leader-rider.

Stripped of its panelling and tourist's paraphernalia, the Leader became the Arrow.

That so few Leaders are seen on the roads today, even at gatherings of classic riders, must be down to their less than sparkling performance, because in every other way they are ideal for someone interested in the club-run side of old biking.

Modern-day problems with the bikes are restricted to a shortage of original spares, particularly of the steel pressings that were used to such great effect in their construction. The main box section chassis of the bike is very strong, but the supporting bracketry can suffer from corrosion if the machine has been left standing for a long time in adverse conditions, and if you have any doubt about the chassis's integrity – if, for instance, there is serious accident damage, think seriously about acquiring a spare one before you purchase the bike.

Unusually, even the seat can rot prematurely because its base is made from plywood, which tends to be ravaged by water retained by the foam of the cushion.

Your choice of tyres will also be limited, as not every manufacturer offers 16-inch covers in the appropriate sizes. Carburettor and electrical ancillaries are by Amal and Lucas, and should be fairly available, even now.

The Arrow

After the Leader, which in common with just about every 'bike for everyman' prior to the Honda C90 was appreciated by the whole world but bought by relatively few, Ariel ditched all the features of their stroker twin that appeal to this particular writer, and turned it into the Arrow. Discarded were the full fairing and its fine screen, the rear skirts with their sensible pannier pick-ups, and the tin cladding that hid the unremarkable engine. Happily, Ariel retained the full rear chain enclosure.

What the Arrow offered was what was left after the asset-stripping exercise, and perhaps oddly – because to my eyes at least, the Arrow looks odd – it was pretty popular with the 250 buyers of the day. It pays to remember that a two-stroke twin always sounds and feels faster than an equivalent four-stroke, and also that learner riders back then could learn to ride aboard a 250.

In performance terms, the Arrow gained over its better-dressed stablemate by having a rather better power-to-weight ratio, and could consequently accelerate and cruise at a slightly higher rate. The handling also gained by the weight reduction, although things could become a little bouncy at higher speeds (don't get excited, we're talking about 65mph here).

Design changes to both Arrow and Leader were of the detail, rather than the fundamental, variety throughout the bikes' production runs, although the Arrow was joined by two slightly developed versions before it was discontinued. The two variants were the 'Super Sports' model, which was far more commonly known as the Golden Arrow – because it was an Arrow, and it was painted gold – and the Arrow 200. Originality in naming models was plainly not an Ariel strong-point, as the Arrow 200 was an Arrow with a 200cc version of the engine, and it was aimed at filling a gap in the insurance classes.

Both of these bikes offer a riding experience that is different from the UK norm of the time. I can think of no good reason apart from nostalgia for buying an Arrow for the roads of the '90s, but the Leader has a lot to recommend it.

Chapter 6

AJS and Matchless

For the sake of this book, almost all of the motorcycles bearing the once-revered names of AJS and Matchless upon their petrol tanks can be considered in the same chapter – because they are essentially the same motorcycles. The highly respected Wolverhampton-based AJS marque was acquired by the London-based Matchless concern before the Second World War, and by the time the 1950s arrived the bikes themselves were pretty much identical. The combined company was known as Associated Motorcycles Ltd (AMC for short) and their AJS/Matchless ranges were good examples of badge engineering in its truest sense.

Prior to their takeover by Matchless's Collier Brothers, the AJS marque had produced some truly fine machinery, winning TT and trials alike with motorcycles that ranged from conventional four-stroke singles to a supercharged water-cooled four. Unusually, AJS also built other items, including a light car, bus chassis and radios! They were an interesting concern indeed.

By the time of the arrival of the classic period, the AMC company also owned the Norton, Francis-Barnett and James marques, but never badge engineered them to the same extent as they had AJS and Matchless. Luckily, perhaps. There was a sensible amount of commonality of parts between the marques where their capacity ranges overlapped, but until the arrival of the AJS/Matchless/Norton 750 'hybrids' in the mid-'60s, the Norton marque was easily distinguished from AJS and Matchless.

I shall write here about the AJS range, and where there is a direct Matchless equivalent (which is usually the case) I shall note the model designation in brackets. In case we both become confused by this, Matchless model names have a 'G' prefix, while AJS models are referred to as . . . Models.

All AJS machines, up to the final demise of the AMC group in 1966, were four-strokes of sound, if conventional, design. AMC machinery was generally held to be robust and reliable enough by the standards of the day, and the company won a good reputation for their competition machinery. Unlike most of their competitors, AMC built and sold pure-bred racing machines, in the stylish shapes of the 350cc AJS 7R 'Boys Racer', its grown-up 500cc Matchless cousin, the G50 (both of them ohc singles), the 500cc Matchless G45, which was essentially a G50 with a roadster-derived twin-cylinder pushrod engine), and the Manx Norton, in both 350 and 500cc forms.

It is, sadly, way beyond the scope of this book to include buying advice for any pure racing machinery, but AMC deserve an honourable mention for taking the time and trouble to market properly developed racers, rather than warmed-over roadsters. If you read a history book or two, it is sobering to discover exactly how many post-war British road-race heroes started out aboard AJS, Matchless or Norton race bikes.

However, AJS and Matchless were also extremely successful at off-road competition, and the machines they campaigned were rather more roadster-derived than were their racetrack equivalents, which had both engines and bicycles of their own. As major rivals BSA achieved greatness when they transformed the extremely humdrum B33 into the salivatory DBD34 Gold Star, so it was when AJS developed their equivalent cooking model, the 18S, into the stump-pulling 18CS scrambler. Like BSA, AJS offered their off-road competition machinery for public consumption, so we will make at least a passing mention where appropriate.

Following the demise of the AMC parent company, the rights to the AJS and Matchless marques, along with Norton and the AMC two-stroke collection, were acquired by Manganese Bronze Holdings, a company with ambitions to become the dominant force in the British motorcycle manufacturing scene. They intended to achieve this by launching a new model (which would become the Norton Commando, of which much more later), but in order to preserve a cashflow while the new machine was under development, it made perfect sense to keep the old marques alive. While Norton, Matchless and AJS machines continued – in rather confused and truncated ranges, it has to be said – AJS-badged (but Villiers-developed) motorcycles with two-stroke engines were offered to the competition fraternity. Because these bikes are occasionally to be seen advertised today, and because the FB-AJS company is still in business building and selling descendants of these two-strokes, we will include them – if only briefly.

Likewise, one of the more interesting – if only because it achieved production of a sort – Great British revivals of the doldrum decade, or the 1980s if you prefer, was that of the Matchless name. These bikes were built by a company with no connection to AMC, but have a small following of their own to this day and are welcomed into the ranks of the excellent AJS & Matchless Owners' Club. So we will include a few words on buying these oddities, too. But that will be later.

The Four-stroke Lightweights

In common with several other British manufacturers after the war, AJS offered the buying public a wide range of models based closely around a very few basic designs. In the case of AJS, there were 'lightweight' and 'heavyweight' bicycles. In the former range the company offered singles, of either 250 or 350cc capacity, and nothing else. In the 'heavyweight' range the company offered both singles and twins. Both ranges varied both their cosmetics and functional details to provide customers with a selection of models from which they could choose their ideal. This makes a lot of sense in production terms, as the expensive components, such as castings, forgings, pistons, gear clusters and the like, along with entire frames and electrical systems and so forth, could be either manufactured or bought in from outside suppliers in quantities sufficient to justify decent price discounts.

The downside of this concept was that it became increasingly difficult to persuade the customer that he should part with his money for a machine with competition pretensions that clearly derived from a common commuter road bike – a bike that was considerably less expensive into the bargain.

To encourage the customer in his purchase, the factory entered its products up against rough equivalents from other factories in the various forms of motorcycle sport. Unfairly, of course, those other factories insisted upon developing their competition machinery until its capabilities were way beyond those of mere modified roadsters – by the use of exotic metals, for instance, the cost of which could never be justified in production models. So, to continue the persuasion, the true, or 'factory', competition machines in reality bore only a superficial resemblance to the competition machinery that Joseph Punter could buy at his local dealer. For a really fine example of this, compare and contrast Sammy Miller's famous – and superbly developed – Ariel HT trials iron, the immortal GOV 132, with the HT Ariel that was offered for sale to the general public. And taking things to absurdity, when Miller was at his most commanding aboard his four-stroke single, Ariel were building only two-stroke roadster twins!

Anyway, in March 1958 AJS (and Matchless, naturally) launched a range of 'lightweight' single-cylinder four-stroke motorcycles to tempt the palate of the public. I put the word 'lightweight' in inverted commas to emphasise that at a quoted 325lb, the bikes are not in fact particular-

Although largely unloved by modern-day classic enthusiasts, AMC's 'lightweight' singles are in fact reasonable to ride. This is a 1960 350cc AJS Model 8 and its braking is a little marginal.

ly light for 250cc machines, with the AJS Model 18S roadster (the full 500cc heavyweight) weighing in at around 385lb.

Predictably, the two 250cc models, the AJS Model 14 and the Matchless G2, were followed in 1960 by a 350cc version, the AJS Model 8 and the Matchless G5. This surprisingly pleasant motorcycle was no sales success, sadly, and had disappeared from the lists – if not the showrooms – by the time the 1963 range was announced.

The Model 14 and its equivalent Matchless survived, increasingly in alleged sports form, until the collapse of the parent company in mid-1966, when it disappeared finally from the scene.

The lightweight engine

The trend in the mid-1950s, when the AMC lightweight was under development, was to combine the engine's crankcases and the gearbox shell, generally referred to as 'unit' construction. The advantages of this developmental process are many. The number of castings is, fairly obviously, reduced, the need for separate primary chaincases can be designed out, the whole power unit becomes much neater, and there is no further need for the messy and cumbersome assemblage of engine plates and spacers so familiar to those of us who have rebuilt non-unit power trains.

AMC, for reasons best known to themselves (I have read a couple of interviews with AMC engineers who offer justifications for their decisions, but have unearthed no real reasons therein), decided to buck the trend for AJS and simply disguised the fact that the engines were non-unit by clothing crankcase and gearbox with a pair of shiny casings. At a stroke, then, they assured that their 250 engine was less compact than the opposition (mainly from BSA, Triumph and Royal Enfield, although AMC stablemate Norton went about

250cc things differently . . .), they assured that it was less economical to manufacture, and that it was less spanner-friendly. Anyone who has adjusted the AJS lightweight primary chain – by rotating the gearbox – will join me in wondering at the sense of this method of construction. Having said that, at least the primary chain was adjustable; that of BSA's C15 was not . . .

AMC also mounted their oil tank, with a weedy 2.5-pint capacity, on the right-hand crankcase wall, inside the outer engine cover. This was not a great idea, as the already small volume of oil got little chance to cool down before being recirculated; the cooling airstream was kept away from the oil tank by that outer casing.

These minor niggles aside, at least the engine was easy to clean, and was generally well constructed, as were all AMC products.

It was a simple pushrod single-cylinder four-stroke, with both valves operated by a single camshaft. The head was twisted slightly off the centreline of the bike, so the mixture entered via a carburetter pointing at the rider's left thigh, and the spent gas exited via an exhaust pipe slightly to the right of the front downtube. Ignition was by a coil and points system, and the lighting side of things was taken care of by an alternator mounted in the primary chaincase. Oiling was effected by the slightly unusual AMC singles' oil pump, which both revolved and reciprocated. It sounds odd and its operation is laborious to explain, but it worked well enough if high oil pressure was not a priority. The Achilles' heel of this power unit is in fact the responsibility of its oiling system, but the pump itself is reliable enough when correctly assembled.

Primary drive was by a single-strand chain via a conventional wet multi-plate clutch to the four-speed gearbox. As mentioned earlier, the gears were carried in a

cylindrical casting, which could be rotated in the straps that retained it to adjust the primary chain. Again, although this way of doing things shows some eccentricity of thought, the gearbox's problems arise from its oiling, rather then from its non-unit construction.

The engine was peppy enough for the time, and when it was stretched from 250 to 350cc, its reliability suffered little. Having said that, a power hike from 18 to 24bhp should strain no half-decent transmission, although the primary chain was improved to a duplex design to cope with it. The 250 should be able to cruise at 50mph, and the 350 has maybe an extra 10 realistic mph on top of that. As always with machines of this age, top speed is at best theoretical, and anyone after outright performance should not be buying one of these bikes!

Problems? Wipac electrics are reviled by many, and rated by others. The Wipac kit is less easy to obtain than the Lucas equivalent, and many of these machines still on the road will have had their electrical components switched to Lucas. Poor reassembly can – as always – reduce reliability and increase lubrication leakage. Oil-tightness is not helped on some lightweights (mainly the 350s, to be fair) by the occasional porosity of the cylinder casting, which can introduce some baffling leaks if you're not prepared for it.

High rates of internal component wear can be attributed to the relatively small amount of oil in circulation, and the wise buyer listens carefully to the engine after it has been warmed up thoroughly. Big ends and main bearings can have unhappily short lives. Likewise, if the transmission is noisy – and third gear is prone to being vocal – beware. The design of the gearbox is such that if its oil level falls much below the requisite 3 pints (yes, 20 per cent more than allowed for the engine!), the gears can run right out of it, because they are mounted rather high up in the gearbox shell. Another failing of the gearbox is its tendency to break selector springs, although that is hardly insurmountable.

Spares for these lightweight machines are in fairly poor supply. They are rarely regarded as true classics, few appear to be in regular use, and there is insufficient demand for the AJS & Matchless Owners' Club Spares Scheme to remanufacture them.

The bicycle

The AJS lightweight bicycle was conventionally tubular, apart from a steel channel section that formed the engine cradle. Wheels were 17-inch, and the front fork was a flimsy affair sourced from the Francis-Barnett and James range of two-strokes. This fork is one main reason for suggesting that potential purchasers should look for either a 350 or one of the later versions of the 250, both of which sported a better AMC 'Teledraulic' (telescopic and hydraulic) version.

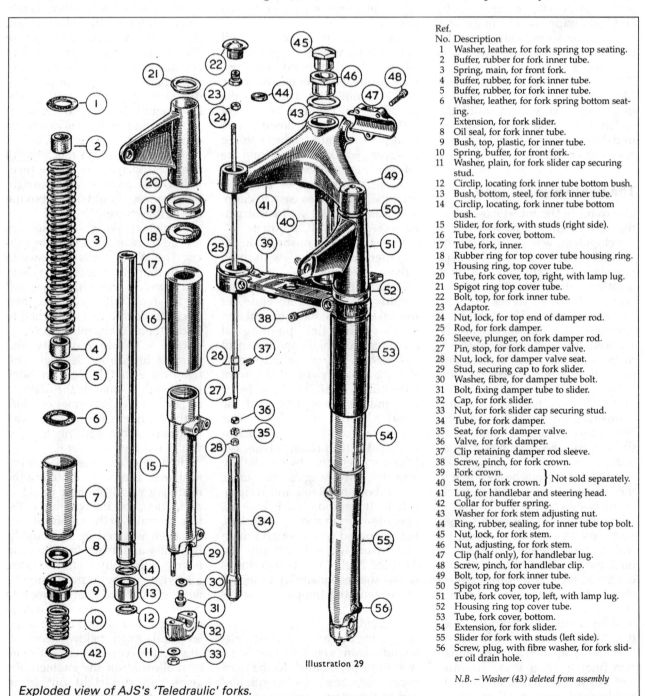

Ref.
No. Description
1   Washer, leather, for fork spring top seating.
2   Buffer, rubber for fork inner tube.
3   Spring, main, for front fork.
4   Buffer, rubber, for fork inner tube.
5   Buffer, rubber, for fork inner tube.
6   Washer, leather, for fork spring bottom seating.
7   Extension, for fork slider.
8   Oil seal, for fork inner tube.
9   Bush, top, plastic, for inner tube.
10 Spring, buffer, for front fork.
11 Washer, plain, for fork slider cap securing stud.
12 Circlip, locating fork inner tube bottom bush.
13 Bush, bottom, steel, for fork inner tube.
14 Circlip, locating, fork inner tube bottom bush.
15 Slider, for fork, with studs (right side).
16 Tube, fork cover, bottom.
17 Tube, fork, inner.
18 Rubber ring for top cover tube housing ring.
19 Housing ring, top cover tube.
20 Tube, fork cover, top, right, with lamp lug.
21 Spigot ring top cover tube.
22 Bolt, top, for fork inner tube.
23 Adaptor.
24 Nut, lock, for top end of damper rod.
25 Rod, for fork damper.
26 Sleeve, plunger, on fork damper rod.
27 Pin, stop, for fork damper valve.
28 Nut, lock, for damper valve seat.
29 Stud, securing cap to fork slider.
30 Washer, fibre, for damper tube bolt.
31 Bolt, fixing damper tube to slider.
32 Cap, for fork slider.
33 Nut, for fork slider cap securing stud.
34 Tube, for fork damper.
35 Seat, for fork damper valve.
36 Valve, for fork damper.
37 Clip retaining damper rod sleeve.
38 Screw, pinch, for fork crown.
39 Fork crown.   }
40 Stem, for fork crown. } Not sold separately.
41 Lug, for handlebar and steering head.
42 Collar for buffer spring.
43 Washer for fork stem adjusting nut.
44 Ring, rubber, sealing, for inner tube top bolt.
45 Nut, lock, for fork stem.
46 Nut, adjusting, for fork stem.
47 Clip (half only), for handlebar lug.
48 Screw, pinch, for handlebar clip.
49 Bolt, top, for fork inner tube.
50 Spigot ring top cover tube.
51 Tube, fork cover, top, left, with lamp lug.
52 Housing ring top cover tube.
53 Tube, fork cover, bottom.
54 Extension, for fork slider.
55 Slider for fork with studs (left side).
56 Screw, plug, with fibre washer, for fork slider oil drain hole.

N.B. – Washer (43) deleted from assembly

Illustration 29

Exploded view of AJS's 'Teledraulic' forks.

Brakes for all the lightweights are unremarkable, although adequate by the standard of their day. The later (1964-on) CSR front brake is the best.

The AJS lightweights offer their rider a surprisingly comfortable 'big bike' riding position, with a good relationship between hands, feet and seat. Properly set up, the controls work well, with tidy and predictable handling, especially on Teledraulic-forked models. They look good too, in a typically late '50s/early '60s commuter way.

Models

The AJS 250 started life in 1958 as the standard Model 14 (the Matchless equivalent was the G2), followed in 1959 by a 'scrambles' version, the Model 14CS (Matchless G2CS). This had a higher compression ratio, internal engine mods and 19-inch wheels to match the off-road cosmetics of the time.

The 350 Model 8 (Matchless G5) appeared in 1960 and vanished again two years later, mourned largely by the rose-tinted brigade. (I have owned two – both were unreliable, leaky, noisy and slow, as well as badly braked.)

For 1962 the sports model, the AJS 14S (Matchless G2S), appeared, only to be replaced a year later by the Model 14CSR (Matchless G2CSR), which is the one to have – if have one you must. The range petered out with the collapse of the company in 1966, despite some re-engineering

Top: *By 1964 the AJS and Matchless lightweight models were becoming handsome and gaining greater performance. This 1964 G2CSR combines low mass, agility, and a reasonable amount of go. The 'stop' is improving too.*

Bottom: *The first post-war AJS frames were based closely on those of the WD G3L.*

that makes the final-year Model 14CSR the best of a dull bunch.

A nomenclature postscript

When things were getting tough for AMC, they leaped straight to the root of their woes and . . . gave their bikes model names to go with the numbers. So, in case you are offered one, here are the lightweights by name:

AJS 14 Sapphire (Matchless G2 Monitor)
AJS 14CS Scorpion (Matchless G2CS Messenger)
AJS 14S Sapphire Sports (Matchless G2S Monitor Sports)

AJS 14CSR Sapphire Ninety (Matchless G2CSR Monitor Ninety)
AJS Model 8 Senator (Matchless G5 Matador)

The Four-stroke Heavyweights

After the end of the Second World War, AJS were in a pretty strong position. Like BSA, and to a lesser extent Norton, parent company AMC had been supplying bikes to the forces for most of the duration. That bike, the Matchless G3L (for 'Light') was regarded by many as the best of the despatch riders' tools, and formed the basis for the first of the civilian models to bark

their way from the London factory when hostilities ended.

The bicycle

One of the favourite features of the wartime G3L Matchless was its telescopic-forked front end, and the AJS range, along with its Matchless stablemates, entered the brave new peacetime world with this advantage right from the start.

Unlike most of their major opposition, when AJS introduced a twin-cylindered model, in the very smart shape of the 1948 AJS Model 20 (Matchless G9), they offered it only with swinging arm rear suspension to compliment the telescopic front. The early rear spring/damper units were known by the same Teledraulic name as the front forks. Again, unlike their opposition, AJS rear suspension was built by themselves, and was not bought in from one of the suppliers (Girling, Woodhead-Monroe and Armstrong were suppliers to other motorcycle manufacturers).

AJS converted the rear end of the rigid frame with which they had launched into the post-war market by simply replacing the tri-angulated rigid rear chainstays with a subframe to carry seat and suspension top mounts, a substantial alloy casting to carry the swinging arm pivot, and a selec-

tion of tubes to connect the bottom of the alloy casting to the front downtube. It sounds complicated, and it would probably have worked out cheaper in manufacturing terms to have designed a new frame, but cost accountants didn't run companies in those days.

So, the AJS (and Matchless!) twins all had a swinging arm frame right from the start, while the opposition twins from BSA, Norton and Triumph, among others, suffered more from the indignities of either plunger suspension or odd ideas like the Triumph sprung hub and the Ariel Anstey Link when they started the drift away from their own rigid frames. The AJS frame handled well enough, too, with its massive construction making light work of the relatively low power outputs of the time. The combination of modern roads, modern rubber and limited ground clearance means that even early AMC bicycles can be cranked over until the undercarriage grounds in perfect safety. Another nice touch is that AMC rear suspension units are as rebuildable as their front forks, and most spares are available.

The singles were also offered with the fully-sprung bicycle, but retained a rigid frame option right through until the appearance of

the 1956 range, which featured a fairly major across-the-range redesign. Why the option? Some experts considered that the rigid frame was better for attachment to a sidecar, while others preferred its simplicity, lighter weight and (slightly) lower cost.

AMC maintained a policy of gradual development of the AJS and Matchless ranges, which has many advantages for the latter-day collector and restorer. Basically, almost any AJS part can be made to almost fit almost any similar AJS motorcycle. So you should not be kept from the road by the unavailability of essential spares. The exactly correct spare may be elusive, but something that fits – and works! – will almost certainly be available.

There are still a lot of AMC motorcycles about that run well and look great but which are less than strictly original in their fittings. Whether this is a good or a bad thing depends upon your own viewpoint, but one of the reasons for my running AJS bikes for two decades was their easily available, almost correct, parts – as well as for their comfort, reliability and fine handling, of course.

The original sprung back end's suspension units, which were known latterly as 'candlesticks', were superseded in 1951 by the rather more famous 'jampots', which were conspicuously fatter than the candlesticks and remained a feature of AJS and Matchless machinery until 1957. A neat touch of both marques' machines until 1963 was that they fitted their rear shocks with clevis lower mountings, rather than with the side mountings used by everyone else. Whether this made a great contribution to their fine

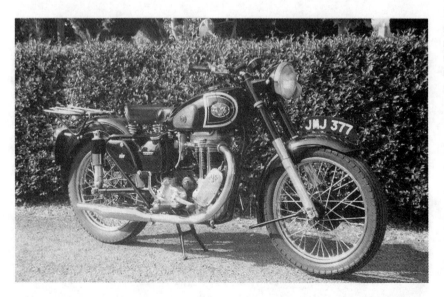

The AMC sprung frame was not long in coming, and this shot of a very fine AJS 18S shows the 'jampot' back end to advantage.

handling is open to debate, but it suggested a commitment to engineering excellence that must have helped in the marketing wars if nothing else.

The brakes also underwent incremental improvements from 1946, until by 1956 they were both mounted in handsome full-width alloy drums. These looked great, and worked adequately by the standards of the day, but dismantling one reveals that the lining area is in fact very small. Those brakes persisted until 1963, when AMC had something of a brainstorm and introduced redesigned hubs for that year only – they followed up for 1964 and the rest of the range's life by fitting Norton brakes along with forks from the same stable. And they are the models to ride if you want the best stopping.

The new-for-1963 hubs finally saw the end of the vintage built-up wheel spindle, long a feature of AMC motorcycles. In this design, the wheel spindle comes complete with its bearings. When replacement is due, the whole assembly needs replacing, rather than just the worn out bearings. Anyone who has rebuilt a push-bike will be familiar with this idea, and its departure was no great loss. As I write this, spindles are available, but sometimes they aren't . . .

As mentioned above, the bicycle underwent continual steady redesign, with far too many year-on-year changes to list here. Significant was the 1957 change

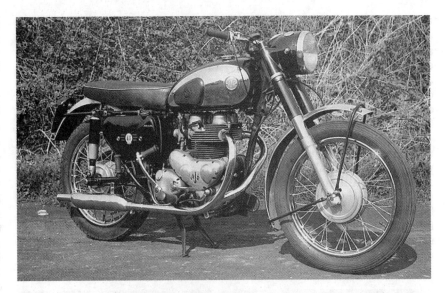

Top: *1957 brought a frame redesign and the introduction of Girling suspension units.*

Middle: *When it arrived for 1960 AMC's full duplex frame (left) was a considerable improvement over the earlier one (right).*

Bottom: *The final roadster frame added Norton front forks and wheels to the AMC package, producing a fine-handling motorcycle.*

from Burman gearboxes (excellent accurate shift, enormous durability, slightly ponderous action) to one of their own design (excellent accurate shift, enormous durability, clean light action), which was fitted across the AJS, Matchless and Norton heavyweight ranges.

Also significant was the redesign of the frame to do away with the curious alloy swinging arm pivot, although that new-for-'56 frame remained of single-front-downtube type, leaving the final major shift to a duplex cradle until 1960. Everything else, from toolboxes to mudguards to electri-cal sundries, underwent a process of steady change, and a dedicated marque history book is the place to discover all of them.

The final change to the heavy-weight bicycle took place in 1964, when, as mentioned above, the entire 'Roadholder' front end from the Norton range was fitted to the AMC frame, along with the Norton rear wheel. This allowed increased across-the-range stand-ardisation for the company, which was steering well on to the rocks by that time anyway, and produced some strange models: AJS singles badged as Nortons (the Norton Model 50 Mk2 and ES2 Mk2, which were AJS Models 16 and 18 respectively), and almost identical twins fitted with Norton engines and badged as everything else (the Norton N15, Matchless G15 and AJS Model 33, in various trims). Some enthusi-asts love these latter-day hybrids, others loathe them . . .

AJS and Matchless heavyweight bicycles all offered the traditional-ly comfortable British 'sack of spuds' riding position, handling that improved steadily until the appearance of the final duplex frame, which is very good indeed, and steering and stopping at least on a par with their contemporary competition.

They suffered, however, as did other manufacturers' equivalents, from being expected to cope with the power output of, eventually, a 750cc twin, while at the same time being offered for sale equipped with a sturdy but unexciting 350 long-stroke single. The strength necessary when handling 50bhp is something of a weight handicap when coping with less than 20bhp . . .

The heavyweight engine

AJS and Matchless offered just three heavyweight engines in the post-war period. These were, per-haps predictably, a twin and a single. But I said three? Yes, indeed – from 1963 until the end of the line in 1968 you could order your AJS or Matchless fitted with a Norton Atlas 750 engine. However, we will take a look at the singles first.

Heavy singles

The AMC single engine entered the post-war market in a very

Perhaps the greatest improvement for the 1964-on twins was the fitment of the Norton 'Roadholder' front fork and its 8-inch, full-width front brake.

strong position. As the WD G3L Matchless, it had been in production right through the traumas of the war, and almost all that was required for the transition to civilian trim was a coat of lustrous black to replace the olive drab, and a lot of polishing for the power train's covers.

The engine's design is typical big Brit: long stroke, iron barrel, iron head, heavy flywheels and pushrods. This low-revving, mechanically quiet power plant, sweet in both 350 and 500cc formats, is one of the charmers from the period. And although conventional in most ways, it does have its quirks. These include an unusual oil pump plunger that both rotates (it's driven at 90 degrees from the crankshaft) and reciprocates (the rotating plunger has an eccentric slot, which moves over a fixed pin, thus reciprocating lengthways), and a quaint drive to the dynamo.

Unlike many designs of the immediate post-war period, the AMC engine does not make use of the Lucas magdyno. Instead, drive to the magneto is by chain from either the exhaust (AJS) or inlet cam (Matchless). You can work out where the mag is mounted on the two marques for yourself! The dynamo, which inhabits a space between engine and gearbox, is driven from a chain running inside the primary chain and sharing the (usually leaky) chaincase with it. This must have made sense to someone, we assume.

The single-strand primary chain, which was only occasionally wrecked by the breakage of a never-adjusted dynamo chain,

Top: *An early post-war Matchless G80 shows off its rigid frame, Teledraulic front forks and twin saddles.*

Bottom: *The late engines – this is a 1966 Matchless version – feature a completely redesigned bottom end, which includes a Norton gear-type oil pump.*

Above left: *For scrambles use only: the last of the 'real' Matchless bikes was the G85CS. These command a high price today.*

Right: *The final AMC twins saw the 750 hybrid power unit slotted into the bicycle of the Matchless G85CS to produce the P11.*

transmitted power via an excellent Burman clutch to an equally excellent Burman gearbox, an arrangement that survived until both were replaced by AMC's own – very similar – design in 1956.

Carburation was, inevitably, by Amal, usually unfiltered and rarely sensitive to either adjustment or wear.

The engine was developed with the urgency familiar to British bike fans, ie remarkably slowly, and almost all the changes were retro-fittable. In other words, as already stated, almost any part from almost any AMC single can be fitted to almost any other. Hence you can occasionally come across very eccentric combinations of major components, a common one being the 500 single that started out as a 350. A hint: AJS 500 singles are always engine-numbered 18 (350s are 16); Matchless 500s G80 (350s G3). The problem with this simple conversion is that unless the flywheel assembly was changed at the same time, its balance will be wrong (the 500 has a heavier piston) and what should be a pleasantly smooth and woffly engine can vibrate like a late BSA twin.

Major changes include the disappearance of the attractive but functionally flawed tin chaincase (actually pressed steel, but tradition refers to them as stannic rather than ferrous in nature) in 1957, and the handsome (but leak-prone) chrome pushrod tubes were cast into the barrel in 1962 (350) and 1963 (500). The tin chaincase's legendary ability to leak its lube can be viewed as a gentle eccentricity in these days of relatively low classic mileages, but beware – running dry will not only wreck the chains but can also wear the clutch rapidly and can almost destroy the big engine shock absorber that lives on the drive-side crank outboard of the sprocket. This shock absorber is a spring-loaded cam that absorbs some of the shocks (really!) from the engine's power pulses. Dry operation can chew the splines of the crank's drive-side axle really badly. Then the engine runs mysteriously roughly, and replacement requires a complete dismantling of the crank itself . . . and great expense.

Alternator electrics with coil ignition replaced the old magneto and dynamo for 1958, which

spoiled (some say) the looks but improved the functionality.

Oddly, just before they went bump in 1964, and given that sales of heavy singles were hardly buoyant, AMC completely redesigned their aged but charming banger engine for 1964. Although visually the changes were less than obvious, in fact the engine's vital dimensions had been changed, to shorten the stroke, and the quaint oil pump had been replaced by a Norton-type gear device. Very few of the 1964-on engine components are interchangeable with the earlier design, incidentally.

The final Matchless-only big single is worthy of a small mention of its own. Right at the end of their existence, the AMC company produced their final scrambler, the Matchless G85CS. In a final (failed) attempt at stemming the onslaught of European and oriental two-strokes, the Matchless big banger gained a new and very fine chassis indeed. It was apparently based upon a chassis from the Rickman brothers, but worked well for AMC. Following the demise of the big singles, Norton-Villiers (who owned the name by then) slotted the 750 Atlas engine into the G85CS bicycle, to produce what must surely be the ultimate UK desert sled, the Norton (or Matchless, if you wished) P11.

On the road

Ignoring their obvious modern-day performance limits, AMC singles are fine to ride. They are flexible, mechanically quiet and handsome to look at. The one to have? Either very early or very late are the ones I recommend. The post-64 short-strokers are quick, agile, revvy and rare; the rigid, iron-head '40s versions are the most charming, gentle and – if you like – classic.

Reliability on today's roads is generally fairly good, although there were a lot of suspect-pattern big-end bearings around for several years, which tarnished the reputation of the 500s. The AJS & Matchless OC is a fine, professional club, and remanufactures most vital spares.

A Matchless-only footnote

There was an attempt at reviving the old name of Matchless in the late 1980s, by L. F. Harris Ltd. These fine folk, who had been building Triumph Bonnevilles under licence down in Newton Abbot, Devon, built a Rotax-engined 500cc roadster under the 'Matchless G80' label. Although a pleasant enough machine, and welcome in the AJS & Matchless OC, the bike was really too expensive to sell well, and indeed did not.

Such problems as these last singles suffered from were mainly down to poor starting, breaking rear wheel spokes and a sometimes fragile finish. The engine was durable enough, the oil-in-frame bicycle was well-built

An attempt was made in the late 1980s to revive the Matchless name. Sadly, although the G80 was a pleasant motorcycle apart from some starting difficulties, it failed to catch on.

and fine-steering, while brakes by Brembo and reliable electrics added to an attractive package.

An AJS-only footnote

Following the collapse of the old London-based AMC company, the reviving Norton-Villiers company decided to continue building AJS motorcycles – but only as two-stroke off-roaders. These were powered by a derivation of the Villiers Starmaker engine, and were even successful in competition in the late 1960s.

Following the collapse of the new Norton-Villiers company, the rights to build bikes bearing the AJS name were acquired by Fluff Brown, down in Dorset most deep, and he continues to offer his own improved versions to this day. So, the last surviving remnant of the once-proud London company (out of Wolverhampton) is a bespoke stroker hand-built in Dorset.

AMC single numerology

All AJS and Matchless singles can be identified by their engine numbers. Indeed, as we have mentioned already with reference to the lightweights, until the early 1960s brought a flush of remarkable model names the bikes were best known by their model numbers. So, with the Matchless equivalent in brackets, here is the AJS heavy single range.

The post-war range began with the 350cc Model 16 (Matchless G3L – L for 'Light') and 500cc Model 18 (Matchless G80). When rear springing appeared, the 16 became the 16S (for 'Sprung', not 'Sports' – do not ever be fooled by this) and the 18 the 18S (Matchless G3LS and G80S). Competition versions were denoted by the addition of a 'C'; hence 16C and 18C, followed by the 18CS (Matchless G3C and G80CS). When rigid roadsters were no longer available, the factory dropped the 'S'. Thus the 18S went back to being the plain old Model 18. It's simple really.

The Heavy Twins

AJS and Matchless twins followed the British tradition established by Triumph in that they were all parallel twins with their valves operated by pushrods. AMC twins broke away from the British tradition in that their crankshafts were supported by three – not two – main bearings, and by having separate castings for both cylinders and both cylinder heads. The design was a very well-reasoned one, and although it did not take to the inevitable capacity increases as well as, say, the Norton engine, up to its limits the AMC twin can hold up its head in any company of classics.

The AJS Model 20 (and, inevitably, the Matchless G9) was introduced for 1949, and came complete with a swinging arm bicycle – as described earlier – missing out the plunger compromise completely. It was a very neat, clean design of engine, with just feed and scavenge lines from and to the oil tank, with all other oilways being internal and invisible. It contrasted nicely with most other twins, and indeed with the company's own singles, in that there was a conspicuous lack of the 'bits stuck anywhere' approach to engine design common at BSA and elsewhere.

There were, for example, no cylinder-retaining nuts clustered traditionally (and untidily) around the base of the blocks. The AMC design mounted both barrels and cylinder heads on four long studs for each cylinder, holding the lot together with nuts atop the heads. The top end was notably oil-tight, largely because the rockers were mounted in pillars formed as part of the head casting itself, and a neat rider-friendly touch was that adjustment of the valve clearances was by eccentric mounting of the rocker spindles – no fiddling with locknuts and spanners here. Thus a rocker cover was exactly that – a cover, completely un-stressed and oil-tight as a result.

Where the engines could, and did, leak their lube was from a gallery between the crankcase mouths, usually after the first

Top: *Following the collapse of AMC, the AJS badge was used on a range of two-stroke off-roaders. They are fiery, fast and fun, as you would expect.*

Middle: *With their all-aluminium engine, towering cylinder and . . . interesting exhaust systems, AMC's big bangers are still fun on the rough.*

Bottom: *The 1952 AJS 18S has only one flaw: its braking is poor for today's roads.*

amateur bottom end rebuild had failed to seal the surface. The movement under load of the centre main bearing's retaining web did not help here.

That centre main bearing, unique to the AMC twin engine, was something of a mixed blessing. It was intended to support the crankshaft, thus making the engine smoother-running than its rivals, but experience and myth supported by 20:20 hindsight suggests that allowing the crank of a large capacity parallel twin to flex may make it smoother. In fact, if you step from an early-'50s AJS 500 twin and on to, for example, an equivalent BSA in similar condition, there is little to choose in the smoothness of the engines. In fact, there is usually more variability between models from the same marque . . .

Like the Triumph twin, the AMC engine incorporated two camshafts, both driven by gears in the timing case. This is a simple, quiet and effective method of operation, although there is a small irony here, in that the early AMC engines were considered to be pretty clattery, and most of the racket came from duff design of the cam followers. Nearly right, then.

The two cylinder heads were made from aluminium alloy right from the start, and were particularly handsome, with their generous cooling fins and domed rocker covers.

Top: By 1955 the Model 18 would stop a whole lot better.

Middle: This very smart Matchless G3LS is a 1956 model. That year saw the last of the 'jampot' suspension units and the introduction of more streamlined styling.

Bottom: This 1959 Matchless G80 was re-imported from South Africa in sound running and standard order. Note the alternator electrics and removable chrome petrol tank panels.

AMC's frames were built with integral lugs to permit the towing of sidecars. This 1955 G9 Matchless is ride-to-work transport for a matchless mechanic.

Carburation and electrics were standard for the time, with the former courtesy of Amal and the latter coping with Lucas's best dynamo and magneto. Alternator electrics appeared in 1959 and spread gradually through the range, with the CSR sports twins hanging on to the magneto until 1964.

The early AJS (and Matchless) twins are very pleasant to ride, with a generous spread of power and a distinctive style. They sound good, too, especially Matchlesses that are fitted with that marque's short 'megaphone'-type silencer. But they can be leakers, from the areas already mentioned and from the notoriously unsealable primary chaincase. This was replaced by a smart alloy case in 1958.

Below, left: *Cross-section of an AMC twin, showing the oil galleries, oil passages and release valve.*

Right: *The AMC engine's valve timing gear.*

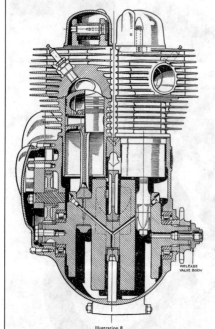

Illustration 8
Cross section of engine showing oil galleries, oil passages, and release valve.

21

Illustration 20

Valve timing gear

1 GEAR WHEEL ON MAGNETO ARMATURE SHAFT.
2 MAGNETO.
3 GEAR WHEEL ON INLET CAMSHAFT.
4 ONE OF THE THREE STUDS RETAINING THE OIL PUMPS ASSEMBLY.
5 INTERMEDIATE (OR IDLE) GEAR.
6 GEAR WHEEL ON EXHAUST CAMSHAFT.
7 DYNAMO.
8 GEAR WHEEL ON DYNAMO ARMATURE SHAFT.
9 STUD, IN DYNAMO BODY AND PASSING THROUGH CRANKCASE AND TIMING GEAR COVER.
10 CRANKCASE DRAIN PLUG.
11 ADAPTOR TO ACCOMMODATE OIL FEED PIPE BANJO PIN.
12 TIMING PINION ON CRANKSHAFT.
13 ADAPTOR TO ACCOMMODATE OIL RETURN PIPE BANJO PIN.
14 MARKS TO SET TIMING.

The first boost to the engine's capacity came in 1956, when the 600cc AJS Model 30 (Matchless G11) was introduced. This engine was still fairly unstressed, proving little quicker, but a little more flexible than its smaller stablemate. After the arrival of the G11 came the option of sportier versions, the G11CS and G11CSR, which together paved the way for the 650 stretch. This was introduced for 1959 as the AJS Model 31 (Matchless G12), and the range included both the 31CS (theoretical off-roader) and 31CSR (a theoretical road-racer). The S versions are rare in the UK, but relatively common in the US.

The 650 version of the twin, which in sports trim was by now a rather rorty, unsophisticated device, far removed from the sedentary earlier models, remained in production until 1966, when the company collapsed.

The factory attempted to satisfy the American taste for ever-greater capacity by stretching their engine all the way out to 750cc, with the Matchless G15/45 (there was no AJS equivalent), but only a couple of hundred were built before it was recognised as being a bad idea. These big twins, and I've been blessed enough to have ridden two of them, are prodigious leakers, unless they are assembled carefully and ridden slowly – which rather defeats their object.

Top: *Possibly the most charismatic of the twins are the CSR sports roadsters. Here, author Steve Wilson makes notes after a brisk ride on a 1960 AJS 31CSR.*

Middle: *In a strange move, AMC redesigned their range for 1963. They redesigned it again for 1964, making this 1963 G12 something of an oddity.*

Bottom: *The final AMC-engine twins are very handsome motorcycles, capable of brisk performance and fine steering. This 1966 AJS 31CSR is a smart bike by any standard.*

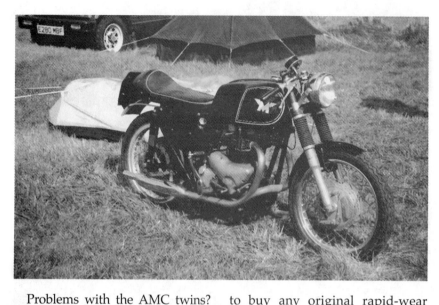

Neatly modified in the cafe racer tradition, this late Matchless G12CSR is capable of keeping up with many modern machines.

Problems with the AMC twins? The early 500s suffer from the unsealable AMC tin primary chaincase, and leak their oil. There are many and various cures for this, including pouring molten tallow into the chaincase, allowing it to set, then adding oil! It is my experience that spraying the primary chain with a good quality aerosol chain lube keeps the chain happy, and after half a dozen applications the gloop that has been thrown off by the chain makes an effective enough seal for the case to hold enough oil to keep the clutch happy – if not the engine-shaft shock absorber. Join the excellent owners' club and join their debate . . .

Original early cam followers wear out rapidly, but the design was changed and you are unlikely to buy any original rapid-wear ones now. Replacement cures the alarming rattle.

If badly tuned, the 650 engines can be vibrators – as can all British twins – and if allowed to continue like this they can shake their fasteners into looseness. Fitting a twin engine into a single frame (which is perfectly possible) means that the frame lug provided to anchor the cylinder head steady is missing. If you are test riding an AJS twin and it shakes like a Norton Atlas, look around here.

Early alternator 650 engines have a continuing reputation for breaking cranks. The crankshaft material was changed in late 1960 (to 'nodular' iron) to prevent this, and everything improved bar their reputation. My feeling is that if an engine has survived for 30 years, and provided that it is driven sensibly and furnished with clean lubricant, it should survive for many more years.

In common with a lot of other designs of engine that use gear-type oil pumps, the AMC twin has a tendency to drain all the oil from the oil tank into the crankcases if left standing for a long time; this is known as 'sumping'. Replacement of the oil pump helps, but draining the sump (it has a large threaded plug for this very purpose) before starting the engine after a long period of idleness is cheaper and equally effective.

If you choose to do neither, I cannot recommend fitting a tap into the oil feed pipes – for obvious reasons – and personally dislike adding anti-drain valves into the oil pipes. So, when you start up after a lay-up, you should not be surprised by clouds of smoke and prodigious oil leaks. Experience suggests that it takes the pump only a minute or two at tickover to scavenge the offending oil, but you can leak a lot in that time.

The oil will come out from a breather hole in the inner face of the primary chaincase, because the crankcases breath through the drive-side main bearing into the chaincase. I have seen chaincases with these holes sealed to prevent the leaks – do not do this!

Another sometimes mysterious oil leak can appear to be from the cylinder base joints. Remaking the joint has no effect – frustration sets in and bikes get sold! The problem

AMC stretched their 650cc twin engine out to 750cc to produce the Matchless – only – G15/45. This machine was not successful, being leaky and fragile, and was replaced by the Norton-engined hybrids a year later in 1963.

Although the early 650 twins have something of a reputation for breaking crankshafts, this 1959 G12 Matchless has never been off the road since . . . 1959.

here is that there is an oil gallery formed by matching grooves in the top of the crankcase halves. If care is lacking when the crankcases are reassembled, this gallery leaks.

The late, 1963-on engines benefit from a high-capacity oil pump (fitted earlier to the CSR sports twins), as well as good 12-volt electrics and sundry other improvements. Thus, once again, the last tend to be the best.

Which brings us to the final family of AMC twins, the so-called hybrids. Associated Motorcycles, the parent company of AJS and Matchless, had also owned the Norton concern since the early 1950s, and when their own twin failed to stretch successfully to 750 it was decided that the Norton Atlas engine should be fitted to the AJS bicycle. This produced a surprisingly pleasant motorcycle, with the Norton engine feeling much less vibratory in the AMC

frame than it did in its own Norton featherbed.

Once again, these bikes were available as the AJS Model 33 (Matchless G15) and as 33CS and 33CSR versions. Interestingly, it was also possible to buy the AJS (or Matchless) as a Norton, in which case you were buying a Norton N15. But what's in a name?

A word of caution. If you are considering the purchase of one of these charismatic hybrids, try to buy one that has its engine and gearbox still bolted into the bicycle. The reason for this is that fitting the Norton engine into the Matchless bicycle involved the use of several spacers, and they fit properly in only one sequence.

Below, left: *In a bid to broaden their range and to satisfy the power-hungry American market, AMC slotted the 750cc Norton Atlas engine into their own model. It was available badged as either AJS or Matchless, and in some versions as a Norton.*

Right: *In its touring guise the 750 hybrid makes an excellent chair-puller. This 1965 AJS 33 is a frequent visitor to rallies.*

Unless you are prepared for a lot of fiddling, it is best to dismantle your own, marking up all of the nuts, studs, washers and spacers that hold it all together.

Following the collapse of AMC in 1966, and its takeover and resurrection as Norton-Matchless (a division of Norton-Villiers), the 750 hybrids remained in production until the establishment of the Norton Commando, even being developed further, ultimately into their final form in the Matchless G85CS-framed Ranger 750. That was – and is! – a very powerful on/off-roader and is well worth considering if you can find one.

The ones to buy? As with the single-cylinder models, I would recommend either the early versions of the twins (for their charm, docility and character) or the very late ones (for their performance, style and modern-day useability). Most wearing components are available, although as less early versions are used on the roads, their spares are becoming harder to find.

The very last, 1964-on, twins are very well sorted, with higher-capacity oil pumps contributing to mechanical longevity, and their 18-inch wheels accepting modern rubber. They wear Norton 8-inch front brakes, which accept the Commando 2ls brake plate, offering very effective braking. And if you think that you detect a hint of bias – well, you're right. I have a great fondness for the AMC twins, and there are currently three of them about the place. A personal recommendation, then.

Top: *Is this the most handsome AJS of them all? 1967 AJS 33CSR poses demurely.*

Middle and bottom: *As long-legged tourers or dirt-track tearaways, the 750 hybrids allowed the ancient names of AJS and Matchless to go out on a high note.*

Chapter 7

BSA

BSA was the biggest motorcycle manufacturing company this country has ever known. Even by modern European standards, they were huge. It has been said that their bikes are runners-up in current 'classic' popularity after those from more glamorous Triumph – please remember that BSA owned Triumph until 1973 . . .

And they owned Sunbeam and Ariel, too, as well as an impressive assortment of other, mainly non-motorcycling, companies. BSA was not a small business, run either by enthusiastic individuals or by a dedicated family concern. BSA was an awfully big business and BSA built an awful lot of motorcycles in a wide variety of styles and a bewildering assortment of designations.

During the Second World War, as well as supplying a vast quantity of weaponry to the Allied Forces (BSA stands for Birmingham Small Arms, in case you didn't know), BSA built more military motorcycles than any other UK manufacturer – over 125,000 WD M20 side-valve singles saw service all over the world. And so, when peace roared back in 1945, they were in a strong position to resume the mass production of motorcycles. And so they did, with their major plant in Birmingham's Small Heath switching over rapidly to the rather brighter and more varied

models required by the civilian market.

BSA developed their business rapidly enough and effectively enough, too. Although it is possibly inevitable that here in today's post-classic nostalgic world we tend to dwell upon the ultimate failure of the classic British motorcycle industry, in fact that industry produced an enormous number of good, sound motorcycles over the 30 years from the cessation of hostilities to the effective end of UK motorcycle mass manufacture in 1975 or thereabouts.

As you might expect, given that BSA produced so many motorcycles, they either enjoyed – or suffered from, depending upon your point of view – a reputation as builders of worthy, but somehow unexciting, machines. And if your memories are full of images of families being hauled around in giant sidecars pulled by plunger Flashes, with their inevitable breakdowns being repaired by beaming AA chaps riding M20-powered outfits, then the above reputation is forgivable. But you should also remember that the Clubmans TT was effectively scuppered because BSA won it all the time, and that even in their dying days the BSA factory's racing triples scored many heroic international race victories. Their competition efforts

were world class, and they were funded by the sale of thousands of bread-and-butter working machines – not by major sponsorship.

In fact, BSA was a large industrial conglomerate run on sound commercial principles. It was only when they inexplicably veered away from a long policy of diversification (they also built cars, guns, bicycles, machine tools . . . and lots more) that things went terminally wrong. In their defence, it should also be remembered that the industrial climate in Britain throughout the 1970s was not helpful for a major concern attempting to make radical changes to its way of operating, and that when the company was finally stalled, it was by an illegal stock market manoeuvre and not by commercial failure.

Having said that, BSA's model development strategy was a conservative one. New models developed incrementally, year-on-year, and there were very few wholly new launches. For instance, all of their unit-construction singles developed from the original 250cc C15 of 1958, and their unit-construction twins used many design cues and similar engineering to the preceding non-unit twin range. Likewise, although the Rocket 3 750 was a wholly new model for BSA, its engine was a development of the Triumph twin's engineering, and its bicycle was a development of the BSA twin range.

Strangely, where BSA had decided to introduce something wholly new, they often used other brand names within the group as vehicles for this new direction. Thus, Ariel was chosen to launch the radical new two-stroke Arrow and Leader twins, while Sunbeam launched the in-line ohc luxury shaft-drive twin rather than the parent BSA company. When BSA did use their own name on entirely new projects, these were usually lightweights and often less than successful; I am thinking particu-larly of the Beeza, Beagle and Dandy here.

The BSA model range in the classic period was very large, and it would be easy to fill this entire volume with details of the year-on-year changes. So, by necessity, there are going to be some glaring omissions – you have been warned! What I will attempt to do is offer some thoughts on the bikes that you are most likely to be considering buying. So, in the same way that the scrambler AJS 18CS merited only a mention in the AMC chapter, Gold Stars will get the same treatment here. If you are seriously contemplating the purchase of what purports to be a genuine BSA Gold Star, or Rocket Gold Star, you need the personal assistance of someone who has expert knowledge. That is sound advice – ignore it at your peril.

BSA's post-war range, as I shall consider it, consisted of the following major lines: side-valve singles; non-unit singles and non-unit twins; unit singles and unit twins; and triples. I shall concentrate on machines of a capacity greater than 250cc, so although I am delighted to make a respectful nod in the direction of BSA's most enduring, and indeed endearing, two-stroke lightweight, the Bantam, its two decades of development are beyond the scope of this volume. Other than to say that if you do fancy buying a Bantam – for whatever reason – bear in mind that they are still common, so their prices are relatively low, and that if you wish to ride one, buy one that has already been restored by someone else. It is currently impossible to recover the cost of a thorough rebuild of the Bantam when it's time to sell it.

The Non-unit Singles

By non-unit, you should under-stand that the engine and gearbox of the power train are completely separate items. In other words, it is possible to remove the engine in its entirety while still leaving the gearbox in place. Unit construction is the opposite; engine and gear-box are built up into a common set of castings, and the whole lot comes out of the bicycle together.

BSA's non-unit singles as

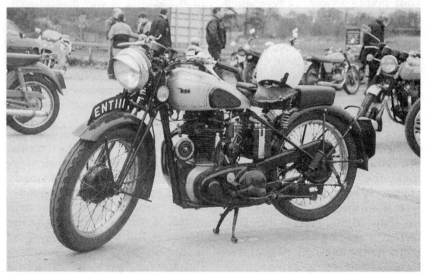

Top: *At the risk of offending many, it has to be said that the pre-unit 250s like this C11 are a little under-powered for today's roads.*

Bottom: *Remarkable as it may seem, some riders still use rigid-framed, girder-forked M33s on the roads of today.*

considered in detail by this volume were all 'heavyweight' – in other words, they were of a rather more substantial build than the more delicately constructed 'lightweights'. The unit replacement for the final 350cc B31 was the 350cc B40, which was a stretched version of the 250cc C15, and therefore a lightweight.

In brief, then, the lightweight non-unit singles consisted of the 250cc C10, C11 and C12 ranges, and although they were all of them worthy enough machines – indeed, their healthy sales provided good profits for BSA throughout the 1950s – they are woefully slow for use on the roads of today. Anyone who regularly rides a side-valve C10 on a busy A road is a brave soul indeed, in my view. They also turn up only rarely in today's press adverts and are something of an acquired taste. When they were new, they were capable of claimed top speeds in the region of 60mph . . .

The post-war BSA range of heavyweight singles began with the 350cc B31 in late 1945, and this was joined by the 500cc B33 for 1947. There were competition versions of each single, too, the 350 receiving the designation B32, and the 500 becoming the B34 – the DB32 and DBD34 Gold Stars, considered by many to be the pinnacle of classic British single-cylinder engineering, started here.

In common with most other British manufacturers, BSA introduced changes on an annual rota

Top: *Telescopic front forks improved the ride of BSA's pre-unit singles, but the rider was still dependent upon the sprung saddle for comfort.*

Middle: *It is unusual to find a genuine Gold Star used as hard and often as this one.*

Bottom: *Not all BSA Gold Stars have sporting pretensions. This one has been used for long-distance touring for many years.*

commencing after the summer holiday shut-down. Also in common with their competitors, the more modern the BSA you are considering, the more suitable it will be for today's roads.

The bicycle

The post-war B31 began its life equipped with a fairly unremarkable rigid frame, but benefited from the fitment of telescopic front forks right from the start. The BSA fork was originally well-known for being noisily under-damped, but this was changed by the time the B33 appeared, and the design served well for many years.

BSA introduced an option to the standard rigid frame for 1949, although unlike AMC they failed to take the big step to providing a swinging arm arrangement. Instead, they offered the option of 'plunger' rear suspension. This offered some minimal rear springing to the customer, without costing the manufacturer a fortune in redesign work; the plunger frame was very similar to the rigid, but with the forging that carried the spring boxes replacing the rigid frame's rear wheel mounts.

As already mentioned, I have never been a great fan of the plunger frame, although so long as you don't expect the steering

The arrival of plunger rear springing was rather cancelled out in comfort terms by the adoption of a dual seat.

precision that is offered by the better rigid and later swinging arm frames, it is not actually dangerous. As always, the problem is wear. With the BSA plunger design, things were not helped by the fact that the whole device was undamped, relying instead upon the notional damping action of grease packing the spring boxes, and thus upon the level of maintenance practised by generations of owners. Removing the covers to expose the springs, as was once popular, merely increases the rate of wear and removes any form of damping, however notional. Worn plungers produce a characteristic weave when riding at any decent speed, and although it can be disconcerting, it's usually safe enough.

The next big change to the sturdy BSA bicycle came for 1955, when the rigid frame was dropped from the range and a proper swinging arm rear suspension was offered. And it was a truly worthwhile improvement.

BSA's swinging arm frame was a lesson from which other manufacturers could have learned a lot. The AMC frame, for example, was a development of the original rigid design, and the contemporary Triumph frame was just plain poor. Only Norton, with their excellent featherbed's full duplex cradle, were better than the BSA offering at the time.

The new frame was very similar for both the singles and the increasingly popular twins, with the former being readily distinguished by a kink in the

When BSA finally adopted a swinging arm frame it was a wholly new affair and steered very well indeed.

lower right-hand frame rail. This is there to clear the bulge in the single's crankcases, which contains their oil pump – and is not unique to Gold Stars, in case someone tries to tell you otherwise.

As the frame developed, so did the brakes, with the single-sided front stopper growing to 8 inches for 1953 before being replaced with full-width aluminium 'Ariel' hubs for 1956. These lasted just two seasons; although they were usually effective enough in operation, they were not as effective as the Triumph type that replaced them for 1958.

The non-unit single engine

The BSA single engine is a thoroughly conventional design in most respects, and evolved slowly enough from its appearance in 1945 to its demise in 1959. It is a very robust power plant, and is capable of covering enormous mileages and enduring fabulous levels of neglect.

As with other British single-cylinder engines of the day, the B31 (and its bigger B33 brother) featured a pair of massive flywheels running in a vertically split pair of aluminium crankcases. Sandwiched between the flywheels was a caged roller big end bearing of generous dimensions with a similarly herculean con-rod running upon it. The cylinder barrel and head were both made of cast iron, were substantially befinned, and the head came complete with cast-in rocker boxes, themselves closed by neat aluminium lids.

The pushrods were operated by a pair of cams driven from the crankshaft, and were housed inside a smart cast aluminium tower that ran up to the base of the rocker box. Adjustment of the valve clearances was effected through a square aperture at the base of the pushrod tower, and was simple and neat, meaning, as it did, that there was no need to

disturb either the petrol tank or the rocker box covers to carry out this chore.

The oil pump was a fine sturdy gear pump that lived at the bottom of the engine in a small sump, from where it propelled its lubricant around the engine then back to the oil tank, which was mounted behind the rider's right knee – again in the classic British tradition. The pump was driven by a skew gear from the crankshaft, and is the heart of the engine's renowned reliability.

Again, in the traditional manner, carburation was by courtesy of Messrs Amal, while sparks and lighting were provided by a Lucas magdyno sitting behind the engine.

BSA made their own transmissions, and the clutch and single-strand primary chain lived inside the traditionally leak-prone pressed-steel chaincase. However, in a break from convention, the BSA clutch lived inside its own case within the primary chaincase, preferring to run dry.

Development was steady rather than spectacular, with a neat design of cast aluminium primary chaincase arriving with a new gearbox, the swinging arm frame and an Amal Monobloc carburetter in 1955. The final big redesign came for 1958, when the magdyno was replaced by a alternator driven from the drive side of the crankshaft. The alternator powered the battery, and the battery powered a coil to provide the sparks. The contact breaker and automatic timing device lived in the space vacated by the magdyno, driven by the same train of gears.

There were of course other changes, but they require more space than we have available to detail.

The B31 reached the end of the road in 1959, and the B33 followed it after the 1960 season. The traditional place of the big single as a tireless, dependable workhorse had been taken by the

increasingly popular twins, and the next generation of singles would be much lighter than the last of the heavyweight generation.

Providing that it has been rebuilt by someone who knows one end of a spanner from the other, and that it has been well maintained, the BSA heavy single is a fine workhorse. The 500cc B33 is the better suited to modern traffic conditions, entirely by virtue of its greater performance.

The weight of the bikes increased quite noticeably with the introduction of the swinging arm frame, which was common to the 650cc twins. As was then usual, the 350cc single engine struggled to provide sporting performance.

Such problems as these engines do have are generally the result of inept reassembly or complete lack of maintenance. Oil leaks were once common, usually caused by poor attempts at sealing the top of the pushrod tower or a failure to fit a gasket to the tappet inspection cover.

Which one to have? The rigid singles have all of the style. They steer very well and are generally more lively than the later bikes. However, they can have rather feeble brakes, and the suspect lighting that I always associate with dynamos. The later singles benefit from the fine handling of the duplex frame, while at the same time suffering from its greater weight. They are better braked, alternator electrics are generally more reliable, but they lack the style of the earlier bikes. The plunger models no doubt have their devotees, too, but I am a little pressed to think of any outstanding virtues.

Model designations

BSA resumed production for peacetime with the basic 350 (71 x 88mm = 348cc) B31 in 1945. A bigger brother 500 (85 x 88mm = 499cc) B33 followed for 1947. The B31 was joined by a rather more sporting

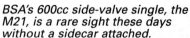

BSA's 600cc side-valve single, the M21, is a rare sight these days without a sidecar attached.

version, the B32, for 1946, and the 500 single was available as a more sporting B34 from their introduction in 1947. The B32 and B34 developed separately into the real Gold Stars of legend, and ran until 1957. The B31 roadster lasted until 1959, and the B33 until 1960.

The Side-valve Singles

As mentioned earlier, BSA built a creditable 125,000-plus motorcycles for wartime service, and the great majority of those were the M20 500cc side-valve. Following the end of hostilities, BSA hastily offered colours other than khaki and pointed their slogger at the civilian market, and thousands of

sidecar drivers in particular bought them. Included in these, of course, were the AA, whose yellow and black combinations were once a familiar sight on British roads.

BSA listed two side-valve singles: the 500cc M20 and the 600cc M21. The larger of the two was not a sports option; its extra cubes offered extra torque and a small amount of extra power.

Riding these once common sloggers should be part of every Britbike fan's education. They are slow, cruising around the 50mph mark; they are thirsty for the available performance too, and they can overheat alarmingly in heavy going. But they offer vast

charm to those with the patience to take time to sample a very different – and totally vanished today – way of going.

Oddly, BSA also produced a 'side-valve single' with overhead valves. This was the M33, which combined the M-series's (in other words, the side-valve's) bicycle with the engine from the B33. The idea was to provide the dedicated sidecar haulier with a plunger motorcycle tug, while offering more developed engine performance than that supplied by the M21. They are rare today but perfectly pleasant.

The bicycle

Although the front frame of the M-series side-valve machines differs from the ohv singles in carrying the crankcases in a very vintage-style 'shoe', they followed the B31 and B33 into the uncertain world of plunger suspension in 1951. And there they stayed, in a world of their own, gaining an 8-inch front brake in 1956, but otherwise suffering little in the way of developmental indignity before their demise in 1963 (the M20 was de-listed in 1955).

The side-valve engine

The bottom end of the B-series engine was derived from that of the wartime M20, although subsequent development of the latter failed to keep pace with that of its offspring.

The 1945 engine continued the wartime theme of cast-iron barrel and head until 1951, when a new alloy cylinder head was introduced – in the interests of better

Once a common sight, combinations like this rigid-framed 500cc M20 are unusual today.

The first of the BSA twins was the rigid-framed 500cc A7. The design changed very soon, making models as original as this one hard to find.

cooling, not greater performance, it should be said.

And basically, that's it. As an aside, BSA recognised the failings of even the 600cc M21 as a power unit for the family sidecar man, and offered the M33 as an alternative. As its designation suggests, this is actually a B33 500cc ohv engine in a plunger side-valve bicycle, and its lack of popularity is demonstrated both by its rarity today and by the fact that it preceded the M21 into the history book, leaving the lists in 1957. Looking back, I can see no way in which the M33 was a better bike than the B33, which must mean something.

On the road

Road performance of both side-valve singles is leisurely indeed. That is not to say that it is dull, providing that the rider plans his routes with a little forethought, avoiding long straight roads like the plague. The bikes are hearty travellers, setting a pace of their own choosing, and turning every trip into a journey. They don't even leak much. Usually.

The Non-unit Twins

The BSA A7 and A10 twins were a pair of very fine traditional British motorcycles, and many indeed are the riders who learned how to handle big bikes aboard them. To many they represent the very best of the 1950s British bikes, and although they are not without fault, they are as good as or better than all of their competitors. If asked to recommend a good all-round motorcycle from the '50s, I

Plunger rear springing helped but a little in smoothing out BSA's early twins.

would have little hesitation in suggesting one of these. Spares are plentiful, there is an active and friendly owners' club and the bikes can hold their own on any non-motorway road. Good enough?

There were in fact two A7 non-unit twins, although surprisingly few folk are aware of it. A 495cc twin was launched in 1946 and lasted only until 1950, when it was replaced by a 497cc twin. This was in fact a redesign of the original twin engine, carried out in the late 1940s to permit both comfortable enlargement to 650cc and to cure some overheating worries with the original engine.

These early twins still appear occasionally in the For Sale ads,

and they are reputedly very pleasant motorcycles. Sadly, although I almost bought one once, I have never ridden one further than around the block. Initially offered with rigid frame and telescopic forks, the early A7 was soon available with BSA's slightly dubious plunger frame, and in that form it bowed out in 1950 when it was replaced by the 'new' A7. Its mechanical specs were too similar to those of the later twins to be detailed here, so we will move on to 1950 and BSA's announcement of their revised twins.

The bicycle

BSA's twin arrived complete with

its own frame, available with both rigid and plunger rear wheel attachments. The frame was a very sturdy duplex affair, and its stiffness was complimented by the BSA telescopic forks fitted up front. I'm afraid that the comments made above regarding the plunger frame as fitted to the singles apply equally to the twins. Although the conventional wisdom has it that the rigid frame was favoured by sidecarists, I personally much prefer it for solo use – steering vagueness is no problem when you're coping with the navigational eccentricities of an asymmetric third wheel!

Be that as it may, and the 'plunger Flash' was an iconic motorcycle during my own youth, 1954 saw the appearance of the very fine BSA swinging arm frame. This was originally destined for export markets, but it arrived in the UK for the following year. And, as already discussed in the singles section above, a very good bicycle was the result.

Development of the bicycle was as already outlined for the singles, with brakes and major tinware changing for both ranges. The twins were available for three years longer than the singles, and the final versions developed a rather more modern, enclosed look than earlier bikes, with the headlamp, speedo, ammeter and lighting switch being mounted in a tin nacelle rather than in a separate

Top: *The first of the truly classic BSA twins was surely the plunger Flash, which was also an accomplished sidecar tug as this 1955 Watsonian combination shows. The bike is seen here in its traditional golden (beige) shade.*

Bottom: *The 'Golden Flash' was also available in black. This plunger twin featured iron head and barrels (which made it mechanically quiet) and a gearbox that bolted to the crankcases (giving a sane method of primary chain adjustment). This example is wearing a later Concentric carburettor.*

Cutaway diagram of the 1951 A10 engine.

bracket-mounted headlamp. The style was leading up nicely to the introduction of the notably more rounded unit models, as retrospect shows clearly.

The non-unit twin engine

In any discussion of classic British motorcycle engines, the inclusion of BSA's A7 and A10 twins is obligatory. Although it is conventional in most ways, the engine is most individual in others. And, most importantly, it is fuss-free in service and always a pleasure to use out there on the road.

In the British tradition, the two pistons rose and fell together inside a cast-iron block topped by a cast-iron head, and were retained by alloy con-rods running on a massive crankshaft. That shaft was supported in two main bearings, with the timing side main being a substantial bush. A train of three gears was driven from the end of the crank; the first intermediate carried a sprocket for the dynamo's chain drive; the second carried a timed breather and drove the single camshaft; and the third drove the magneto. An eccentricity of the design was its inclusion of an outer timing case, which enabled the dynamo chain to run in its own grease-filled compartment, as well as making space for the gear-type oil pump.

The single camshaft, located behind the cylinders, operated the valve gear via four lengthy pushrods that ran up a cast-in tunnel between and behind the bores – a neat arrangement. The valves themselves were operated by rockers mounted in an aluminium rockerbox, and their clearances could be effected through a pair of access openings.

As ever, the electrics consisted of Lucas magneto and generator, and the mixture was metered into the combustion chambers by an Amal

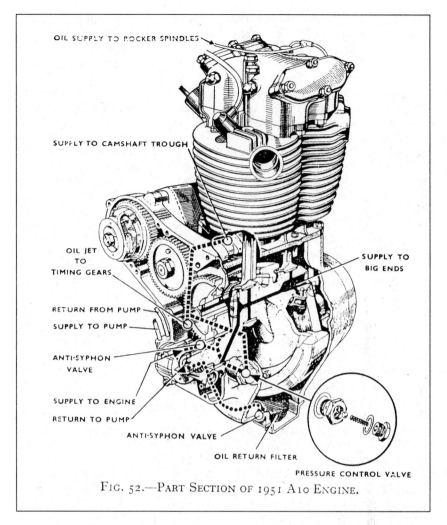

FIG. 52.—PART SECTION OF 1951 A10 ENGINE.

carburetter. This was a remote float Type 6 until 1955, when it was replaced by a 376 Monobloc – still mounted complete with a pressed-tin drip-shield to protect the magneto from fuel.

One very neat touch of the rigid and plunger-framed BSA twins was the method of mounting the gearbox. Unlike most others (Royal Enfields and the Mk3 Norton Commando honourably excepted), BSA did not rely upon pivoting of the gearbox to effect adjustment of the primary chain. They sensibly bolted their gearbox to the engine's crankcases, and adjusted the duplex primary chain via an internal tensioner. Sadly, progress, in the form of the swinging arm frame, brought with it a movable gearbox and single-strand primary chain.

I have previously declared that these engines are fine, strong workers and have an army of followers – not all of them members of the BSAOC! But they are not without their failings.

Unlike the AMC engine, the BSA twin continued BSA's tradition of boasting fasteners everywhere. The barrels were held down by a battery of studs and nuts, as was the cylinder head, as were the rockerboxes. And every time the engine was stripped, for whatever reason, the possibility of damaging one of the threads on one of these fasteners increased. I have shared many miles with several A10s and a couple of A7s, and none of them has been oil-tight, particularly from the top end when worked hard. BSA themselves recognised this, and increased the strength of the engine's construction as they upped its performance over the years.

Another slight madness of the design was that relocating the pushrods into their rockers after head removal was a truly fiddly job. Again, BSA recognised this and sold a comb-like tool to hold the pushrods in place while the rocker box was lowered on to the head. If you lacked one of these – and many of us did – it was fiddling, cursing and inevitable oil leaks from the inevitably damaged rocker box gasket. Ironically, Ariel's Huntmaster, a re-working of the BSA design, sported an access hole in the top of its rocker-box. My last A10 wore an Ariel rockerbox . . .

And speaking of cylinder heads, BSA offered an alloy head for the sports versions of their twins from 1954 onward. A nice touch was that the touring Golden Flash kept its iron head almost to the end, along with the mechanical quiet that was a welcome characteristic of the older design.

BSA's gearboxes are robust and accurate enough, although their clutches once had a reputation for weakness. Indeed, back before classic days, when these were cheap working bikes, a fairly common modification was the fitting of a Triumph clutch, and a kit was

available from specialist dealers to accomplish this. These days, when few old bikes are driven to their limits, BSA's own clutch should cope.

The big change to the 500 and 650 design came in 1958, when the bottom end was re-engineered. The bikes gained an improved crank, along with more robust mains to support it, and the cylinder block gained bigger fins and a thicker base mounting flange.

By the time the non-unit twins were being supplanted by the unit models they were well established as being an integral part of British motorcycling. They may not have equalled Triumph's reputation for being rev-happy fliers, but they certainly steered a lot better than 1950s Meriden twins, and the engines were generally rather less rattly, too.

On the road

Generations of family men hauled those families about with BSA Flash power, and if you are looking at a bike that appears to have pulled a sidecar (good giveaways are the remains of side-car lugs on the frame and improbably low gearing), expect serious wear to all the bicycle's bearings, and do not be surprised by a twist to the front forks. I

found this the hard way on my last Flash; it was impossible to point the headlamp down the road ahead, such was the twist to the forks. The bike steered well enough, though, despite this.

The engine itself has only one major weak point. That is the timing-side main bearing, which is a bush, and which controls the flow of oil to the big ends. As the bush wears, so the oil pressure drops, and the bush usually wears because servicing has been neglected. A conversion is available, using a complex but effective dual bearing, and further details of this will be available from BSA specialists. The conversion itself is offered by SRM Engineering of South Wales.

Recommended buys are . . . well, all of them, really. There are no true duffers, and although it should be remembered that if a bike is worn out then it is worn out whatever the badge on its tank, most of the wearing parts on both 500 and 650 twins are available – as is the specialist knowledge to make them run well. I have particularly fond memories of an unkillable old Flash (which boasted a plunger engine in a swinging arm frame, with Ariel yokes and a Norton front wheel!) and a very quick but ecologically disastrous Shooting Star, loyal fliers both.

Model designations

In brief . . . The basic A7 500cc twin was originally called just that. The sporting version was called the Star Twin until 1954, when it became the Shooting Star. The end of the road for the 500s came in 1961.

The basic A10 650cc twin was the Golden Flash, which was originally available painted gold all

By 1959, BSA's A10 was fully developed. It had good brakes, a willing engine and great looks.

over, including the frame. For the 1953 and '54 seasons we were offered the Super Flash, but the sporting A10 became the Road Rocket for 1955. In turn, the Road Rocket was supplanted by the Super Rocket, which was joined by the Rocket Gold Star for the final 1962–63 season.

The A10 was to prove a hard act to follow . . .

The Unit Twins

When BSA introduced their redesigned twins, in both 500 (A50) and 650cc (A65) capacities, the motorcycling world was rather less than completely bowled over. The snag was that although the A10 and A7 twins were getting a little long in the tooth, even by the standards of British motorcycle design, they were very popular with the riding public.

As the 1950s drew to a close, there was a school of thought within the industry that had observed the popularity (and high sales) enjoyed by the scooter-style of two-wheeler. It was apparently felt that the neat, clean lines of the Vespas and Lambrettas, along with their fashionable image, were the keys to a whole new market, and that 'real' bike sales would boom if only they were more neatly styled . . . were less threatening in appearance, perhaps.

This led to a couple of the major manufacturers (and several of the

Top: *Road Rocket cafe racers were once common. This 1956 model has been well customised.*

Middle: *Top of the pre-unit heap, the final development of the A10 was the Rocket Gold Star; vibratory and very expensive today.*

Bottom: *The first of the unit construction A50 and A65 twins were notably smoothly styled. Many owners updated theirs with 12-volt electrics, better brakes and a more interesting fuel tank. Like this one!*

slightly unglamorous two-stroke builders) adopting some pretty bizarre styling cues in their quest for 'smooth' styling. The Triumph 'bathtub' is well known, and Norton's light and heavy twins were offered with skirts for a while. Strange thing, fashion. Especially when viewed in retrospect.

Happily, BSA built a scooter and left their motorcycles looking like motorcycles. What they did to their bikes was to modernise them, taking their styling away from the trad approach, where nuts, bolts, adjusters and widgets were prominently on show, to a notably smooth, bulbous theme. Engine and gearbox were built as one, with smooth egg-like forms replacing the angular mechanismo that had gone before. Wheels became smaller, lowering the seat height, and although all the engineering was derivative of the earlier machines, it was immediately evident that the motorcycle had been designed as a whole. And there is absolutely nothing wrong with that. Most of the maintenance and accessibility problems that beset modern-day rebuilders of classic machinery can be traced to the manufacturers' attempts to continually evolve their existing designs, rather than starting afresh. Anyone who has attempted to remove the cylinder head of a

Norton (aka Matchless) P11 without first removing the engine from the frame will know exactly what I mean!

So. It is 1962 and BSA are introducing their new main motorcycle range. The old order has gone, taking with it magnetos and dynamo, and the new order has tramped in, bringing with it alternators and coils. If you charted major British motorcycle model changes across the years, you might notice that Lucas (the suppliers of most UK motoring electrickery) appeared to dictate many of these changes – but in reality, Lucas's own changes were all part of a continual drive to reduce costs, and that drive was a result of a continual demand from their customers for cheaper components. Market forces, as usual, in action.

The unit twin engine

The engines of the new 500 and 650 were identical below the cylinder barrel, differences mainly being limited to differently dimensioned holes in the blocks and different cylinder heads up top. And the bicycles were almost identical too, with the 500's front brake being 7 inches rather than the 650's 8 inches in diameter, which is a little odd, given that the bikes weighed much the

same. And had very similar performance, truth be told.

Returning to the engine, examination of appropriate engineering drawings reveals that although the A65 and A10 engines look entirely different, in fact the design principles behind them are very similar. The basic layout of the bottom end of the unit motor follows that of the earlier effort in that its crank is mounted between a ball main bearing on the drive side and a bush main bearing on the timing side. Why was this, given that the timing-side bush was a known area of weakness on the outgoing A10? No idea. Cost, probably.

Likewise, the single camshaft is mounted to the rear of the crankshaft, driven from it by a pair of gears and carrying the engine's main breather. The pushrods run up between the barrel to the rockerbox, where they work their magic with the valves. And here is one of the more sensible developments of new from old. Unlike the A10, the A65 carried its rockers in pillars cast into the main cylinder head casting. This meant that the rocker box cover was just a cover, was under no load, and should not leak. From an owner's point of view, valve clearance adjustment becomes much easier (no silly little hatches through which hapless spannerjack is expected to waggle feeler gauge and two spanners), as does locating the pushrods into their various rockers after a head-off rebuild. This neat design also tidied up the appearance of the engine's top end. It's just a shame that BSA failed to go the whole hog and retain the whole top end by studs running straight from the head to the crankcase – but they no doubt had their reasons.

The other, very obvious, difference twixt A10 and A65 engines

As the '60s progressed BSA tuned their unit twin, offering it in alternate sporting guises.

was that the crankcases themselves included provision for the gearbox. Hurrah! At a stroke, a whole load of spannering angst was dispelled, with adjustment of the primary chain being accomplished by the civilised application of spanner to a slipper tensioner, rather than by swivelling the whole gearbox backwards (and then, of course, discovering a sudden need to adjust the final drive chain). BSA also fitted their unit twins with a triplex chain (one which has three sets of rollers built across its width, rather than just one row – simplex – or two rows – duplex – and which should transmit more power for longer before requiring adjustment). A long-time owner of an A50 Royal Star of my acquaintance once told me that he had only needed to adjust his primary chain once in 20,000 miles of commuter use.

The A65's primary chain, the alternator and the clutch all live together under the cover on the left (drive) side of the engine, and unless the engine is worked very hard indeed by classic standards, they should last a good long time. However . . . if a unit BSA twin is abused and badly maintained, the primary area can take a pounding. If you are looking at a bike that sounds uncommon clattery from deep inside, stop the engine (please!) and insert a digit through the hole thoughtfully provided, both checking the tension of the chain and the amount of oil on it. If it is both dry and slack, contemplate some restorative expense; a slack dry chain can rattle an alternator stator to pieces, can lose rollers that will grind up both alternator and clutch plates, and can knock spots off the clutch via its chainwheel. Unit Triumphs can do this too.

The unit BSA engine has a short-

er stroke than its predecessor, and tends to be a better breather and a happier revver as a result. And, as already mentioned, things electrical were taken care of by a Lucas alternator, to provide charge for the battery, and by Lucas coils, to provide sparks. Neither alternator nor coils feature moving parts (excepting the alternator rotor, but these are generally robust and reliable enough), so tend not to break down. That the dreadful voltage regulator box also departed with the dynamo is a cause for celebration, as they were poor things that suffered badly from vibration and misunderstanding. Fans of dynamos should at the very least replace their voltage control boxes with more modern alternatives.

Ignition faults can usually be traced to the points assembly, which lives under a circular cover in the timing case. Because of the design, originally only one cylinder could be timed, and any inaccuracies in construction or assembly could result in the timing for the other cylinder being inaccurate. This situation persisted until 1968, when a better design eliminated this. I have also seen the points' housing filled with oil

after the failure of the oil seal, and with water after the vigorous application of a power washer. Ignition complaints are inevitable in both cases. Sensible modern man fits electronic ignition.

Carburation was again supplied by Amal, initially through the fine Monobloc instruments, changing to the slimmer Concentric in 1967–68, depending upon the model.

The engine's development proceeded fairly briskly, with performance versions following the original tourists into the showrooms. Generally, the more the performance envelope was stretched, the less pleasant became the engine, and as noise, vibration and harshness mounted, BSA responded by improving the oil supply to prolong the life of the internals, then increasing the sizes of the joint faces in attempts at curbing the oil leaks. High performance models usually boasted twin carb heads, and the traditional inability of the home bodger to balance twin carbs has resulted in some fiercely ill-running Lightnings over the years.

The last big developments to the engine came for 1970, when every-

The 1971-on oil-in-frame machines are generally underrated. A shame, because they can go really well.

thing was beefed up (and many parts from then on are not interchangeable with earlier equivalents, please note), including an increase in the diameter of the cylinder block retaining studs to 3/8 inch and an increase in the size and strength of the flange that was bolted to it. A good parallel with the 'big flange' A10 barrel there for hobbyists.

With the introduction of the new oil-in-frame bicycle in late 1970, development of the twin effectively ended (as did production of the 500, in fact), as BSA's much discussed collapse starved resources. But, as is so often the case, the last engines were the best – at least for anyone wishing to use their old bikes on modern roads. Having said that, driven gently the A65 and A50 engines are all pleasant enough and are capable of high mileages. They may lack some of the charm of the A7 and A10, but they do boast (mostly) reliable electrics . . . And a lot of them were built, which means that there are still many running, which in turn ensures that spares supply and specialist knowledge remain available.

A final footnote is provided by the very rare 750cc A70 engine. This was intended for racing in the USA, and was apparently spectacularly vibratory in use.

The bicycle

Readers may note that I have departed from the pattern of the rest of the book in discussing the unit engines before the appropriate bicycle. I did this because the unit engine's tale follows directly from that of the non-unit. And, having said that, it should also be

Top: *The last of the twin engines was sturdy, reliable and a good ride, and the late bikes can be made to stop well, too.*

Bottom: *Clarity: all the clocks you need.*

said that the bicycle did exactly the same.

The design of the A50 and A65 bicycles was very similar to that of the preceding twin, with obvious dimensional changes brought about by the accommodation of the new power plant. Wheel sizes also dropped, down to 18 inches, and the wheelbase miraculously shrank by 2 inches, making the whole motorcycle noticeably smaller.

As already mentioned, BSA had joined in the rush for 'smooth, modern' styling, and the tinware certainly demonstrated this. The mudguards were all smooth curves, deep valances and few stays, the petrol tank was bulbous and smoothly curved, while the grubby bits (oil tank, coils, carburetter, tool compartment) were all hidden away behind vast, bulbous, smoothly curving side panels. This was possibly the very first British motorcycle that looked as though it had been designed so that it could be effectively cleaned with a hosepipe. Cleverly, although it relied upon much of the experience gained with the non-unit twins, it looked very different.

Happily, the new bikes rode well enough too, with the only real complaints being that the centre stand's operating lever grounded too early on left-hand bends, and that the 500 should have had the same brake as the 650.

As ever, we don't have room here for listing all of the year-on-year, model-by-model changes, but the pace and pattern of development were typically British, and major surprises were few. As the engines' development was primarily to improve performance, then reliability, then performance, and so forth, the development of the bicycle echoed this. So, briefly, the A50 received the 8-inch brake in 1965; two-way damping of the front forks appeared in 1966; decent 2ls front anchors (from Triumph) were fitted in 1969 (a year earlier for the A65L and A65SS sportsters), with the design of the forks changed to suit; and a whole completely new bicycle appeared for the 1971 season.

This new BSA bicycle was to be common for all BSA twins, and all Triumph twins that were not 500s. The frame's major areas of new-ness were that its large-diameter top tube carried the engine's oil, it was startlingly tall and it was painted grey. Many are those who claim that the grey was a sort of pretend nickel-plating, but you believe this at your peril. Grey paint looks like grey paint, even to stylists of the 1960s . . .

The new chassis also boasted new forks, with their stanchions sportingly exposed to show off their chrome, and new hubs and brakes at each end. These brakes, the famous 'conical hubs', were either BSA's best or their worst, depending upon who you talk to. I have owned several BSAs and Triumphs fitted with them, have ridden many more, and have found that when well set-up (ie by following the instructions in the manual) they work very well.

The rest of the machine reflected the fact that BSA had clearly identified the USA as their primary market. Hence all of the skimpy mudguarding, exposed chromium and polished alloy. Hence also the small petrol tanks and wide handlebars. Ironically, although the bikes were roundly criticised by some for all of these features when they were new, and although they continue to be roundly criticised by some today, their styling, riding positions and general brash character make them absolutely perfect for today's classic scene. For, let us face it, most old Brits are kept off the road in the winter, mainly being ridden for short distances when the weather is at its most clement. And as they are almost invariably ridden slowly, the high, wide and indeed handsome bars are no problem.

BSA's late twins represent one of the few bargains available in the world of the classic British bike, in fact.

The final changes to the bicycle added a 4-gallon petrol tank to the original 2.5-gallon one, chopped some of the height out of the riding position and changed the standard colour back to black. Sadly, the day of the BSA twin was over, although new machines were still available after production ceased in 1972.

On the road

All of the various BSA unit twins are good riding machines. The braking on the earliest A50 500s is a little marginal for today's roads, but braking abilities improved as the years rolled by. There are also all manner of export market oddities available in the UK since the great repatriation of the late '80s and early '90s. If I was to make recommendations, I would suggest that exhibitionists and polishers should buy the export market sportsters, which look beautiful in their gaudy colour schemes and muscular stance, while riders should avoid the twin-carb models, and especially the high-compression twin-carb models. One of the most vibratory experiences available to modern man is riding a Spitfire Mk IV with maladjusted carbs and a loose headsteady.

The A50 in its touring form is a very underrated motorcycle. Almost all the wearing parts – both power train and bicycle – are designed to handle the stresses of the 650s, and as a result this is an almost unburstable machine. OK, it is unlikely to top the ton, but it won't shake your feet from the footrest either. Likewise the A65T Thunderbolt, from any year, which is like the A50 – only more so.

As a personal choice, I would choose the latest A65T, with the UK 4-gallon tank, low bars and single carb. I would pay to have the engine rebuilt by an expert recommended by the BSA

Owners' Club, and I would have them incorporate the timing-side main bush modification offered by SRM Engineering. Oh yes, I would also fit a halogen headlamp and the disc front brake from the Triumph T140 Bonneville, which uses the same front forks. One very sweet motorcycle.

Model designations

The cooking 500cc A50 Star was available from 1962 until '65, when it became the Royal Star, and lasted until 1970. Goodbye A50 at that point. The first sporting A50 was the A50C Cyclone, which ran from '64 to '65, when it became the A50W Wasp (on the way, from '64 to '65, an even sportier version, the A50CC Cyclone Clubman was available).

The touring 650cc A65 Star ran from 1962 until '65, when it became the A65T Thunderbolt, retaining this proud name until the end of the line. The sporting A65 Rocket was offered from '63 to '65, while the A65 Lightning Rocket (just for the Americans) and the A65 Lightning Clubman and A65 Spitfire Hornet (for the Americans again) were around from '64 to '65. Quite rare, those. Meanwhile, the British market sportster was the A65L Lightning, which ran from '64 until the end of play, being joined by the A65H Hornet (mainly for export) for '66 to '67, and the A65FS Firebird Scrambler from '68 to '71. The UK

Top: *The mass repatriation of a few years back saw many American models returning to the UK market. This 1966 export A65T is hardly standard but would have been cheap.*

Middle: *The grey paint on the frame, revealed by the peeling off of the black coat above it, shows this re-imported A65T to be a 1971 and not a 1972 model.*

Bottom: *Underrated but great fun to ride are the 500s, like this 1968 Royal Star. Smooth and unburstable, they represent good value.*

super-sportsters were the A65SS Spitfires, in Marks II, III and IV forms (no MkI, oddly, unless that was the '64–'65 US model Spitfire Hornet) in 1966, '67 and '68 respectively. Finally, the 750cc A70 Lightning 750 was the swan-song, but they were never sold in the UK, and you wouldn't know if you'd got one anyway because they were badged (and the engine cases stamped) as A65L Lightnings.

The Unit Singles

Both before and after the war, BSA sold a vast number of ride-to-work utility motorcycles. Most of these were of relatively low capacity, sturdily built and ideal for their intended commuter role. That is actually to say that their performance was adequate for the urban and country roads of the time, but would be rather lacking on the new dual carriageways and motorways of the coming decades. The world was changing, changing fast in terms of personal mobility, and the decision-makers within BSA recognised that as well as anyone.

So it was, presumably, that the decision was taken to discontinue the line of worthy heavyweight singles at the end of the 1950s. Although the twins moved on into a second iteration, with the modernised unit models, the big working single was seen as being dead, and BSA vacated that market sector, leaving it to AMC, Panther and Velocette. The hand of Triumph's Edward Turner is often seen in this change of direction,

Top: *The most sporting of the unit twins is the Spitfire.*

Middle: *The Spitfire is durable, too. This 1967 example was used for despatching in London for many years.*

Bottom: *The arrival of the unit-construction C15 marked a turning point in British bike design.*

BSA STAR 250c.c. model C15

The first stretch of the engine produced the 350cc B40. This is a 1962 example.

and indeed all of the unit BSA singles are derivative of his original design for Triumph, the Tiger Cub (or, to be more accurate, the Terrier, which preceded it).

Although the big BSA single was effectively deceased, a small irony is that the 'light' C15 replacement for the utility lightweights, the C10, 11 and 12, was eventually developed until it displaced the full half-litre capacity. It should also be remarked that although it is fashionable to criticise Turner's simple single design, few engine designs have withstood a capacity increase of a whole 100 per cent.

The C15 Star, when it appeared in late 1958, was as much a departure from what had gone before as

were the unit twins. Its styling was similarly neat, smoothed off and bulbous. Its engineering was conservative and conventional and it predictably adopted the new Lucas electrics, with coil ignition and an alternator charging the battery. Again like the twins (which had yet to appear, of course), the C15 had been designed as a whole; it was not merely a new engine sitting uncomfortably in an old frame.

The 250cc C15 Star was soon followed by the 350cc B40, and the variations on a unit single theme continued with bewildering rapidity: there was the C15T (for 'Trials'), the C15S (for 'Scrambles') and the SS80 (a sporty roadster) for

the 250s alone within the first few years. This both provides a happy hunting ground for anyone who fancies owning a unit BSA single, and a minefield for anyone attempting an accurate restoration!

The unit single continued right until the end of the BSA name – and slightly beyond, when the last of the 500s was badged for a short time as a Triumph (the very rare TR5MX). It is without doubt an object lesson in how much development can be bestowed upon a simple original design, and anyone riding both a 1972 B25SS then a 1959 C15 Star would be hard pressed to describe similarities. Except one – the characteristic whine of the valve gear . . .

The bicycle

The C15's frame was a neat but simple design featuring a single top tube and a single downtube that spilt into two to form a cradle beneath the engine. The rear subframe, which carried the seat and the rear suspension, was bolted to the main frame – nothing at all unconventional there. Front suspension was by courtesy of a set of telescopic forks, while the back wheel was suspended from a swinging arm.

The wheels were just 17 inches in diameter, which helped the overall diminutive stature of the bike, and they were braked by a pair of 6-inch full-width drums. The 'working' nature of the machine was demonstrated by its deeply valanced, heavy mud-

The final stretch of the unit single took it out to 500cc for the B50SS Gold Star. Pokey motor, low mass, trick styling and good brakes almost outweigh the difficult starting.

guards, and the oil tank, battery box, air filter and gubbins were all tucked neatly away into a full-width compartment beneath the front half of the seat.

The smooth design cues of the bigger BSAs were continued to the headlamp design, where the light itself, the speedo, switch and ammeter were all fitted into a neat nacelle.

Early C15s and B40s steer perfectly well by the standards of the time, and for their available performance. If they have serious flaws, the original front fork is less than sturdy, the swinging arm bushes are prone to wear and, to be honest, the brakes are not the best, which can make for worrying moments on modern roads. However, it is hard to get into trouble with a standard C15 because the engine's output is low and the undercarriage decks long before the tyres reach their limit. As the years passed, so the whole bicycle was improved, and by the late 1960s developments from the works scramblers had transformed the faintly dull C15 into the seriously pokey – but well-steering – B50SS.

As already stated, development proceeded apace, with more appropriate and hopefully more effective forks and brakes appearing on the more sporting versions, along with less effective and more appropriate mud-guarding and lighting. Having said that, the basics of the bicycle remained fundamentally close to the original until the introduction of a new frame for all the singles for 1971, although things did improve on the high-speed steering front with the introduction of a newer, better fork (from the twins) with the Barracuda in '67. A new, and rather better 2ls front brake followed the following year.

BSA's modernisation of their unit single saw its transformation from simple Star to virile Barracuda.

The new frame followed the twins' design in so far as it also carried the engine's oil in its tubes. It also conformed to the new, more modern approach to suspension design, as outlined in the twins' section.

Where the single's frame differed from the that of twins was in the retention of the single-downtube layout (the front tube was used as the main oil reservoir, with the oil filler being behind the steering head, rather than under the nose of the seat as on the twins), and in the method of rear chain adjustment. The twins tensioned their final drive chains by conventional pulling of the rear wheel nearer to the end of the swinging arm, but the singles employed a cam and peg approach, where the whole swinging arm was moved backward. This was the better system, being born from heavy competition use, and it was impossible to get the rear wheel out of alignment due to poor adjustment.

The brakes for the new machine were also common to the twins, and earlier comments thus apply, apart from the fitting of a 6-inch sls, rather than the more usual 8-inch 2ls, front brake to some 250s.

Rather sadly, the range ceased when BSA stopped production,

and although off-road versions were available – as CCMs – for some time, the roadster singles died with the factory closure.

It should also be mentioned that the genuine competition models (which started with the C15T and C15S) boasted a lot of cycle parts that were different from those on the roadsters. Be careful, should you be looking at a bike described as being a C15S, for instance, that it is the genuine article, and not a stock C15 with the tinware thrown away and an alloy petrol tank . . .

The unit single engine

Although BSA's unit singles shared the same egg-shaped styling as the unit twins from the same stable, they share almost none of their engineering. Which is because – as already mentioned – the design was a development of an existing Triumph single. However, although this fact gets blamed for the faults of the early unit power plant, that's not really fair, given that the design proved to be capable of being stretched out to a whole 499cc!

The heart of the engine, its crank assembly, was slightly unusual for a four-stroke single in that the big-end bearing was a plain bush rather than the more usual roller

bearing. The flywheels were conventional, and the crankshaft itself was supported by a ball main bearing on the drive side, and a bush on the timing side. The single camshaft was driven directly from the crank and a skew drive powered both the oil pump and the cam to the points, the housing for which was mounted at an angle behind the cylinder. The pushrods ran up to the rocker box through a separate chrome-plated tube outside the barrel, and through a cast-in tube in the head. The rockers themselves ran on spindles, which in turn were mounted in the rockerbox, a casting separate from that of the head.

Primary drive was by a duplex chain, which had, unusually, no provision for tensioning, through a completely conventional clutch, to the four-speed gearbox. This was also entirely conventional in its operation, although the shift pattern was Triumph's down-for-first method.

Carburation was handled by an Amal Monobloc, and the 6-volt battery was charged by an alternator mounted inside the primary chaincase and driven by the crank. Sparks were by coil.

The engine's failings are generally down to poor maintenance or to over-optimistic views of its performance capabilities. In common with any engine that runs a plain big-end bearing, the oil supply is critical to its longevity. If the oil is allowed to run low, or is not changed regularly, the life of both the plain bush timing-side main bearing and the plain big-end bearing will be seriously reduced.

Most C15s were condemned to being ridden by younger riders early in their careers, and a lot of their reputation for less than sparkling reliability stems from the poor levels of maintenance characteristic of that breed of rider. When you add to this that the early design really did fall down in terms of narrow joint faces, which failed to keep the oil sealed inside; some awkward top-end fastenings and a timing housing that could (and did) loosen, rotate and mess up the timing; valve inspection caps that (rather like those on Triumph twins, but less badly) were prone to vibrate loose and fall off . . . you end up with a machine that could rapidly become a heap if poorly maintained. When new, which is when the Press tested them of course, they were fine.

From there things went upward pretty rapidly, and although we don't have room here to list all the changes, inevitably some are more important from the point of view of the 1990s rider.

By 1962, the inadequacy of the plain big end had been recognised, and a roller bearing was introduced, at the same time as a tensioner for the primary chain – except for the base C15, which had to wait until 1964! For 1965 things really improved, with a thorough redesign. The points tower behind the barrel disappeared, to be replaced by a set of contact breakers mounted behind a cover on the timing case and driven by the camshaft.

Things looked up again in '65, when all of the unit singles received a bottom end based on the 441 Victor scrambler, complete with a ball race for the timing-side main bearing, and the larger oil pump from the twins.

The bottom end was altered again in 1969, when the drive-side main bearing was changed from a ball race to a roller bearing, and the con-rod was strengthened. By this stage the performance of the singles was in a totally different league, and they were reliable enough providing that maintenance schedules were followed religiously. If oil changes, in particular, were neglected, expensive noises were the inevitable result. And that situation has not altered today.

On the road

The performance of the C15 Star could never be described as invigorating, and its braking is unimpressive on today's roads. With most BSA models, it is something of a truism to declare that they really did get better as they were developed year by year. So I would suggest that should you be contemplating the purchase of a unit BSA single – for riding, not

Workhorses, like this 1966 C15G, are still plentiful and cheap. Sometimes they're reliable, too.

One of the best customers for BSA was the Military. This is an Auxiliary Fire Service WD B40.

showing, as ever – start looking at bikes built after the middle of 1966, with an engine number beginning 'C15G'; they are much stronger than earlier versions. Personally, I prefer the final, oil-in-frame singles, with their mad lozenge silencers, indicators, decent electrics, good brakes and fine steering.

The bigger versions are well worth looking at, too. Again, the B50 is an excellent on-the-road tool, having a lot more punch than the 250 but with little weight penalty to hinder the handling. The problem with the 500s is starting them, and fitting modern electronic ignition systems improves things greatly.

A special mention should be made of the forces' model, the WD B40. Ignore the very early ones, which struggle with a very odd carburetter, and look for the latest you can find. With their scrambles-type frame and sound post-'66 engines, they can make very effective classic workhorses. They were once very easy to find, but pre-'65 trials enthusiasts have converted huge numbers into pukka weekend off-road kit. Their only real problem for road use – apart from the obviously limited performance – is the gearing chasm between third and top.

Spares for the singles are not exactly bursting from the shelves, but the specialists can supply most wearing parts. In addition, prospective buyers should remember that BSA built many thousands of their singles, and exported a high proportion of the late ones. If a rare spare is genuinely unavailable in the UK, a

For those wanting a little more poke, the unit engine proved capable of a stretch to 440cc, as seen in this B44 Victor scrambler.

couple of North American dealers can often help.

Model designations

The first unit single was the C15 Star, which lasted all the way from launch in 1958 until 1967. It was joined by the sportier C15T and C15S off-roaders from '59 until '65, with the SS80 Sports Star joining the squad in '61 until it too passed away in '65. The C15 Sportsman was a one-year wonder from 1966 until '67, when it was supplanted by the C25 Barracuda – also for one year. The C25 was

replaced by the B25S Starfire in '68, and that survived until the new range in 1970, being joined by the B25FS Fleetstar (a fleet model, would you believe?) in '69; it maintained its model designation through the new launch of 1970 and lasted until the end in '72. The final 250s were the B25SS Gold Star and B25T Victor Trail, the oil-in-frame models that passed on in '72.

The first stretch of the design was to the 350cc B40 Star in 1961. This survived until 1965 (two more years for the WD version), and the sporty B40SS Sports Star joined in '62, also

dropped in '65. The 440cc stretch began with the B44 GP Scrambler ('57–'67), and continued with the B44VE Victor Enduro Trail, which began in '66 and was supplemented in '67 by the B44VR Victor Roadster, itself replaced in '68 by the B44SS Shooting Star, as was the B44VE by the B44VS Victor Special Trail. Finally, the full 500s, the B50SS Gold Star, B50T Victor Trail and B50MX Victor Scrambler, were the last oil-in-frame singles, surviving until 1973.

The Triples

By the mid-1960s it was obvious to the motorcycle trade that the

whole world order was changing. The advent of the motorway age had rendered obsolete most of the output of the British manufacturers, for the simple reason that few of their motorcycles would stand being cruised at 70–80mph for long periods without something unpleasant happening to their internals – assuming that the rider hadn't been shaken insensible by the vibration first, in some cases.

The BSA Group's answer to the coming demand for greater sophistication and sustainable performance was a 750cc three-cylinder motorcycle. It is a sad comment on the management

failures endemic in whole sectors of British manufacturing industry at the time that the idea that a three-cylinder engine, based on pre-war technology and engineering, built on old-fashioned machinery and requiring skilled labour to achieve acceptable build quality, could somehow challenge the Japanese in an open market. The Japanese were building new designs, engineered for automated production on the most modern production lines in the world. To assume that the British produce described above could compete on unit price or sustainable performance with the likes of Honda's CB750 was a mistake. A fatal mistake.

However, the three-cylinder machines, built by BSA as the A75 Rocket 3, and by Triumph as the T150 Trident, were – and remain – charming machines. They are also eminently suited to the crowded roads of today, with fine acceleration, good cruising ability, excellent handling and adequate brakes. And in any case, it is not the brief of this volume to analyse the cause of the collapse of our bike industry.

That industry produced many charismatic motorcycles, several of which are the stuff of legend, and priced to match. Their high price renders many of them unsuitable for most classic riders, but not so the BSA triple. Because of their lingering reputation as flawed motorcycles, which can consume a lot of money to maintain and which can appear dauntingly complex to those used to more conventional twins and singles, prices remain surprisingly reasonable. Also, another good point in their favour is that owners tend to be dedicated riders rather than polishers, and as a result a lot of developmental improvement

The 750 Rocket 3, which appeared in 1968, was a great riding machine.

The final version of the Rocket 3 was the Mk 2, seen here in UK guise.

has taken place since they ended production.

Early Rocket 3s (and their Triumph equivalents) were the victims of some rather remarkable styling. It appears that although the marketing men at BSA had understood that the two-wheeled world was changing, they had failed to recognise that motorcyclists are a strangely conventional lot, and that they embrace radical change only when it is plainly linked to high performance. Thus the early Rocket 3s, with their slabby petrol tanks, strange panelling and desperate Dan Dare silencers, were viewed more with wonder and suspicion than with wonder and delight. The world was not rocked upon its axis by the massed opening of customers' wallets.

But the triples were – and remain – good machines to ride. I know, I have one . . .

The bicycle

The Rocket 3 bicycle was completely conventional in function, even if its aesthetic accoutrements may have disguised the fact. The main frame was a duplex cradle, where the front downtubes curved all the way around to the top of the rear suspension units. It was a sturdy frame and was capable of steering well up to the limits of the day's tyre technology with no cause for concern on the part of the rider.

The front forks were of the same type as currently fitted to BSA twins, as were the brakes, the front being the 8-inch Triumph type 2ls unit. The engine's lubricant was cooled by a radiator mounted under the nose of the petrol tank,

The Export Rocket 3: last of the line.

and this was styled by the addition of a pair of alloy covers, complete with side reflectors to satisfy US legislation, and the tank itself was an unusual squared-off shape with badging that was unique to the model.

The side panels were voluminous, containing battery, toolbox, oil tank and half of the air filter housing, and the whole thing was set off by a pair of what were probably the most remarkable silencers ever to grace a British motorcycle.

Although the styling of the Rocket 3 became less flamboyant, especially for the UK market, changes to the chassis were restricted to the replacement of the

front forks for the 1971 season with the exposed stanchion type fitted across most of the rest of the BSA and Triumph ranges. The conical hub front brake accompanied the forks.

The triple engine

The Rocket 3's power plant was in fact a development of the Triumph twin engine, and owed nothing to the BSA twins alongside which it was sold. For this reason, and to avoid excessive duplication, its engineering description is contained in the Triumph section of this volume.

Although most working parts of the BSA and Triumph triple

engines are identical, several major castings are not, as the BSA's cylinder block was canted forward at 15 degrees to the vertical, and the timing side was styled to look more like the BSA twins than the Triumph ones.

Carburation was by three Amal Concentrics, a Lucas alternator provided charge for the battery, and three Lucas coils supplied sparks to the cylinders.

Changes to the engine during its production run from 1968 to 1972 were mainly intended to increase its smoothness and ability to retain its oil. Most Rocket 3s were built with four-speed gearboxes, although a final few were built with a five-speed cluster. These can be distinguished a) by having five gears, and b) by an engine number beginning 'A75RV'. There were no major engineering alterations that are within the scope of this book.

On the road

The Rocket 3 vies for the title of the first British superbike with Norton's Commando, and justly so, as they were both highly individual answers to the problems besetting Britain's traditional motorcycle builders. The expression 'superbike' was coined for bikes like these: they were of much higher apparent performance than their predecessors; they looked radically different; and they were intended to be the start of a whole new era of purely leisure-orientated motorcycling.

Riding the Rocket 3 is unlike riding any other BSA. The whole machine has a presence lacking in any parallel twin, and its performance is exhilarating without sounding mechanically

Was there ever a more handsome motorcycle than this 1969 A75R? It looks good, it stops and steers well and it has a most charismatic motor.

life-threatening. Although it is perfectly possible to fault any motorcycle ever made, anyone contemplating the purchase of one of these models should try to view them as they appeared at the time – reading contemporary road tests is always a good idea. Then consider that a well-assembled Rocket 3 can hold its own with most traffic on modern roads today and a measure of what its designers and engineers achieved is possible.

The triples have their own owners' club, and the supply of most spares is good. If you are tempted by a Rocket 3, I suggest that you try both an early one, with the wildly odd styling, and a late one, with the (sometimes) better brakes. But if it is outrageous style you want, try a Hurricane X-75, which although badged as a Triumph is in fact a BSA . . .

Chapter 8

Norton

Although Norton were never the biggest of British motorcycle manufacturers in terms of the sheer numbers of the bikes they built, their reputation in the classic marketplace reflects the high esteem in which they were held throughout the post-war period, and, indeed, the esteem in which they were held up to their demise in the chaos of the mid-1970s – and again 15 years later . . .

This reputation was largely due to their long and distinguished history as world-class racers. The Norton list of famous victories and remarkable achievements against seemingly insuperable odds is unrivalled, especially when viewed against a financial background that looks horribly like imminent bankruptcy for much of the time. In one of history's little ironies, that tradition carried on from Rem Fowler's class win in the very first 1907 TT race, right up to Steve Hislop's win in the 1992 Senior TT on one of the doomed rotary racers. Heroic failure – Norton in a nutshell.

Like Associated Motorcycles and BSA, Norton had also benefited from large contracts to supply the Allied forces with motorcycles throughout the Second World War. It is another small irony that, despite their unparalleled history of race track achievement, the War Department

chose to purchase a plodding side-valve model, the 16H, from Norton.

However, once hostilities had ended, Norton, like the other British bike builders, returned to the production of civilian machines. Their range was initially singular, both side- and overhead-valve, but they really needed a twin to compete in the post-war world, and the 500cc Dominator duly arrived in 1949. That engine proved to be one of the major stayers of the motorcycle world, surviving in expanded and developed forms for almost three decades!

The post-war history of Norton is the post-war history of the whole industry. It is a long, difficult tale of occasional brilliance countered by a depressing litany of failure brought about by management that was mediocre at best. It is a sadly familiar tale to anyone interested in British commercial history, and it does not bear repeating here. More happily, while the various companies producing motorcycles bearing the Norton name floundered around on their paths to ultimate failure, the motorcycles they produced were disproportionately rewarding and involving to own and ride. Which is another reason why the marque remains highly thought of to this day.

Norton, unlike BSA and AMC,

was rarely its own boss. The company founded by James Norton was acquired by AMC in 1953, moving from their traditional Birmingham base to the AMC plant in London in the early 1960s; a significant number of the engineering changes following that acquisition can be explained by a gradual rationalisation of the four-stroke ranges owned by the London parent. When the AMC company itself ran on to the rocks in 1966, the wreckage was acquired by Manganese Bronze Holdings, who again rationalised the ranges they had acquired, slimming down to just a single four-stroke model range within three years, and moving the base of operations again, this time to Andover and Wolverhampton. When the final mid-1970s convulsions of the industry turned into its death throes, witnessing the effective demise of BSA, the long, lingering decline of Triumph and the end of Norton production, it was to take a lot of commercial courage – and manoeuvring – by the holding company to keep the name alive until their radical rotary-engined model was (allegedly) ready for production almost ten years later.

Sadly, even the rotary revival, while not without its moments – like the TT victory referred to earlier – almost inevitably succumbed, not altogether to

Pre-war Norton singles were often sporting and had a certain elegance of line. This is a 1938 ES2.

commercial failure, but to the collapse of the corporate structure that supported it.

For the sake of this volume, I shall consider the machines that are likely to be of interest to classic enthusiasts everywhere. So, we shall take a look at the singles, from 16H through to ES2 Mk 2, and the twins, from Model 7 to Commando Mk 3, from Jubilee to Electra, and rotaries from Interpol 2 to F1 Sport – but we will ignore the overhead-camshaft singles, the Internationals and the Manxes, which are offered for sale so rarely and are so specialist that they deserve more thought than we have space for. Any reader contemplating the purchase of a camshaft Norton should consult one of the acknowledged experts in the field; failure to do this will almost invariably result in considerable unnecessary expense.

Although at the time of writing, in mid-1997, exactly 90 years after Norton's victory in that distant first TT, the company owning the rights to the famous old name of Norton is still trading, there appears to be little likelihood that any new motorcycles bearing that name will be built. Another sad end, then, but a sad end preceded by many notably successful motorcycles.

The Norton aficionado is well catered for in terms of spares supply and enthusiastic clubs, and the bikes bearing the famous name are almost all good riding machines. They are well worth considering, with a style and character all their own.

The Singles

Although when considering the

This 1946 Model 18 shows how little had changed immediately post-war.

heavy singles from BSA I separated ohv from side-valve and lightweight from heavyweight, when looking at the Norton singles (Norton did not sell lightweight singles) I shall lump both engine types together. My reasoning is simple: when Norton restarted civilian production for the 1946 season, they offered just two models, the ohv Model 18 and the side-valve 16H, and they were effectively the same bicycle fitted with different engines. Why 16H? Yet another question for the classic bike trivia quiz! In brief: before the war Norton offered some of their models in alternative Home and Colonial trims. The latter usually boasted a little more ground

clearance and exotic mudguarding among other changes intended to make the bike more suited for the rougher roads of the empire and colonies – hence the 'Colonial' bit. With the return of peace, the 16C was forgotten, presumably in the interests of production rationalisation – it is unlikely that the Norton management were making a geopolitical statement!

Further models soon followed, these being the ES2, which was pretty much like the Model 18, but fitted with plunger rear suspension as standard (it was an option on the Model 18), and the side-valve Big 4, which boasted a capacity of an impressive 634cc – truly a giant among side-valves. Later on came

By 1950 the Norton bicycle had gained 'Roadholder' forks up front and plunger springing at the back. This not very standard 1950 ES2 has been fitted with a later 19S engine.

the Models 19R and 19S, and 50 . . . but more of that later.

The nomenclature of Nortons can be something of a mystery to the uninitiated, but makes some sort of sense if viewed with a knowledge of their pre-war models. Happily, space is too short to elaborate, but when a model appears with a designation that makes no apparent sense (I'm thinking of the Model 50, specifically, a name that refers entirely to a pre-war bike but which resurfaced in the mid-'50s), don't worry about it.

The bicycle

It is often supposed that the post-war Norton side-valve single, the 16H, was the same as the wartime WD 16H, but in fact it shares its rigid frame with the ohv Model 18, not with the WD model. The main difference lies in the complete cradle of the later frame; the front downtube of the earlier version ended at a forged 'shoe', which bolted to the front of the crankcases.

Norton's singles also launched into the peace with girder front forks to match their rigid rear ends – cutting-edge design they were not, which contrasts neatly with their 'The World's Best Roadholder' advertising claim. This changed for 1947, when the subsequently famous 'Roadholder' front fork was introduced across the range. They also offered the unlovely plunger form of rear wheel springing, as an option on the side-valves (the 16H had been joined by the 634cc Big 4 by then) and on the Model 18, but it was standard on the ES2. The rigid frame carried right on until 1955, mainly for sidecar pilots, and by then carrying only the 19R 600cc ohv engine, the side-valves having passed away a year earlier.

The rear suspension changed again in 1953 for the singles with the introduction of a swinging arm version of the ES2. This was not, sadly, the famed featherbed, which was already in production but only for the Model 88 twin. No, the singles made do with a traditional lugged-type of single-downtube frame, which was at least rather more comfortable than the plunger and rigid versions, and which modernised the bikes' appearance. Better brakes and handsome full-width hubs to take them came in too (in 1954), as did a whole host of tinware changes. These bikes sold only slowly, and if concours originality is important to you, you should ensure that all of the components are present and correct when you buy; they will be hard to find later.

The side-valvers passed from the lists for 1955, with the impressively long-stroke (82 x 113mm!) 597cc Model 19 taking their place in both rigid (19R) and sprung (19S) forms. The 19R was short-lived, and was dropped by the end of the year.

Between plunger and featherbed frames Norton produced a single-downtube frame with a swinging arm. These bikes were intended as workhorses, and some remain in harness today.

Above, left: *The arrival of the featherbed also produced what some have called the safest motorcycle in the world. Norton's legendary handling is more than a match for the less than outrageous power of their 350cc single. This is a 1960 Model 50.*

Right: *The singles went off-road too. Here a 500T is put through its paces.*

The brakes were improved again for 1956, and if originality is unimportant to you, I'd suggest fitting this 8-inch anchor to any earlier tele-forked Norton to make it stop better!

The single-downtube frame changed again for 1957, losing its antique front engine cradle in the process. And, just to permit later historians the luxury of pondering the 1957 frame change, for 1959 the singles (down to two now, the 350 Model 50 and the 500 ES2) were fitted into the acclaimed featherbed.

Finally, for their last couple of years the singles shared the introduction of the 'slimline' featherbed for 1961. The slimline machine was so called because the factory accepted customer complaint that the original featherbed – while steering with a unique precision – was rather wide between the knees of shorter riders. For the slimline, the duplex top frame rails were pulled in tighter as they ran towards the back of the petrol tank.

From a modern perspective, it is important that prospective Norton buyers understand that the non-featherbed swinging arm Nortons share little in the way of tinware

with the featherbeds – even the later front forks are almost entirely different, being shorter than earlier versions, and well modified to boot. Thus, with bewildering originality, the shorter forks are commonly known as 'short Roadholders'. You can probably work out that the earlier ones immediately became the 'long' ones.

The single engine

Norton's single engine has a heritage stretching back for years. This is particularly great news if an enormous heritage is important to you – if it isn't, be comforted instead by the thought that Norton Motors certainly knew how to build singles by the outbreak of peace in 1945.

The engine itself was of completely conventional construction, and was capable of covering great mileages with the reliability associated with low revs, low compression, and large main and big end bearings. The big end was a roller bearing, clamped between two substantial flywheels, with the whole of the crankshaft assembly running in a pair of roller bearings carried in a pair of

vertically split, aluminium crankcases. The timing side of the crank drove a pair of camshafts, themselves turning in bushes in both the crankcase and the timing cover, and a skew drive from the crank drove the oil pump. This was a gear type of considerable robustness, which supplied oil under pressure to the bearings that needed it. An extension of the inlet camshaft in turn drove the magdyno by means of a chain running in its own compartment outside the main timing chest.

By the post-war years, the bottom end – as described above – was common to both ohv and side-valve singles. The top ends, not too surprisingly, were different.

On the side-valve engine, the cams operated a pair of tappets, which in turn drove the valves. In the ohv single, the cams drove tappets that worked pushrods, which then opened the valves. On the ohv single, the two long pushrods were enclosed by a handsome pair of chromed pushrod tubes, which ran up to the rockerbox. The rockers themselves ran on spindles mounted in the boxes. Valve clearances were adjusted in a

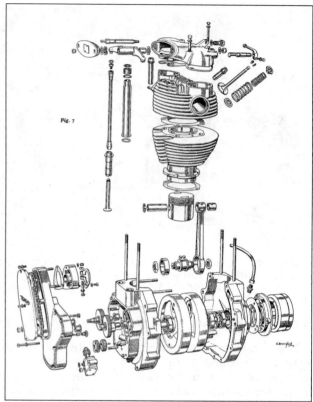

Fig. 7

Left: *The Norton single engine in all its glory.*

Above: *The single engine – exploded.*

tappet chest immediately above the crankcases on the side-valve, and through an opening in the rockerbox on the ohv.

As ever, carburation was by Messrs Amal, with sparks and DC current provided by a Lucas magdyno.

The Norton side-valve engine is not unlike equivalent models from other manufacturers in terms of its performance and robust nature. The ohv engine, likewise, is well engineered, pleasant and an adequate performer, but is a touring engine, not a sportster. Buyers should remember this when they feel likely to become carried away by the glamour of the Norton name at the point of purchase. Sellers, naturally, should do the exact opposite.

As ever, the changes over the models' lives were steady rather than spectacular, and the ohv models were always in front of the side-valvers whenever development loomed.

The gearbox changed to a 'laid-down' format for 1950 for all models and, following the demise of the side-valves, the ES2 and Models 19 gained an alloy head for 1955, along with a 376 Monobloc carb to replace the earlier remote float chamber device.

The rigid Model 19R departed in 1956, the year that saw the appearance of a 350 (71 x 88mm = 348cc) Model 50, while the following year brought in a new cylinder head, along with a host of other more minor changes. More important was the introduction of the AMC-type gearbox and its clutch, which was, however, still housed in Norton's traditionally leaky tin chaincase.

The year 1959 introduced the bright new world of Lucas 6-volt alternator electrics (along with the excellent featherbed frame), and

waved goodbye to the Model 19S. The points lived in a housing that replaced the old magneto, and were driven by a chain from the inlet camshaft as before.

The singles left the range late in 1963, apart from an odd interlude for 1965–66, when the famous names of ES2 and Model 50 re-entered the lists. These bikes, the ES2 Mk 2 and Model 50 Mk 2, were in fact G80 and G3 Matchless machines badged as Nortons, and with their engine numbers stamped accordingly. So, rather inappropriately, ended a long and proud line.

On the road

Despite their unrivalled racing heritage, Norton's non-ohc roadsters are pretty pedestrian in performance terms. Anyone expecting an ES2 to have more performance than, say, a contemporary BSA B33 is in for some disappointment. Having said that, they are charming, generally reliable and boast the charisma of the name on their tanks. They look nice too.

All the singles should be able to maintain an adequate A-road cruising speed, although overtaking safely becomes something of an artform. Motorways are just tiring, for both bike and rider, and it is wise to rediscover the pleasures of careful route-planning should you anticipate covering long distances on one of these machines.

It is also sensible to bear in mind that a lot of Norton singles spent their early lives hauling families around in sidecar splendour. It is therefore a good idea to check the geometry of the bicycle by observing whether or not its wheels are in line. Remarkably, misalignment of the wheels does not always destroy the steering precision, and it is easy enough to compensate for it when riding, but a bike like this should fail the MoT roadworthiness test.

Modern-day riders should also remember the limitations of the lighting systems of the older singles, and will be unable to forget their braking deficiencies. Happily, as already mentioned, the later front brake fits the earlier telescopic forks, and that is a good stopper. It is also easy to forget that while featherbed Nortons handle with astonishing ability, the steering of a swinging arm Model 19 is not in the same league.

Possibly the most desirable of the singles are the later, featherbed models, and herein lies a small modern irony. Many of the Model 50 and ES2 singles had their

Top: *A 1963 Norton catalogue, the last to feature singles.*

Bottom: *When is a Norton not a Norton? This 1965 Model 50 Mk 2 is in fact a Matchless G3 with Norton badges.*

The first of the Norton lightweight twins was the 250cc Jubilee. Despite their 'handsome' styling, the bikes were let down by weak forks, feeble brakes and occasional electrics. This is a 1960 De-luxe example.

engines ditched by cafe racers of the 1960s and '70s, to be replaced with Triumph or other twins – and I have come across two Norton twins that started life as singles, oddly. And just as the single engines were thrown away, with them went the touring tinware, to be replaced by the alloy guards, racing tanks, clip-ons and rear-sets of the cafe racing set. Only latterly, with the discovery of the 'classic' bike, has the genuine charm of the original singles become recognised, and the bikes themselves have somehow become more desirable. This can produce some remarkable situations at auction, where prices achieved by original singles can be as high as those

managed by the sporting twins. Bear this in mind should you be offered one at a low price, if you would really prefer a twin; a little wheeling and dealing does no one any harm.

The Lightweight Twins

In common with many other British manufacturers, Norton correctly identified the need for a range of smaller-capacity models to handle the demand that would follow the 1960 250cc learner limit. Unlike all of the other four-stroke marques, Norton's light 250 was a twin, the Jubilee.

By the time of its release in 1959, the AMC ownership of Norton

was readily apparent to anyone who cared to look, and the new twin carried its Norton engine in a bicycle largely sourced from lightweights built elsewhere in the AMC empire. Thus there is a considerable similarity between the Norton lightweight bicycle and that used for the AJS and Matchless lightweight singles and the James and Francis-Barnett two-stroke singles. This common sourcing (which was an indicator of intelligent management, no matter the protests of marque enthusiasts) extended to the Wico-Pacy electrical systems, to the brakes, and indeed to the gearbox; the new Norton twin shared much of its transmission internals with the AJS lightweights.

The Jubilee was not a resounding success, and even with the benefit of rose-tinted hindsight it is hard to claim otherwise. It was something of a short-stroke revver, and even though its handling was good enough, the hated lightweight forks were roundly condemned. It was also not the most reliable of machines.

Happily, the inevitable stretch to the 350cc Navigator produced a much nicer motorcycle, one that benefited from the addition of the front fork and brake from the heavyweights, as well as the bigger engine.

Finally – and most unusually for a British machine of the period – the small Norton underwent a second stretch, to 400cc, and gained an electric starter. Sadly, despite this attempt at offering a

Rather better than the Jubilee was the 350cc Navigator. The extra power and 'Roadholder' front end improved things significantly.

The drive-side view of this almost original Navigator shows off its enclosed chain drive and the clumsy styling of the rear enclosure. The lightweight engine itself was well designed and remains the only unit-construction Norton twin to date.

modern motorcycle to compete with the Japanese invasion, the Norton lightweights disappeared when the AMC parent collapsed in 1966.

The bicycle

Although the lightweight chassis was shared with others of the AMC lightweight ranges, it is a competent handler, especially when fitted with the heavyweight 'Roadholder' front forks. Which does not mean that the 250cc Jubilee is a poor handler – it is not . . .

In common with the AMC two-stroke lightweights, the front frame tube was a steel pressing, as was the seat pillar. The rest of the metalwork was steel tubing. The forks and wheels were straight from the Francis-Barnett parts list, while the tinware was Norton's own.

In line with the late-1950s fashion for enclosure, the Jubilee was offered with steel panelling that shrouded most things aft of the cylinder block. It was also burdened with a voluminous front mudguard of quite remarkable unattractiveness, and a rear chain enclosure, which was at least sensible. Happily, the Standard option, which appeared in late 1960, offered the little Norton without the enclosing tin sheet, and it looked better for it, and when the 350cc Navigator appeared for 1961 it was available in both forms.

The Navigator also boasted proper Norton forks and front brake, and when the electric-start Electra ES400 joined the lightweight list in 1963 it added the heavyweight rear brake as well.

This diagram of the Jubilee frame illustrates its unusual construction.

And so far as lightweight bicycle development went, that was largely that.

The twin engine

There are those, myself included, who see the Norton lightweight engine as representing a great lost opportunity. The design shows a lot of thought and is altogether a lot more modern in its engineering than the only four-stroke twin rival, the 350 unit twin from Triumph.

Designed around an unusual crank design in which the central flywheel was of narrow section but large diameter, the Norton 249cc engine was, at 60 x 44mm,

very short-stroke for its day. The top end showed a lot of AMC twin thinking, with that engine's separate cylinders and heads, twin camshafts and neat valve clearance adjustment. It was also of proper unit construction, and in its larger capacities could be a rewarding performer. Sadly, less than perfect execution and inadequate electrical systems gained the engine a reputation for oil leaks and unreliability that has persisted to this day.

The crank was mounted on a ball race timing-side main bearing, with a roller on the drive side, and the big ends were conventional split shells. The timing side of the

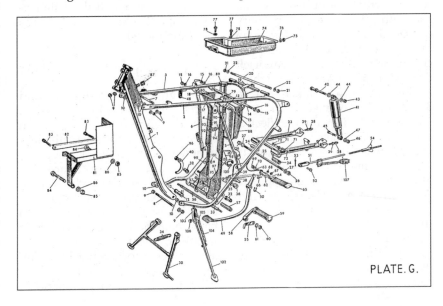

PLATE. G.

The final lightweight development was the 400cc Electra. The prominent extension to the primary chaincase carries the drive from the electric starter to the crank. Quite a few of these unusual bikes have been re-imported from America.

crank drove a normal Norton gear oil pump, and an intermediate gear, which in turn drove the two camshafts, with the ignition points assembly driven by an extension of the inlet camshaft. The cams themselves operated unusually long tappets and short pushrods, which in turn operated the valves. The rockers were carried on spindles, which in turn were mounted on pillars cast into the head, in the AMC twin fashion, with that engine's adjustment method.

The cylinders were cast iron, and the heads were aluminium. Carburation was by Amal Monobloc, and ignition was by coil, with current supplied by an alternator living in the primary chaincase. A duplex primary chain drove a conventional multi-plate clutch to a four-speed gearbox, itself derived from the AJS lightweight.

The engine was taken out to 349cc for the Navigator in 1961, and again to 383cc for the Electra, and the only major engineering change was that the previously separate cylinder blocks were cast as one to improve oil retention.

The Electra's electric starter drove the crankshaft via a chain that ran inside the specially extended primary chaincase, the top of which carried the starter itself. It often worked too, and the electrical system was improved to

12 volts to handle it. The Electra also gained a pair of handlebar-end direction indicators. Stirring stuff indeed for 1963.

The engine's major failings were vibration, mechanical noisiness, especially from the timing gear, a seemingly almost inevitable tendency to leak its oil when thrashed and when hot, and rapid wear of the gearbox. It was unusual for its day in that it needed to be revved fairly briskly to deliver its best, and when extended like this it became unreliable. Things did improve with the larger engines, which did not require the revs demanded by the 250. In a confused approach to marketing strategy, Norton sold their almost-a-sportster 250 learner's express as a touring model . . .

On the road

Although the Navigator and Electra are interesting machines, both to own and to ride, they can still be fragile, and the availability of new wearing spares is not good. This makes them hard to recommend for riders who want to get the maximum enjoyment from their bikes; when stretched on a back road the Navigator can be a fair flyer, but it only really cracks along when worked hard high up the rev range.

I ran a Navigator for about a

year, and enjoyed hammering it through the Border lanes, where its top end was more than a match for a friend's equally high mileage (but rather younger and of more modern design) Honda CB350. The Norton's brakes were far better than the poor single-disc front effort on the Honda, too, and its drastic oil consumption was just our little secret . . . Sadly, all this British superiority vanished when the Norton transformed itself into a 175cc single, a piston crown having broken away from the rest of the piston. After replacing the piston it smoked (and clattered) rather too much, so I swapped it for a 500cc Triumph 5T, which was slower, had worse brakes, and didn't handle at all well . . .

The real sadness of these bikes is that they were never taken further, because the design had a lot going for it. In fact, AMC did build prototypes of unit-construction twins with a similar layout, but they never saw production. Just think how much fun a really short-stroke, high-revving big twin could have been.

The Heavyweight Twins

For the sake of this book, we will consider Norton's heavy twins as Commandos and not-Commandos. It may be that the Commando was really only a development of the Atlas that went before it, but I feel that it is worth a section of its own, so we will have one.

When it arrived in 1949, Norton's twin was joining a marketplace that was growing crowded with twins from other manufacturers who were keen to steal sales from the trend-setting

Triumph. Norton's 500cc Model 7 was a handsome enough motorcycle, but it started life in what was plainly the ES2 bicycle, and was burdened by a high cost compared to the products of the mass producers. So it sold a little slowly.

The arrival of the featherbed frame with its string of racing successes, fine handling and striking looks, changed all that, and thereafter Nortons because increasingly devoted to a twin-based range. By the time of the introduction of the Commando – as radical a motorcycle as had been the first featherbed Dominator – all Norton motorcycles were four-stroke twins. Sadly, the Commando engine, although a pleasure to ride with, was a well-stretched development of the 1949 original twin, and it proved unable to match either the performance or the unit costs of its Japanese rivals. Unsurprisingly, really.

The bicycle

The first Norton twin engine, the 500cc Model 7, was carried in a plunger bicycle that was fundamentally that of the ES2 single. It boasted 'long Roadholder' telescopic forks and 7-inch brakes that were standard period Norton, but the petrol tank and mudguards were all its own, which can be something of a problem for originality freaks in this day and age. The plunger frame of the Model 7 survived the introduction of the revolutionary featherbed-framed Model 88 in 1953, gaining the swinging arm rear end (the not-featherbed mentioned in the singles section) as the ES2. Indeed, in a seemingly

unlikely move that parallelled the introduction of the Model 19S 600cc single as a sidecar-puller's delight, the 500cc Model 7 was replaced by the 600cc Model 77 in 1956 – also for this famous sidecar pilot! The engine for the 77 was that from the newly introduced 99 (are you following this?), with a numerological eccentricity that has endeared itself to enthusiasts for years.

The non-featherbed branch of the Norton twin family ended when the 77 was de-listed in 1958 – apart from the single-season appearance of the Nomad. This was a US market desert racer with lights, featuring a tuned 600cc engine in the old lugged frame from the Model 77, and clothed in off-road regalia. The Nomad lasted only one year but the idea was a sound one, and resurfaced in 1963 when the Norton-Matchless hybrids were created, again largely for the US market.

Norton were unusual – but not unique – in offering their twin engine in more than one bicycle at the same time. They presumably reasoned that following the introduction of the featherbed-framed 88 for 1952 (initially it was for export only, as were so many good things at the time) there would still be a demand for the older twin. And in any case, the firm did not recommend their new

frame for sidecar duty, while the older lugged design was nothing if not robust.

With the introduction of the new frame, Norton lifted the public interest in their twins at a stroke. Here was a world-class racing chassis, fitted with one of the newly fashionable twin engines. How could it fail? It didn't, being popular from its introduction until its demise a decade and a half later. The mystery of the early twins is that the factory chose not to race them – although their advertising occasionally showed a drawing of a racing twin alongside the roadgoing machine that was actually offered for sale.

Things improved further with the introduction of the 8-inch full-width front brake in 1954; a year later the bolted-on rear subframe, which carried the seat and the mountings for the rear shocks, was replaced by a welded-on assembly. The 'laid-down' Norton type of gearbox was replaced by a new one, common to the whole of the AMC range in 1956 (for the '57 season), and an alternator replaced the E3 dynamo for 1958 models.

Although all of these changes were improvements (despite the bluster of dynamo diehards), I'd hate to suggest in any way that the earlier featherbed models are any less desirable than the later. What I would say is that the arrival of the

Although most of the Dominator twins were fitted with the featherbed frame, the less sporting rider was catered for too. This 1957 Model 77 was intended, allegedly, for sidecar use.

featherbed range of Norton twins (and ultimately singles as well) immediately made the earlier lugged-frame models look – and feel – dated.

The next change to the bicycle, the introduction of the 'slimline' featherbed, in turn made the earlier (suddenly dubbed the 'wideline') frame and its associated cycle parts appear dated. The change in 'beds took place in 1960, and brought with it a style that defined 1960s classic Nortons, lasting until the 1968 introduction of the Commando. Only minor changes were introduced for the slimline bicycle until its demise in 1970, most of the efforts of the parent AMC group going into ever more powerful engines, the collapse of 1966 and the engineering thrust that resulted in the Commando – which we will treat in a later section of its own.

In an aside to the 'bicycle' side of things, I should mention that Norton fell victim to the style for enclosed motorcycles that had been pioneered by Triumph with their famous 'bathtubs'. As well as inflicting a weighty load of non-essential sheet metal upon the early lightweight twins, Norton similarly burdened their newly introduced slimline heavyweight twins. The panelling on the De-luxe Dominator 88s and 99s enclosed the carburetter, then ran back all the way to provide a mounting for both the numberplate and its lamp. The immediate and lasting success of the enclosed models is reflected in the fact that they were off the price lists for 1963 . . .

The twin engine

Norton's twin engine, a design

Top: *The 'wideline' featherbed Dominator is arguably one of the best-looking machines of its day.*

Bottom: *The final featherbed, the rather more comfortable 'slimline', was the last word in British bike steering for many years.*

Above: *The first heavy twins were all-iron low compression 500s, and were originally fitted into Norton's plunger bicycle.*

Right: *The twin engine.*

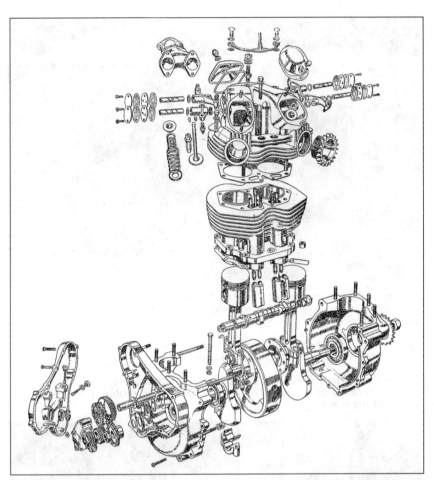

generally credited to Bert Hopwood, is one of the most long-lived motorcycle power units of all. From its introduction as the 1949 497cc Model 7, the same basic plot underwent an impressively lengthy series of capacity increases until it bowed out as the 828cc (badged as 850) Commando engine almost three decades later. At the risk of upsetting Norton twin fans everywhere (and I include myself in that number), I would suggest that the fundamental reason behind this longevity was a shortage of resources with which to develop a replacement, rather than a tribute to a particularly ground-breaking piece of basic design work. Norton failed to embrace the many advantages offered by the adoption of unit construction, even for their new flagship Commando range, and bearing in

Fitting the Dominator engine into the featherbed bicycle was a stroke of genius.

mind that a unit engine must have a lower unit cost than a non-unit equivalent, the conclusion is an obvious one.

Having said all that, the Norton twin is an engine of immense character and charm, and is perfectly capable of providing today's classic rider with plenty of powered excitement.

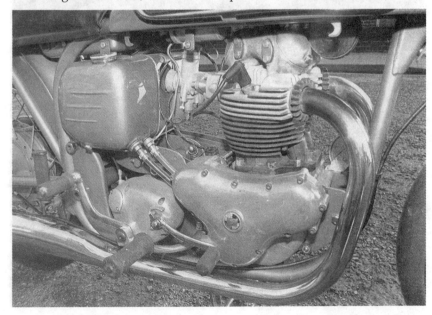

Above: *The 600cc stretch of the twin engine, to produce the Model 99, provided a welcome performance boost. This 1959 example looks splendid in silver.*

Right: *An unsung hero. The 88SS with its twin-carb cylinder head is a rare sight today and is still a good machine to ride.*

Below: *The Atlas engine was also used in Matchless cycle parts to produce a range of hybrids. This high-pipe P11A is probably the most exotic of the breed.*

The Norton engine bears some superficial similarity to the BSA twin, which is unsurprising, given that much of the design work is credited to the same man, Mr Hopwood. The Norton engine is more developed than the BSA A7/A10 unit, however, lacking the latter's twin timing covers and gear drive to the camshaft.

The two con-rods are carried by shell big-end bearings on a conventional crankshaft, which features a central flywheel and a pair of supporting main bearings, a roller bearing on the drive side and a ball race on the timing side. One of the Norton's unique features is that its single camshaft is mounted in the crankcase in front of the cylinder block, driven by chain. On early twins, the camshaft itself carried a gear to drive the dynamo, which was mounted in the traditional position in front of the engine. The extension of the timing chest that carried the dynamo drive providentially looks rather like an add-on, which was easily lost with the changeover to alternator electrics – unlike, for example, the AMC twin engine, which carried an empty dynamo cradle until its demise.

Rather less happily, when the

engine was – in its Commando incarnation – converted to carry the contact breaker assembly in a timing cover bulge, driven by an extension off the camshaft, the original ignition housing was left looking rather redundant. Until, of course, the electric hoof of the final Commando was inserted to both provide occasional starting services and fill an embarrassing gap.

As the camshaft was driven by a chain running forward from the intermediate gear, so the magneto was driven by another chain running backward from the same source. Anyone familiar with the behaviour of worn chains echoing around in a timing chest could be forgiven for expecting the engine to be something of a rattler, but it's not, unless terminally worn, despite the fact that a tensioner for the cam chain was not fitted to the early dynamo engines.

The camshaft drove four (long) pushrods through a tunnel cast into the iron cylinder block, and operated the valves in the normal way. Unusually, the rockerbox was cast integrally with the cylinder head, which makes for a good chance of oil-tightness and a certain fiddling when it comes to seating the pushrods to their rockers.

Lubrication was taken care of by a gear-type pump mounted conventionally in the timing case. Oil from the oil tank was pumped via a neat arrangement into a passage in the timing cover, then into the crank to lubricate the big-end bearings. A crucial part of this simple system is a small rubber

Top: *Those who have owned many classic bikes consider Norton's 650SS to be at least the equal of Triumph's Bonneville.*

Bottom: *The biggest stretch of the old engine in its featherbed phase was the 750cc Atlas. There was no real performance increase over the 650SS, and it was too vibratory for some.*

taper washer, which must always be replaced whenever the timing cover is replaced – along with the oil seal upon which the end of the crank runs, sensibly.

A branch line from the return pipe to the oil tank took oil upstairs to the rockers, with that oil draining back down to the bottom end after it had performed its lubricating and cooling duties.

Carburation was supplied by Messrs Amal, with 6-volt dynamo power to the lights and a Lucas magneto supplying the sparks.

Once under way, development proceeded at the traditionally British gentle pace, with the 497cc (66 x 72.6mm) engine originally used in the Model 7 and the 88, 88 De-Luxe and 88SS, stretching to 596cc (68 x 82mm) in 1956 for the 77, 99, 99 De-Luxe, 99SS and N15 Nomad. A further stretch, to 646cc (68 x 89mm), gave us the engine for the 650, 650SS and Mercury models, while the final hike to 745cc (73 x 89mm) gave us the Atlas engine that powered a fine range of final pre-Commando Norton, AJS and Matchless models: Nortons Atlas, N15, P11 and Ranger, Matchless G15s, and AJS 33s. Then, in late 1967, this fine old design went into a truly Great British Hopeful, the Commando. More of that later.

Although, like most other Brit twins, the Dominator engine started life with an iron head to match its iron cylinder block, a smart alloy head arrived for 1955, along with an Amal Monobloc 376 carb to replace the earlier Type 6. The AMC gearbox, itself a development of the earlier Norton design (which itself was a development of an earlier Sturmey-Archer design, etc), arrived for Norton, AJS and Matchless heavyweights in 1956, and the cylinder head was redesigned to provide better cooling around the exhaust ports for the following year.

It was all change on the electrical front for 1958, when the Lucas RM15 alternator took over from the E3 dynamo to provide current for lights and sparks, with an 18D distributor timing the latter (unless a magneto was still fitted, in which you just got the alternator).

The head was redesigned again for 1960, and SS versions arrived for 1961. These boasted a pair of carbs, along with polishing of the head's ports and combustion chambers and a siamesed exhaust – and a magneto – to supply power figures of 36bhp for the 88SS and 44bhp for the 99SS. That year also saw the introduction of the 650 engine, but initially for export only, the 650SS appearing in the UK for 1962.

Twelve-volt electrics arrived for 1964, along with the final stretch of the Dominator engine, dragged out to 745cc for the Atlas. Atlas engines, incidentally, are always recognisable by the presence of a breather pipe on the drive-side end of the camshaft tunnel. Interestingly, the Atlas engine offered the same 49bhp as did the 650, but its delivery was rather easier, and the spread of power is very noticeable if you are able to step straight from one bike to the other.

The 88 and 99 engines disappeared for 1966, and the surviving 650 and Atlas engines gained a revised drive for the oil pump, which doubled its delivery.

The end of 1967 brought with it the announcement of the Norton Commando, and the Dominator saga was nearing its conclusion. However, one of the sweetest of the featherbed twins arrived for just the last year or so in the shape of the single-carbed 650 Mercury. These machines, the last of the featherbed Nortons, were listed until 1970, and are very rare now; they are as pleasant as they are scarce.

On the road

All of the Norton heavy twins are rewarding to ride, charismatic to live with and highly prized – and therefore highly priced – in today's classic world. Although the non-featherbed models are willing performers, and competent in the steering department, it would be wrong to suggest that a plunger 88 steers any better than a plunger BSA, or that a swinging arm model 77 is going to run rings around a Triumph Thunderbird of the same year. Until the appearance of the featherbed bicycle, Norton's twins were worthy examples of the parallel twin world, but they were not dominant, either on road or track. Likewise, for today's rider the earlier Norton twins are competent, handsome, unusual and good to ride, but they are not particularly inspiring.

The featherbed changed all that. The new frame raised the obsolescent racing Norton singles back into international contention, and its contribution to Britain's motorcycling heritage is hard to exaggerate. If the Triumph twin was the definitive British motorcycle engine, then the Norton featherbed was the definitive frame – it was inevitable that they would find themselves grafted together.

But just how good is the featherbed? Really . . . Well, let us just say that to anyone familiar with the handling of other contemporary roadsters the featherbed offers safe cornering at very high speeds, and it comfortably out-performs all the engines fitted to it by Norton Motors. Although I have read more recently of those who consider that the Atlas engine was capable of making the very stiff frame flex, resulting in high-speed instability, I do not share this view. If the frame has one fault, it is that it is quite possible to reach the limits of the tyres' adhesion without the increasing yaw that is common with lesser frames. At this point the experienced rider recognises that he or she has a slide and compensates; less competent riders can fall off. A

A definitive classic Norton: the 750 Commando.

good demonstration of this is available to anyone who can get the chance to tackle the same set of clear bends on a Norton Atlas (with featherbed) and a hybrid Matchless (same engine, Matchless bicycle). The latter offers by far the more exciting ride, while being appreciably slower than the Norton. But in any case, if you are riding that hard on a Norton on today's roads, you are nuts; buy a more modern machine that can offer better brakes and better rubber.

All of the Norton twins have their fans, and I am one of them; I have owned and ridden most of them over the years. It is quite difficult to select any particular model, but the 'wideline' 99 owned by a friend and colleague is an excellent machine to ride, with good looks, great steering and performance that is well up to today's A roads. Although the Atlas has a reputation for excessive vibration, I prefer it to the 650SS, which is often harsh. The final featherbed, the Mercury, is something of an unsung hero, however, should you be lucky enough to be offered one.

The Commando

The collapse of AMC, and with it Norton, in 1966 saw the eventual emergence of a new company, Norton-Villiers, and as the new firm began the daunting task of bringing profits for its shareholders from the wreckage of the old industry, it became clear that the range of motorcycles they had inherited were not really capable of further development. OK, the Norton-AMC hybrids, mentioned in the AJS and

Hanging in there: the secret of the Commando's success lay in its unique isolation of the engine's vibrations from the rider.

Matchless section (Chapter 6), were useful in that they turned out to be pretty fine motorcycles as well as permitting the clearing of a lot of inherited component stocks, but it was plain that something new was needed.

It was the fault of the expanding motorway network, which offered the long-distance rider new opportunities for sustained high speeds, and expense when the engine let go. It was the fault of the Japanese, who unsportingly, and with no mind for our great heritage, offered better motorcycles, often at lower prices. It was the fault of the management, who siphoned company profits to the shareholders rather than investing in long-term

development strategies. It was the fault of the workers, who went on strike when they felt like it. It was the fault of . . . actually, whose fault it was is unimportant. When the new team at Norton moved in, they found that they did not have a model that could realistically be sold into the modern market with any hope of medium-term – let alone long-term – success. So they developed a new model – and fast!

Norton management accepted that in order to make a profit they had to sell a lot of motorcycles. The trouble was that selling large numbers traditionally involved offering a complete range of models: touring models, sporting models, export models, etc, as well

Above, left: *Long-distance hauler: the vast fuel capacity of the Commando in its Interstate guise gave it tremendous range.*

Above, right: *Taking the engine out to 850cc provided more torque but no more power. One of its more unusual uses was powering Norton's factory custom, the Hi-Rider.*

as a range of capacities and engine types. The new company had neither the time nor the resources to develop such a range. Instead, sensibly, they recognised that they needed to develop a single machine that could be sold as several different models with only relatively low-cost cosmetic changes. They needed a power train/bicycle package that could be dressed up and sold as a tourer, a sportster, even a chopper and a production racer without undue compromise.

The new model was the Norton Commando, one of the most charismatic and popular post-war British motorcycles. It was both staggeringly successful and remarkably flawed. It was nearly right – bold yet conservative, new yet traditional – and it was the best the new company could manage.

The bicycle

The Commando was based around a solution to one of the preceding twins' major faults –

The final version of the Commando, the Mk 3, featured disc brakes at both ends and an electric starter. This 1975 model was originally a Police Interpol machine. Police riders appreciated the bike's torque and smoothness.

vibration. The effects of a large-capacity parallel twin engine's high-speed vibration on both rider and componentry was well known (the rider gets shaken to bits, things fall off), and in the absence of an alternative engine, a way of either reducing the vibration or its effects was essential if Norton were to have a motorcycle that was at least superficially modern. Rubber mounting was seen to be the answer, and the famous Norton Isolastic system was the result.

The Isolastic system was simple in concept, but remarkably effective in operation. The engine, transmission and swinging arm pivot were all carried in a steel cradle that was attached to the rest of the machine at three points. The major component of each of these points was a rubber mounting, which absorbed the engine's vibration by preventing any metal-to-metal contact between engine and bicycle. It works, too, as many a rider can confirm. The secret of the system's success is that mounting of the swinging arm pivot in the engine cradle. This maintained the alignment of the gearbox and the rear wheel, which would otherwise have varied every time power was applied had just the engine and gearbox been rubber-mounted, as the engine tried to pull the back wheel toward it. The cost of mounting the swinging arm in this way was notionally reduced steering precision, as the swinging arm pivot moved in relation to the steering head. This was compensated for by limiting the

Top: *The final Roadsters were handsome indeed. This one has benefited from an upgraded front brake – a useful mod.*

Bottom: *The transformation of the Dominator and Atlas into the Commando was a great leap forward in sophistication.*

Sadly, plans to introduce a new version of the Commando for 1976 came to nothing.

sideways movement of the rubber-mounted componentry, and the Isolastic units were adjustable to maintain that limit. The ideas here are that most vibration from a vertical twin is in the vertical plane, and that any of this movement transmitted to the swinging arm pivot should have no noticeable effect upon the rear wheel's behaviour. Rear wheels move vertically anyway.

The main member of the frame was a single large-diameter top tube from which the power train was effectively suspended at the rear. The front forks were the familiar 'Roadholders' and rear suspension was by equally familiar Girling units. Styling was modern and unusual for the time, with the Fastback tank, seat and tail looking very up-to-date indeed. Ironically, the styling of the Commando became more traditional as the years rattled by.

Front-wheel braking was provided by fitting a smart twin leading-shoe mechanism into the drum from the older bikes, and rear anchorage operated the earlier brake by cable, which at least made it delicate in operation.

The basic bicycle was available dressed up in several guises to provide the range of models mentioned earlier. The basic machine was originally dubbed the Fastback, and featured an integrated design of tank and seat that looks distinctive to this day. That was joined by the Roadster, more conventionally styled in the tank and seat department, and the first to feature the famous 'pea-shooter' kicked-up silencers, and the 'S', which was similar to the Roadster but with a very American high-level exhaust system and a smaller headlight. More interesting to us UK touring types was the Interstate, which carried a very well-styled, massive 5-gallon fuel tank (and which was modded for police use as the Interpol). Norton would, amusingly, also supply the Hi-Rider soft chopper, a factory custom before the term was invented, as well as a production racer. The rarest road bike was the John Player Special, which was a roadster dressed up in sporty fibreglassware to resemble the company's real racers.

Things improved on the braking front (or not, according to some) with the arrival of a disc front brake for 1972. And things improved on the safety front (or not, according to some) with the arrival of direction indicators for the same year. And things improved visually (or not, etc) for 1971 when the exposed-stanchion front forks appeared. Other than that, the basic bicycle changed remarkably little throughout the Commando's life, and most componentry is interchangeable.

The power train

The original intention had been to use another, more modern, unit-construction power plant, which had been under development at the time of AMC's collapse, but that development was nowhere near complete, and would have taken more time and more money than the company could afford. So they decided to use the existing Atlas engine, which offered plenty of power and which was completely familiar both to riders and to those building it.

Things in the power train were tidied up, however, with the earlier twins' ancient and notoriously leaky pressed steel primary chaincase being replaced by a smart alloy effort. This was a little remarkable in that it was sealed by a long rubber O-ring rather than a gasket, and held together by just a single bolt. Primary drive was by a monster triplex chain, rather than the single-strand effort that was a little prone to premature wilting under the torque of the Atlas. The gearbox was the familiar Norton four-speeder, but the clutch was unusual, being controlled by a single diaphragm spring instead of the customary collection of small coil springs. That worked well, too.

The engine itself came with twin Amal Concentric carbs, fitted with proper air filtration, better breathing arrangements and a Lucas ignition system that included a capacitor to permit running with a completely flat battery. Most importantly, the venerable engine had been canted

A worthwhile modification for any Commando owner who wishes to smooth his twin still further is to replace the twin carbs with a single one.

forward in the frame, which at least made it look more modern.

As ever, development involved components, either individually or in groups, rather than wholesale redesign, and I shall mention the more significant here.

In a famous abberation, Norton offered a tuned version of their ancient power unit when they introduced the 'Combat' engine for 1972. Equally remarkably, the tuned engine was first offered in the Interstate touring model. The thinking there is a little elusive, in retrospect.

The Combat engine was a tuned version of the standard 750 lump, and is famous mainly for the remarkably short life of some of its more major components, like the main bearings. It is safe to suggest that any Combat engines still running have been remedied by now, and the cures are still readily available from Norton specialists. The Combat fiasco, which severely tarnished the reputation of the Commando and its reputation as the first of the 'superbikes', was a blow to the company, not least because sales of the bike were halted while a solution to the short-life engine scenario was being found. But it could have been worse . . .

Long after the demise of the Commando, an ex-employee recently told me that the same 1972 model year was to have seen the introduction of an electric-start Commando. This, along with the disc front brake, would have shown that Norton were at least attempting to keep up with the Japanese, whose big bikes already

The first the public knew of Norton's rotary renaissance was the appearance of Police Interpol 2 machines on the roads of Britain.

featured these luxuries. However, the original design of starter was to have driven the engine through suitably strengthened timing gears, rather as the later Triumph Bonnevilles, in fact. However, kickback from the engine could – and did – wreck the entire timing gear assembly. Happily, the fault was identified and production halted before it had begun.

In any case, 1973 saw both the introduction of the old Dominator engine's final capacity hike in the form of the 850 (actually 829cc, at 77 x 89mm) Commando, and the departure of the 750. Happily, any ideas of increasing the engine's power output along with its capacity were ignored, with the

850 putting out the same 52–53bhp as the 750. This gives a very pleasant feel to the engine, and the 850s are more relaxed and quieter than the 750s; for many this is therefore the version of the Commando to buy. My own favourite appeared a year later.

The last conventional Norton appeared in 1975, when the final, Mark 3 version of the Commando was introduced. Much work had been done to the bike, and the new model featured an electric starter, driving through the train of gears in the primary chaincase, a left-foot gearshift and a rear disc brake. Other detail work introduced at the same time is often ignored by historians, but for

this scribbler the self-adjusting primary chain, the revised Isolastic mountings and the anti-drain valve fitted into the oil feed make this the Commando I recommend to folk.

After several false stops, Commando production finally ceased in 1978, and another great name appeared to be part of British history. But the story isn't quite complete yet.

On the road

For many, the author included, the Norton Commando is the definitive British twin. Others have their own favourites, but in support of my argument I would remind readers that the Commando won the coveted *Motorcycle News* 'Machine of the Year' award no less than five times.

Commandos can be something of an acquired taste, and riding one with its isolastics way out of adjustment, with a badly tuned engine, a clutch that both drags and slips and requires the muscles of Hercules to operate, as well as a front disc brake that appears to be completely non-functional and

steering that offers new meaning to the word terror . . . well, riding one like that can be a little off-putting. And I have ridden several similarly sad offerings over the years, not all of them ex-police high-mileage Interpols, either.

The faults of the Commando are well-known to the owners' club, and they publish an excellent booklet of service notes for the bike. If you are contemplating buying a Commando, join the NOC and buy that book first. Really.

Then ride one in good order. You will soon discover what all the fuss was about, and why the bike won so many awards. Performance – even motorway performance – is fine, the engine's power characteristics are perfect for open roads, the handling matches the performance, and the steering is predictable enough.

But Commandos do wear out, and after quite low mileages if maintenance is not up to scratch. Dismal steering can result from a combination of worn head-races, worn-out forks and worn-out swinging arm bushes. The latter is always one area to look out for, as the lubrication arrangements

offered by the factory were sketchy, to say the least.

Disc front brakes seem strangely variable in effectiveness, but can be replaced with upgraded ones, and fitting a single carb conversion usually improves the engine's behaviour no end. This is one classic bike where a decent service record really is a good thing to consider when buying. I have owned, ridden and rebuilt several Commandos, and run a Mk 3 Roadster to this day. A personal recommendation then.

The Rotaries

Uniquely, Nortons failed to accept that they were finished after the end of Commando production, and continued to develop a rotary-engined machine for several years afterwards. This bike had originally been a BSA project back in the very early 1970s, and had passed to Norton when BSA Triumph collapsed and NVT was formed. Despite a severe lack of funding, Dennis Poore, Chairman of the company that had actually owned Norton Motors since the 1966 AMC collapse, kept faith

Below, left: *The air-cooled rotor motor, an elegant engineering solution to the old problems of vibration and complexity.*

Right: *The first civilian rotary, the air-cooled Classic, was strictly a limited edition.*

with the project through the dark days of the early '80s.

The concept of the rotary, or Wankel, engine is an appealing one. This type of engine has remarkably few essential moving parts, making for lightness and low cost; and as it has none of the reciprocating engine's stop-go piston behaviour, it is also very smooth in operation. The geometry involved in the Wankel cycle is complex to explain, but basically instead of a conventional piston forming a combustion chamber in combination with the cylinder head, the rotary engine relies upon a three-sided rotor moving eccentrically within a fixed figure-of-eight-shaped housing to provide a moving chamber with varying volumes. It's murderous to explain in print – look at a diagram or a model! Take it from me, the engines work. The appeal is that there is no valve train, no con-rods and none of the assembly complexity associated with conventional four-stroke engines. The problems come in the cooling and rotor-sealing areas. Norton solved both, with some elegant engineering in the best tradition of brilliant minds working with tiny resources.

After many years of rumours and cancelled launches (allegedly), riders from several police forces, starting with the West Midlands, were to be seen whirring about the place on odd-looking – and very odd-sounding – motorcycles with the words 'Norton' and 'Interpol 2' on them. Most of those lucky enough to ride them were impressed, and several hundred machines were sold to the police and military, where they lined up with the then current BMW R80RT whose fairing design they had copied.

Ownership of the company changed again, and in 1987 the first publicly available rotary was announced. This was the Classic, essentially the police-spec Interpol 2 with the fairing and police ancillaries ditched in favour of a new tank, side panels and dual seat. This was a wholly new model. It used no parts from previous Nortons (although the gearbox was based around that of the Triumph T160 Trident, an indicator of its mixed pedigree), being designed very much as a whole. It is maybe amusing to consider that the last wholly new Norton had been the Jubilee light twin. Or maybe not.

There is another small irony here. The factory built a couple of batches of civilian bikes for one of its aborted launches; these were mostly converted to police trim and sold as Interpols. The Classic was a stripped-down police model sold as a civilian machine . . .

Following the sell-out of the entire build of 100 Classics (actually, slightly more than that were built, but we won't quibble), Norton announced their next new model, the Commander. Once again designed for fleet use, the new machine ran a liquid-cooled version of the rotary engine in a similar frame to that of the Classic. Whereas the earlier bike had used Italian Marzocchi front forks, Brembo brakes and Radealli wheels, the Commander took its running gear – and much besides – from Yamaha's XJ900. It also hid all of its mechanicals beneath the most comprehensive fairing seen on a British motorcycle; the fairing included integral panniers, storage compartments and daytime running lights, and was particularly effective in protecting the rider from the elements.

The rear of the fairing was redesigned for 1991 to permit the fitting of Krauser panniers for civilian riders, but sales were slow, because in truth the Commander was rather too obviously designed as a fleet motorcycle. Indeed, I have read a memo from one senior manager at the time to another demanding that the Commander be re-worked extensively before being offered for civilian sale. However, development effort was by then going toward the next launch, the super-sporting F1, and the inevitable irony here is that the Commander was never as successful in winning fleet orders as its Interpol 2 predecessor.

The F1 featured the liquid-cooled engine mated to a Yamaha gearbox and mounted in a Spondon aluminium chassis, using

The fully faired water-cooled Commander made a fine touring motorcycle.

The last production Norton, to date, was the F1 Sport.

top-spec White Power suspension and clothed in one of the most beautiful sets of fibreglass bodywork seen on a motorcycle. Sadly, although its performance was impressive enough for a 588cc motorcycle, it was a craftsman-built high-specification machine, and its price reflected this. Even the JPS-sponsored race team's track achievements and Steve Hislop's TT win failed to raise sales to profitable levels, and despite the introduction of a rather cheaper and less radical F1 Sport model, production ceased after a distressingly short run.

By this stage a combination of poor sales and misguided management ventures had robbed the company of the capital it needed to survive, and by 1993 production had ended. At the time of writing, the factory is open for servicing and spares sales, and there is the inevitable talk of rescues, but talk is exactly that – talk.

On the road

Norton's last motorcycles are radically unusual to ride. The engines are very smooth and rather smoky, as they burn their lubricating oil, and they sound distinctly strange to anyone used to conventional British four-stroke twins. Add to this their peculiar mechanical noises, especially on the over-run, and you can almost forgive the British riding public for failing to buy them. However, the engines – especially the water-cooled ones – are powerful enough, they have a tremendous spread of torque, they are very reliable if used intelligently, and all of the bikes are practical, too. Does this sound biased? It should – I run a Norton Commander, which I bought new, for my everyday transport, and have never felt tempted to trade it for a more modern machine.

The handling on the Commanders is a little on the wallowy side, but the air-cooled Classic and Interpol 2 steer with the best, while the F1 and F1 Sport were among the best-handling roadsters of their day.

Faults? The engines' longevity is dependant upon the use of the correct lubrication, and ex-police machines have a tendency to being worn out when sold. Gearboxes can be noisy and some spares are scarce.

The rotaries were a somehow appropriate end to a long and distinguished marque. They were late arriving, they went out and won races, and they were largely ignored by the buying public . . .

Chapter 9

Triumph

There are those who will argue that Triumph is the greatest of the British marques. Indeed, judging by the fact that the famous name is still appearing on the tanks of new British motorcycles at the time of writing, it is difficult to contradict this viewpoint.

Triumph were there right at the beginning of motorcycling in Britain, and, as ever, supplied the British forces with two-wheeled transport throughout the First World War. However, unlike most of the other successful post-war mass manufacturers, Triumph were almost prevented from exploiting the supply of their products in the second great conflict because the Germans bombed their Coventry factory. So, while Triumph in fact offered a perfectly suitable military machine (the 3HW, of which they built almost 50,000), they were unable to supply the vast numbers achieved by BSA. On the other hand, when hostilities ceased, Triumph were working in a new, modern factory fitted with at least some new, modern machinery, rather than the elderly premises occupied by most of their competitors. And, although their wartime military mounts had been singles, Triumph were also familiar with the new classic British bike design, the engine configuration with which British sportsters would soon become

almost completely identified – the vertical twin.

Triumph were the first British manufacturer successfully to introduce this design of engine, in 1937, and motorcycles based around this original Speed Twin, and bearing the Triumph name, would remain in production for almost exactly five decades. Which is long enough for anyone, surely?

Triumph, the company itself, was sold to BSA in 1951 and was able to benefit from the economies of scale that the merger offered, while at the same time remaining truly a marque in its own right. It was aided in this by the fact that Triumph man Edward Turner, designer of their ubiquitous twin, was appointed head of BSA's Automotive Division in 1957.

In a direct contrast to the actions of AMC, whose AJS and Matchless marques were distinguishable mainly by the badge on their fuel tanks, BSA kept their equivalent marques, BSA and Triumph, very distinct until the last gasp. There was a reasonable – and sensible – degree of component sharing in the electrical, carburating and braking departments, but the two marques shared neither frames nor engines. Even their last successful major new model, the three-cylinder BSA Rocket 3 and Triumph Trident, used very different frames and engine major castings. Even had the BSA parent

survived, however, the writing was on the wall for the marque individuality that every rider claims to value . . . but does not wish to pay for. The final range of twins from both BSA and Triumph, the famous 'oil-in-frame' models launched in 1971, shared everything apart from the engines, and the single-cylinder models were separated by finish. Had the BSA Fury and Triumph Bandit – the new 350cc twins that the company attempted to launch in 1971 – made it into production, they would have been virtually identical.

The downside of Triumph's binding to BSA was that when the BSA Group began its doomed slide toward closure, it took Triumph with it. The convulsions of the whole industry in the early 1970s saw the formation of the famous Meriden Co-operative, as the workers at the Triumph factory acquired control of their company and attempted to go it alone, without the bulk purchasing powers of a larger company and without its development resources.

What this meant, from this book's point of view, is that from the emergence of the Meriden Triumph co-op until its demise in 1983, Triumph were very much a single-model marque. That machine, the 750 twin, was the last of the old, classic, British bikes.

The co-op did their best to disguise their reliance upon just one antiquated engine design in a world of increasing technical sophistication and ever-higher performance, but the end was inevitable. One of the world's most famous motorcycle lines came to an end – but the Triumph marque itself, remarkably, survived.

When the Meriden co-op was finally wound up in 1983, two remarkable events took place. First, the new owner of the name and rights, John Bloor, licensed the old twin for a further lease of life, and second, he announced that a completely new Triumph range would be built at another location in the Midlands. This was no idle dream – he kept both commitments. Another 1,200 or so Bonneville twins were built by L. F. Harris Ltd in Newton Abbot, Devon, keeping the Triumph name visible, and brand new Triumphs rolled out of a brand new Triumph factory in 1991. Wonderfully, the new Triumphs, which carry many of the model names made famous by the old company, have turned out to be sales successes, and this is one piece of the British bike industry that can end on a high note.

The Singles

Although the Triumph name is most commonly associated with

Top: *The first post-war Triumph single was the Terrier. They are very rare now, and rather slow. This 1954 example has remarkably spindly forks and plunger rear suspension.*

Middle: *The Terrier was replaced by the Cub, which at least felt like a real motorcycle to ride – agile, nimble and surprisingly nippy. Many riders have a fondness for machines like this 1963 T20 Sports Cub.*

Bottom: *The last Triumph singles were BSAs in disguise. This is a 1969 TR25W.*

its parallel twins and, latterly, with the three-cylinder Tridents, they also produced two ranges of single-cylinder motorcycles. The first, the well-known Tiger Cub, and its predecessor, the Terrier, lie outside the scope of this book. Although both are pleasant enough bikes to ride, at 150cc and 200cc capacity they have very restricted performance, and are of limited appeal to those who intend to ride their classics on modern roads.

Amusingly, for historians at least, the singles that we do cover are relatives of the Tiger Cub, and were intended to replace it as an entry-level Triumph for 1968 . . .

Triumph offered a 250cc model that was that year's BSA 250 with Triumph cosmetics. The bikes were in fact built at BSA's Small Heath factory, rather than at the Triumph works at Meriden, and many are the tales of perfidious goings-on by the BSA workforce, who were allegedly not too appreciative of building bikes for their Triumph rivals. Whether you choose to believe them or not is up to you, but in my experience the reliability of BSA and Triumph singles is indistinguishable.

So it was that the BSA B25 became the Triumph TR25W Trophy, gaining a distinctive fuel tank, a higher-level exhaust pipe, different side panels and sundry cosmetic changes, including Triumph logos on a couple of castings. The only functional difference was that the Triumph was fitted with the front end from the Tiger 90 350 twin, but BSA fitted that to their own singles for 1969 anyway. For a brief technical description of both engine and bicycle, please refer to the BSA chapter.

When the last BSA oil-in-frame

250 was introduced, there was also a Triumph version, mechanically identical but with Triumph cosmetics. This was the T25, available as T25SS Blazer and T25T Trail Blazer, which differed at the front end. The T25T lost the conical-hub 8-inch front anchor and 18-inch rim, replacing them with a 6-inch sls front brake laced into a 20-inch front rim. It also lost a tooth on the gearbox sprocket and boasted a front mudguard mounted on the bottom fork yoke, rather than on the sliders. Along with a 4-inch-section knobbly back tyre, these changes were intended to make the Trail Blazer more credible as a notional off-roader – and indeed these bikes are good trail irons, with excellent performance from the bicycle. The engine, however, was really a little too rev-happy for serious off-road work; ironically, the 'plonk' that most weekend mudlarks of the time preferred is nowadays largely ignored by today's equivalent models, so maybe BSA/Triumph were a little ahead of their time!

In a singular postscript, BSA badged their B50MX 500cc single as a Triumph (the TR5MX, or Avenger) for the 1973 American market, distinguishing the two marques by fitting the Triumph with the most bizarre silencer arrangement seen on a British

production motorcycle. Some of these bikes have been re-imported from the USA, but they are pretty rare in both countries.

On the road

All of these machines are pleasant enough to ride. For preference, I would recommend the later oil-in-frame T25SS, with its better braking. Buy the latest you can find, as a lot of the earlier unreliability problems were overcome with the later models. You can also fit the larger fuel tank available from the BSA equivalents, should you be serious about covering the miles . . .

The Non-unit Twins

Triumph's twins were the first commercially successful British parallel twins, bursting on to the UK motorcycle scene before the Second World War. They were so immediately, and obviously, successful that they set a design trend that would continue to form the backbone of the British industry until its final collapse in the mid-1970s. Prior to Turner's Triumph Speed Twin, the mainstay British bike had been a single-cylinder model, with variety and minority interest being supplied by V-twins, two-strokes and a few oddities like

When BSA introduced the oil-in-frame bicycle for their singles, the Triumph equivalent followed suit. This 1971 Blazer SS is a Triumph in badges only.

the Matchless V-4s. After Turner's triumph, the mainstay British bike soon came to be an ohv parallel twin, with variety and minority interest provided by singles, two-strokes and a few oddities like the BSA-Triumph triples. This was a defining motorcycle.

Whether the trend set in stone by this engine was good or bad for the industry as a whole is a moot point, and is possibly best left to historians, but it is actually impossible to exaggerate its impact. The basic design stayed more or less constant from its introduction in 1937 until its demise in 1987 – although its

capacity grew by 50 per cent and it gained unit construction of engine and gearbox along the way.

So many Triumph twins were built and sold in so many places throughout the world that finding spares is rarely a problem. Indeed, there are those who suggest that spares are more widely available now than when the machines were new . . . Whether this is fact or fantasy is largely irrelevant to my suggestion that a Triumph twin is probably the easiest introduction to the classic bike world. Which from a personal viewpoint is a little ironic, as I have never been a great fan of them.

As with BSA, so there are two categories of Triumph twin: the non-unit construction models and their successors, the unit construction machines. Unlike BSA, however, Triumph also produced middleweight unit-construction twins, in 350 and 500cc capacities.

The bicycle

Not only were Triumph at the front of the field with their twin engine, but they also entered the peacetime world with telescopic forks hanging from the front of their motorcycle. So when peacetime production resumed the range boasted at least two unique selling points: the twin engine and the telescopic forks.

The rest of the bicycle was utterly conventional, with a rigid rear end and a sprung saddle to ease the rider's posterior. However, rear-wheel springing to match that up front was quite plainly the coming thing, and late in 1946 Triumph offered their (in)famous sprung hub. Like the plunger back end, this was a way of selling rear suspension without the expense of tooling up a new frame. And like the plunger, it is difficult to engage the rose-tints of nostalgia and suggest that the sprung hub was a great idea. It wasn't, and can steer particularly alarmingly, especially when well worn. If you must have one, that is your decision, and I would suggest that you allow some professional other to risk life and limb by dismantling it for that vital overhaul.

Happily – well, almost – Triumph introduced a swinging arm frame, initially for the Tiger 110, for 1954. The other models followed as stocks of the rigid frame ran out, and all should have

Triumph's 1950s' sportster twins have a poor reputation for roadholding, but given a firmer throttle hand they steer predictably – if not well.

The late 1950s heralded the new era of unit construction . . . and the dreadful 'bathtub'. Triumph's 350 Twenty One compares rather unfavourably with the Velocette 350 Viper behind it.

been wonderful. Sadly, despite the protestations of Triumph fans that persist to this day, it could not be claimed that Triumph steering was up there with Nortons, or even Ariel . . . or Royal Enfield. Some unkind souls refer to the Triumph frame as 'instant whip', but I'm sure that's cruel. What is true is that if the rear end was under better control with the swinging arm, that merely showed up the weakness of the spindly front fork. Not for nothing were Triton specials once so popular.

Triumph's braking was also nothing to tear up the tarmac, although both front and rear drums were adequate and grew in width as the '50s progressed.

Things did look up in late 1959, when Triumph introduced not only a new main frame but also a much better front anchor. The revised frame featured twin front downtubes, and steered rather better than the earlier one, while the brakes gained floating shoes, which improved things. Sadly, some of the new frames were a little delicate, mainly when in harness, and an extra tank rail was added for 1961.

However, by that stage the range was being up-dated with unit-construction engines, and when the unit 650s appeared their frames had reverted to a single-downtube design.

Tinware for Triumphs changed at the same rate as for everyone else, although Triumph were the first of the big four-stroke manufacturers to introduce rear enclosures for their bikes. These vast steel pressings, which gained the bikes various nicknames (like 'bathtubs', or 'Lancelot's horse'. . .) appeared with the unit-construction 350 and 500cc twins in 1957, and spread to the larger

touring pre-unit twins apace. Whether you like it or not is up to you, but original pressings are now scarce (because most youthful second-hand buyers threw them away) and the quality of some of the replica parts is variable, so beware when buying. In fact, the worst that can happen even with poor pattern parts is that they fall off (which would be an improvement) or that they rot and vibrate (both of which are irritating rather than life-threatening).

The non-unit twin engine

It is impossible to argue that the Triumph twin engine is not the definitive British post-war power unit. It just is. It was the first on the scene – and the last. There had been other parallel twins before it (and plenty after), but this was the first successful one and the longest-lived. Its secret is simplicity, which, allied to pretty lightweight construction, earned it a reputation as being eager for revs and responsive to the throttle. Both are true of the non-unit design, and remain true for the unit engine until emissions and noise regulation strangled it in the mid-'70s. But that's a way away at this point.

Turner's twin engine was designed around a central

flywheel, which wore a big-end journal on either side and a main bearing outside those. The pistons rose and fell together in the approved (British) manner, while power was taken off the left end of the crank (viewed from above) and ancillaries driven from the right.

The engine boasted two camshafts, driven by gears from the crank, and a double-plunger oil pump, the two plungers of which were motivated by an odd sliding block, itself driven by a protrusion from the inlet camshaft. This was a strange, elderly design that survived until the very end, admittedly with many modifications. When worn – and oil pumps do indeed wear, although few riders appear to realise it – the pressure can get very low. This wears the rest of the engine and is probably the reason why so many old Triumphs are famous rattlers.

For many years Triumph fitted their engines with an oil pressure indicator, a button that protruded when the oil pressure was good and high. It was once common for these buttons to return to their resting (no oil pressure) position when the engine and its oil was hot, which should have sent everyone scurrying for the spanners to avoid blow-ups. Oddly, the very robust twin could

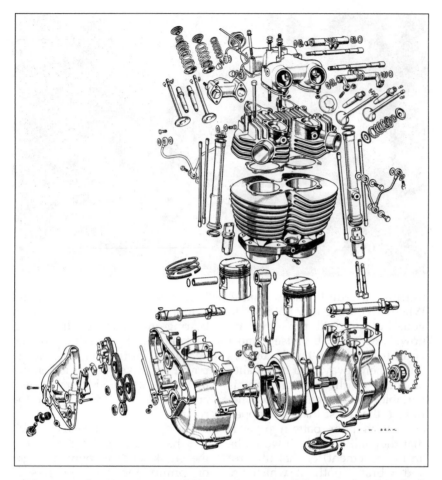

The pre-unit engine revealed.

rattle away for many, many miles like this, and when time came to sell, it was a simple matter to refill the oil tank with straight 50-weight oil. In one case of my knowledge, a bike was topped up with EP140 (a truly gloopy gear oil) for reasons of poverty and sales desperation, and it ran on cheerily with its new owner for a couple of years! Do not do this . . . Happily, today's riders can fix the age-old Triumph oil pump situation by fitting a proprietary gear pump. This is a good idea for all Triumph twins, and is recommended.

Petrol was breathed into the engine by (usually) Mr Amal's finest, and sparks were provided by a magneto mounted behind the cylinders, while dc current was supplied by a dynamo mounted in front. Both were gear-driven from the crankshaft via the camwheels. Each camshaft operated its valves via a pair of short pushrods, which ran up to the head through a pair of chromed tubes. If there was a single feature of this engine that should have been changed early in its life it is these external pushrod tubes. Even today, with modern technology, it can be a complete pain to seal them, and although they may all look the same, they are not. If you are looking at an engine that cannot hold its lube, be wise and ignore the seller's suggestion that the seals have dried out. Check that both seals and tubes are correct for your engine.

The rockers are housed in a pair of separate rockerboxes, which are held to the head by an assortment of fasteners. This is another design feature that should have been changed in the early years, and if you're looking at an engine that is smothered in oil at the top end, it is quite likely that some of the rockerbox retaining devices have stripped their threads. The circular inspection covers fitted to the rockerboxes of most models prior to the appearance of the 750 engine also had a tendency to explore the scenery all on their own, but that situation was improved by the addition of little clips to hold them in place. It defies belief that Triumph persisted with this separate rockerbox nonsense until the introduction of the TSS in 1982, but persist they did, and they held on to those separate pushrod tubes until the very end of production.

In the early engines, oil drained from the rockerboxes back to the crankcases via external pipes, and when these engines are old (as they all are) and worked hard (as they all used to be) they can leak oil from the joints of these pipes. This is merely irritating, and should be viewed as evidence of poor maintenance. A bright side? Certainly – the engines are all willing workers and are charming in use, and Triumph never wasted their customers' time with the leaky pressed steel chaincases so beloved of other manufacturers. No, the smart cast aluminium primary chaincase, featuring its trademark streamlining of the bulge over the engine-shaft shock absorber, is both attractive and functional. Sadly, the primary chain itself was still tensioned by swivelling the gearbox in its mounting plates, but you can't have everything.

Drive was taken through a good, solid clutch to a conventional four-speed gearbox, and from there to the rear wheel.

Until the appearance of the Terrier in 1953, Triumph's entire range was based around this twin engine, and by 1950 it was available in 350, 500 and 650cc capacities, the 650 being the Thunderbird, new for that year. The 350, which was dropped for

The 1956 Tiger 100 featured this beautiful all-aluminum engine. The close-pitched fins afford it a definite style.

1951, is rather neglected these days, which is a bit sad, as it is a very pleasant – if leisurely – machine to ride. However, the 500 and 650cc engines were the most popular with riders, and their development proceeded once again at the traditional British pace – gradually.

In addition to the Speed Twin or 5T, Triumph offered a pair of sporting 500s, the Tiger 100 and the TR5 Trophy. Both of these could be specified from 1951 with alloy barrels and heads, and the story of how the barrels from a wartime aircraft generator were modified for competition bike use is legendary – and possibly apocryphal.

A little less legendary was the fitment of an SU carburetter to the 6T Thunderbird from 1952. This was apparently an attempt to improve fuel economy, and it must have worked, because it lasted until 1959. The T'bird was inevitably joined by a sporting 650, the Tiger 110 for 1954, and the size of the main bearings was increased to cope with all this extra performance in 1955. The T110 was joined by a notional off-road sportster, the TR6 Trophy, for 1956, so offering the same range of models in the larger capacity as in the smaller. And of course most of the cycle parts were the same – and were often interchangeable, which is why you do need the company of an expert if you are buying a bike with a supposedly sporting pedigree. It is very easy to transform a humble (but very pleasant) 5T Speed Twin into a fake TR6 Trophy and to ask a

The 650 touring engine, with its cast iron block and head, is not the thing of beauty that the T100 is. However, alternator/coil electrics provided a degree of civilisation.

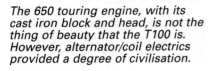

premium price for it. Wise buyers do their homework well before parting with money.

In an odd, if adventurous, move, Triumph introduced a semi-automatic clutch for their bikes in 1958. This was the once-notorious 'Slickshift' gearbox, in which the clutch was actuated by moving the gear lever. They were strange to use, proved unpopular with riders, and are pretty rare today as many riders removed the mechanism. If you ride one you will understand why, especially if your riding style is sloppy enough to find that you unconsciously rest a toe on the gear lever between changes. If you do, you achieve permanent clutch slip, which is not too useful.

The 500cc bikes were replaced by the unit-construction models for 1959, and the final few years of the 650s really are the ones to have. That year also witnessed the introduction of the most charismatic Triumph twin of all, the T120 Bonneville – basically a Tiger 110 with twin carbs and a big reputation. Once again, should you be buying one ask expert advice, as these bikes are also too easy to fake.

The pre-unit range ran to a close when the new unit-construction 650 was launched in late 1962.

Model designations

Triumph launched their post-war offerings with the 350 (55 x 73.4mm = 349cc) 3T and the 500 (63 x 80mm = 498cc) 5T and T100 in 1946. The 3T lasted until 1951, when legend has it that demand for the 6T Thunderbird

Top and middle: *The pace of change at Triumph was less than meteoric. Spot the difference between the 1956 TR5 and the 1958 version of the same bike.*

Bottom: *Our overseas cousins preferred the more macho styling of the TR6C Trophy, seen here in 1966 form.*

absorbed all the factory's capacity. The off-roader TR5 Trophy arrived in 1949, along with the track-oriented T100C; all the 500s survived until 1958 and the arrival of the unit-construction engine, apart from the T100, which lasted a year longer.

The 650 (71 x 82mm = 649cc) 6T Thunderbird sprang into the showrooms in 1950, and was joined by the T110 for 1954 and the TR6 Trophy for 1956. The non-unit 650s lasted until 1962, apart from the T110, which departed a year earlier.

On the road

All Triumphs are fun to ride, providing that they are not completely worn out, of course. The 350s are charming but a little pedestrian, unless you compare them with their single-cylinder contemporaries, whereupon they can become quite attractive. But the Speed Twin was one of the definitive motorcycles of its age, and although the continual development did indeed improve it over the years, it was pretty much right to start with. The Tiger 100 and Trophy models are today much more highly priced than the humble all-iron 5T, and although they are very pleasant, the price differential is difficult to justify.

As was the case with BSA's A10, the Triumph 6T Thunderbird was desirable from the date of its launch, and the model's huge popularity with police forces the world over is an indicator of the design's basic strength, as well as

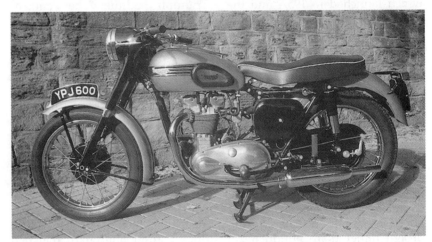

Top: *The 1954 500c Speed Twin shows off Triumph's styling at its best. Also revealed are the spindly forks and small front brake.*

Middle: *A definitive sports motorcycle of its day, the 1956 Tiger 100 is shown here in all its glory.*

Bottom: *This early Thunderbird shows off its handsome headlamp nacelle – but the forks and brake are less impressive.*

its performance. The traditional Triumph weakness lies in their steering, with spindly front forks and weak swinging arm pivots being the root of this. Happily for many, Norton saw fit to offer their somewhat pedestrian 350 and 500cc single engines housed in their very fine featherbed bicycle, and the Triton was the inevitable result.

The Unit-construction Middleweight Twins

Unusually for the time, Triumph offered two distinct ranges of unit-construction twin-cylinder models: the 350 and 500cc range, which launched in 1957, and the 650 and 750 range, which launched in 1973. In an attempt at minimising confusion, I shall take a look at them in two parts, beginning with the middle-weights, which came first.

As already discussed in the BSA section, the engineering and cost justifications for introducing a unit-construction engine design are simple enough to understand and, like BSA, Triumph took the opportunity to revamp their range completely. Also like BSA, they effectively 'unitised' their existing design rather than introducing a wholly new one, and some of the flaws of the original were carried over. So, in the same way that BSA

stuck with their weak timing-side main bearing, so Triumph persisted with their external pushrod tubes and separate rockerboxes, thus maintaining their hard-won reputation as champion oil leakers. Similarly, they also retained the double-plunger oil pump, ensuring a healthy supply of rattles when the engine was well worn.

Triumph also took the opportunity offered by the introduction of new models to offer the public a whole new 'Triumph' look. And so a small legend in the great and varied world of classic biking was born, in the unlikely shape of the Triumph 'bathtub'. The trend, as perceived by several other manufacturers as well as Triumph, was supposedly away from the trad Brit 'nuts 'n' bolts' school of motorcycle design towards a more enclosed, cleaner style. Triumph went a long way down this road when they launched their new 350 and 500cc machines in 1957, complete with a voluminous skirt that enclosed the whole machine aft of the engine. They retained the handsome headlamp nacelle (from which the Owners' Club named its magazine, incidentally) and also fitted a front mudguard matched in its vastness only by Royal Enfield's Airflow device – and then spoiled the streamlined effect

rather by tacking on a rear numberplate that looks very much an afterthought. In fact, the appearance wasn't unpleasant, it was just unusual. And unpopular, ultimately.

Which means that should you really need to possess a standard bathtub Triumph, the chances are that you will need to scout about to find original tinware, because when my friends and I were learning to appreciate great British engineering in the late 1960s and early '70s, we threw all the enclosure away, fitting instead wobbly alloy mudguards, uncomfortable clip-on handlebars and badly made rear-set foot rests. Such is the way of things, and a lot of these messed-around machines are still coming to light and being offered for sale. Sound advice is to buy a thoroughly worn-out machine, complete with all its original tinware, and restore it. Buying a machine with a sound power plant but lacking all the original fittings is going to be by far the more expensive route to an original bathtub Triumph.

The enclosed look lasted only until 1962, when the sports models began to lose their bathtubs and reverted to a more conventional stripped-down and sporty look.

Right from their introduction the unit twins were nearly right, and although they initially maintained the Triumph tradition of second-league steering, they improved steadily through the 1960s. The early experiments with 'energy transfer' ignition systems proved only that it was unreliable and misunderstood, and by the time the touring models faded away in 1966 the smaller unit

For 1961 the Thunderbird gained a rather better duplex main frame and a considerably better front brake. With its tank-top grid, jukebox badges, alloy head and alternator, it was a pretty well perfected motorcycle, but was burdened by the bathtub.

By 1965 the Thunderbird had acquired unit construction and was losing its enclosure.

twins had gained a deserved reputation for being quick, entertaining and reliable. By 1969 the 350 had reached the end of its line and the 500 twin was one very fine and highly recommended motorcycle. The sadness was that in the face of Japanese mechanical and marketing sophistication its days were numbered. Whatever, a good, late Tiger 100 makes a sound proposition even for the crowded roads of today.

The middleweight unit twin engine

No one boasting a familiarity with Triumph's pre-unit twins could have been surprised by the design of the unit-construction engine. The basic principles were identical, with the same pair of gear-driven cams operating pushrods to operate the valves. The changes made by fitting both engine and gearbox into a common set of castings were improvement enough to justify the new design, although why the opportunity was not taken to dispense with the leaky external pushrod tubes remains a mystery.

The notion of unit construction was in its early days too, as although the major components of the power train shared their castings, the engine, gearbox and primary chaincase were all still quite separate. This has its advantages, mainly in that the different requirements of those components could be met by appropriate lubricants, but the resulting complexity of the castings must have made them expensive to produce. The shame is that despite being comfortably profitable at the time, Triumph

By 1963, happily, the 350 (the Tiger 90) was also losing its bathtub.

appeared unable or unwilling to re-tool sufficiently to permit full unit construction on Japanese lines, with horizontally split crankcases.

The new engine was much more compact than the old, and was altogether more modern in appearance. And, as ever, unit construction did away with the need to tension the primary chain by tilting the gearbox backwards and thus necessitating subsequent adjustment of the main chain. In fact, and not a little remarkably given their reputation as builders of real riders' machines, Triumph failed to provide the primary chain with any method of adjustment at all until 1960. As

you might imagine, this can greatly enhance the twins' reputation for being proficient rattlers.

The crankshaft followed the basic layout of its predecessor; both pistons rose and fell together, with their shell big ends placed on either side of a central flywheel. The crank itself was supported by a ball race on the drive side and by a plain bush on the timing side. As previously, drive was taken from the left-hand end of the crank via a duplex primary chain to a conventional clutch and equally conventional four-speed gearbox. As ever, carburation was performed by Amal instruments, although dynamo and magneto

had disappeared, their roles being assumed by a crank-mounted Lucas alternator and coil ignition. The latter was initially timed via a distributor mounted rakishly behind the cylinder block, but the bikes to look for are those with the points assembly mounted in the timing cover and driven from the exhaust camwheel. Even though early Lucas contact breaker assemblies are not famed for their strength and accurate timing, they were a definite improvement over the distributor; the latter can shake itself to pieces, and even come loose, which can give rise to interesting engine behaviour. And contact breaker assemblies were cheaper too, which is why they were introduced.

Sadly, oiling was still handled by the plunger pump, and as I've said before, if you really want to enjoy hard riding and long life from your Triumph, you should give serious consideration to its replacement.

Engine development proceeded briskly enough, with improvements to performance, mechanical quiet and oil retention being announced from time to time. In fact, these engines are robust enough, although the 500 could be very noisy and vibratory when thrashed – which they often were. Like their pre-unit ancestors, the unit twins have a tendency to become raucous when worn, but can also endure low oil pressure with commendable stoicism. If you are looking to buy one, listen to a decently rebuilt engine, note how mechanically quiet it is, then listen to a worn one. The difference is very plain, as is the variance in vibration levels. Note also that original Triumph silencers were effective at their job; too many modern-pattern substitutes are so noisy that they tend to mask the engine's rattles. Remember that an engine will still run if you put your hand (in a glove, please) over the silencer's exit and the noise level drops to the point at which you can hear

untoward mechanical cacophony.

The arrival of 12-volt electrics in 1965 was a notable improvement, and the introduction of a revised cylinder head design for 1967 increased the rider appeal. Sports models from 1967 onward benefited from an understanding by the factory that high-performance Japanese motorcycles were on their way to compete in Triumph's traditional market, and much emphasis was placed upon improving both performance and reliability. What was actually needed was a new model range – quite possibly the ill-fated Bandit/Fury 350 twins – but in the meantime Triumph produced their best 500 twins as their time ran out.

These later Daytonas ride quite differently from their Tiger 100A predecessors, with slightly feeble low-speed performance and a pronounced power step at around 3,500rpm to provide performance comparable to the new wave of Japanese middleweights. Sadly, this valiant attempt could only succeed at the expense of decreased engine flexibility, while the competition had the benefit of more modern design and technology to provide both high outputs and good low-speed performance.

Another cost of the steady increase in power output is reduced component life, and later engines can be oil drinkers and smokers. This generally indicates wear in the valve gear, which although simple and inexpensive enough to repair, should be borne in mind when price negotiations are taking place.

A worthwhile improvement came along for 1969, when the timing-side main bush was finally replaced with a ball race, and the ball bearing on the drive side was replaced with a roller. These changes may not sound too thrilling, but if you want to be able to thrash along with modern traffic on a classic 500 Triumph, these are the ones to look for,

because their engine – or at least the bottom ends – are up to it.

Major engine mods to the 500s ended with revisions to the breathing (again, in the quest for oiltightness) for 1970, the 350 having passed from the lists a year earlier. Which is not to say that the 500s built thereafter are not worth having – they are. The collapse and confusion in the whole BSA/Triumph group, along with concentration of engineering effort on the aborted 350cc Bandit and Fury twins, took most of the engineering effort. And in fact, generally speaking, the later the engine, the better it is, because detail improvements carried on throughout the chaos.

An excellent example of this is a simple alteration to the rockerboxes that greatly simplifies the application of feeler gauge to the valve/rocker interface. This arrived in 1971, and is so simple that you have to wonder why it wasn't part of the original design.

The 500 twins soldiered on until 1974, but production was not resumed when the Meriden Co-operative restarted Triumph production.

The bicycle

As previously stated, when Triumph's new 350 and 500cc twins appeared in the late 1950s, they boasted a lot of modern enclosures and shared the same, or very similar, rolling chassis. Beneath the swoopy tinware, however, lay a very basic bicycle, a bicycle that could never be claimed to be one of the greats in handling terms.

The basic frame design was a development of that used on the 200cc Tiger Cub, which possibly explains its poor handling when housing a 500cc twin, and although it was conventional enough in its use of telescopic front forks and a rear swinging arm, both of these major hinges are badly supported, and the roots of the poor handling lie there.

The front fork, itself a little spindly and wear-prone, pivoted in a steering head that was supported – in the conventional way – by the front downtube and the upper frame rail. What was odd design, particularly in a bicycle intended for a sporty 500, was the lack of triangulation to provide rigidity. The upper frame rail, instead of running to the top of the steering head to support the top race there, joined the front downtube at the *bottom* of the steering head, and followed it upward. The twisting force here during hard fast cornering can be imagined.

Triumph attempted to brace this strange 'swan-neck' design by incorporating bracing into the fuel tank, which bolted to the frame at the steering head, and at the seat nose to offer some sort of triangulation, but this was only partially successful. It was rendered completely unsuccessful by the tendency of coffee shop cowboys to fit later, more handsome Triumph tanks or the fibreglass racing varieties that were so popular. Triumph in fact recognised this weakness, and fitted a bolt-on bracing strut – but that was for off-road Americans, not arriving for the home market until 1965!

To further add excitement to the Triumph twin experience, the other hinge, the swinging arm pivot, was based around a simple lug on the seat downtube. The inherent weakness of this very lightweight design should have produced a bike that was notably lively – and so it did. Wear in both hinges combines with wear in the front fork to offer the modern-day rider a truly unusual riding experience.

Having said that, if you are content to use your classic Triumph for gentle Sunday trundles, don't worry about it. Once the bike's 'lightness', to quote contemporary road tests, is familiar, it ceases to be much of a worry.

Both wheels were fitted with conventional 7-inch single leading-shoe brakes, which were adequate for the bike's performance.

The enclosure gradually departed, as I've already said, and an improved front fork arrived for 1964. Developments to Triumph's ranges followed a familiar pattern. Engineering and style changes arrived first on the sporting models, following later on to the cooking versions – presumably as stocks of old components were used up. As on the engine side of things, development was steady rather than inspiring until the mid-'60s, when the arrival of the Japanese manufacturers concentrated minds a little and the pace of improvement hotted up.

The big improvement arrived for 1967 (after only a decade of poor handling) when a new frame was introduced. This was a great step forward, and was a direct result of racing experience. The steering head was properly supported with a full triangulation, and the swinging arm

pivot was transformed into a piece of solid engineering. From this point, the smaller twins' handling was up there with the best of the rest of the middleweights.

The arrival in 1969 of the 8-inch front brake from the 650s to compliment 1968's revised front fork greatly improved the bikes' stopping powers, and we suddenly have a classic 500 Triumph fit for modern use. Then most things went quiet on the major improvements front, as mentioned in the engine section, while the company concentrated on its new range for 1971. But of course there were the endless year-on-year detail changes, just to frustrate and fascinate today's rebuilders.

The last change for the middleweight twins' bicycle came with the introduction of the TR5T, also known as the Trophy Trail or Adventurer, for 1973. This was a real BSA/Triumph hybrid, using the frame design of the BSA oil-in-frame singles to produce a Triumph-badged off-roader. And a very pleasant machine it was too.

More detail on the oil-in-frame bicycle can be found in the BSA unit singles section (Chapter 7), but I should point out here that the main frame used for the Triumph twin is not identical to that used for the singles, and although it is

After the demise of BSA, Triumph fitted their willing 500 twin engine into the bicycle of BSA's street scrambler singles. This produced the surprisingly good TR5T Adventurer.

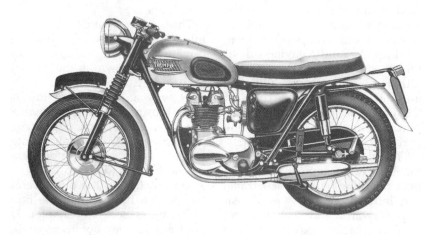

350 c.c. TRIUMPH TIGER 90 (T90)

possible to build your own by dropping a 500 twin engine into a single bicycle, that route is fraught with fiddle and frustration.

A final note on what might have been is offered by the existence of a Daytona that never was. The 500 twin was to have gained the complete front end from the bigger twins for 1974, and several were built, leaking on to the market following the collapse of BSA and NVT. I have ridden two of them, and the disc brake and heavier front fork work well with the rest of the 500's bicycle. But the 500's day was done by then, as the Co-operative presumably recognised, and it was a new engine that was needed, not a new front brake.

Model designations

The 350 (58 x 65mm = 348cc) Twenty-One (or 3TA) was the first unit twin, arriving for 1957. Its sporty sibling, the Tiger 90 (T90), joined it in 1963, and although the original 3TA passed from the lists for 1966, the T90 survived until 1969. The 350 was joined by the 500 (69 x 65.5mm = 490cc) for 1959, which also ran on until 1966. The Tiger 100 (T100A) appeared for 1960, being redesignated the Tiger 100SS for 1962. The Tiger 100 changed its model number again for 1960, as the T100, becoming the Tiger 100 (T100S) and Daytona (T100T) a year later. These models were succeeded by the Trophy 500 (T100C) and Daytona (T100R) for 1971. The Trophy 500

Top: *The one that got away. Had the 500 twin remained in production it would have gained the disc-braked front end of the Bonnevilles for 1974.*

Middle: *1964's Tiger 90. An altogether more attractive motorcycle than its predecessors.*

Bottom: *The end was approaching by 1971 when this T100C was produced. It really is a classic bike and it's a pleasure to ride today.*

was replaced by the Adventurer/Trophy Trail (TR5T) for 1973.

On the road

There is no doubt in my mind that the later Triumph 500s are the best. The later engine is a much more willing device than the earlier, its electrics are far more reliable and the whole motorcycle holds the road with great confidence and is stopped by anchors up to the power of the 650s. In short, the 1969-on Tigers, Trophies and Daytonas are very desirable motorcycles.

As mentioned above, the earlier machines suffered from poor (read 'cheap') design on the bicycle front, and from unreliability (read 'cheap') electricals. Although this is indeed a criticism (the AMC products, and indeed many contemporary BSAs, for example, were better-built), it should be viewed in context. Triumph were leading the world, and their nemesis, the Japanese manufacturers, were not yet major players in Triumph's traditional markets. Triumph accepted the challenge offered by the incomers in the mid-1960s and their models improved rapidly as a result.

And did the early unit twins handle badly, as their reputation suggests? Yes they did, and getting a first-year Tiger 100 around a fast corner requires dedication and technique. The trick is simple but not always easy to apply: the rider must keep the power on all the way around the corner, preferably opening the throttle. A need to shut off or – horrors! – brake while cornering can lead to some memorably gymnastic riding experiences.

The last of the Daytonas are surprisingly highly tuned; the single-carbed versions are much more flexible and easier to ride, especially if you need to journey through traffic. Starting is easy on the late machines (if you are offered an early model still fitted with energy transfer electrics, pass by), and they make fine all-round riding companions. And the final TR5T is still a handy green-laner, although its very low gearing is an impediment if relaxed A-road riding is your aim.

The Heavyweight Unit Twins

By the time the big twins underwent their unit-construction transformation for 1963, Triumph had learned several lessons from their experience with the smaller ones. Right from the start, the unit 650s came with conventional alternator/coil electrics, for instance, and without the voluminous panelling that burdened the 350s and 500s for so long.

Like the smaller Triumph twins, the 650s bore enough resemblance to the non-unit twins for their lineage to be evident – and reassuring. Again like the smaller twins, there was little in the way of new technology involved and therefore nothing to scare away a technophobic potential purchaser. Triumph's unit 650s were the bikes that their competitors needed to beat every time, and the fact of the Triumphs' success is reflected in the vast numbers that survive to this day. Whether they were actually better motorcycles than their contemporaries is a matter of debate, but this is the most successful British motorcycle of all time.

When you are contemplating the acquisition of a Triumph twin for yourself, their ubiquity should be turned to the buyer's advantage. If you are unconvinced by the bike you're looking at, walk away. There will always be another on offer. If you are selling one, it works to your advantage too, in that you can reassure your trembling customer that a quarter

Below, left: *The last of the smaller twins featured grown-up front brakes.*

Right: *The last of the hot roadster 500s (this is a 1972 T100R Daytona) in a suburban setting.*

of a million Bonneville buyers cannot be wrong. Allegedly . . .

Several of the more unusual 650 Triumphs were built for export, and for space reasons alone must largely be ignored here. However, we cannot ignore the existence in the UK of large numbers of Triumph twins that started their lives on roads under foreign skies. Indeed, it sometimes seems that the majority of the bikes offered for sale in today's classic mags are in export trim. If you are offered Triumphs that appear to be original but appear non-standard in detail, do not despair – they are probably re-imported models from the USA, where many slightly odd bikes were sold, and where even the models offered on the East and West Coasts differed. It is worth bearing this in mind when looking at the earlier models in particular – the unhappy energy transfer ignition system, for example, was an option in some overseas markets.

The heavyweight unit twin engine

As was the case with the middleweight twins, the design of the unit-construction engines followed broadly similar lines to the non-unit ones. One notable

The unit 650 twin engine.

exception – and worthwhile development – was the introduction of an extra stud to assist in holding the cylinder head to the block. By the time the pre-unit T120 Bonneville arrived with its extra performance, gas sealing at the head-block joint was becoming an issue. The nine-stud head can be fitted to earlier engines, but only in conjunction with a matching cylinder block – obviously enough!

Otherwise, much was as before, with the same lost opportunity to design out the traditional Triumph leak-prone pushrod tubes and rockerboxes as on the smaller twins. And like the smaller twins, the 650 engine was a notably handsome unit, as well as being revvy and willing to work hard.

Development proceeded in the traditional British way, with power increases followed by attempts at curing the subsequent vibration and oil leaks. In fact, as I have said before, the single-carb Trophy and Thunderbird are generally easier bikes to live with than the slightly temperamental Bonneville, although there is also an odd extra alternative.

Triumph sold a huge number of their 650 twins to police forces, not only in the UK but also overseas. The police bike, the TR6P (or, more romantically, the Saint – for 'Stop Anything In No Time') is an excellent compromise between the touring TR6 and the twin-carb T120 Bonneville. Saints in standard mechanical trim are quite rare now, as the first act of many first civilian owners was to convert them from obviously high-mileage ex-police (and therefore of low resale value) models into more desirable, if slightly bogus, civilian machines. Although all owners always have the right to do exactly whatever they may wish to their own bikes, the Saint's combination of Bonneville cam and single-carb

head made for a fine roadburner, especially with the lowered and differently spaced gear ratios of the police machine.

The first giant leap came as soon as 1964, when the Thunderbird gained 12-volt electrics; the rest of the range followed over the next two years. This is of particular relevance today as it permits the use of a modern halogen headlight without the need to change the whole system over from 6 to 12 volts.

After this, the 650s followed the familiar pattern of a myriad annual mods that inevitably upped the quoted horsepower by a point or two, while oil leaks were also cured annually. A particular improvement – at least from today's point of view, because the spares situation is easier – was the shift for 1968 from Amal Monobloc carbs to the more compact Concentric version. Performance of both models, oddly, remained broadly similar, year on year, while that of the TR6 (the Thunderbird passed from the lists in 1966) drifted towards that of the T120 as commonality of components increased. However, just as an extra indicator that the engine was becoming a tad stressed, by the time the 1969 model was announced, with its redesigned crankshaft, the factory was admitting that the principal reason for this introduction was to counter ever-increasing vibration.

In fact, many are those who consider the 1969 and 1970 650s to be the pinnacle of this engine's development, and many of that year's changes combine to make the bike more desirable: things like the wider joint faces introduced at the same time as the fittings changed their threads, and which increased the oil-retention ability; like the better crank mentioned earlier; like the increased oil pump capacity; like, oh, another solution to the perennial leaky pushrod tubes.

But this was by now a fully developed motorcycle in either single-carb Trophy or twin-carb

Bonneville versions. The engine and the bicycle complimented each other, with fine power matched by fine steering, and the machine is worthy of its current iconic status. It was plainly time to change things.

The changes when they came are mentioned in more detail a little later, but centred around an entirely new bicycle, the oil-bearing frame and its associated ancillaries that Triumph twins shared with their rivals from BSA, the parent company. The 650 Triumph engine itself underwent the continuing series of detail developments, with a new cylinder head appearing for 1972 (and new rockerboxes too, which finally did away with the grand old Triumph twin tradition of scattering rockerbox inspection covers throughout the land!).

A five-speed gearbox arrived for 1972, and the engine gained a capacity boost to 750cc for the following year. Unusually, the extra capacity arrived in two stages, with the first 750s actually having a capacity of 724cc, the more impressive 744cc arriving a few months later. If you have a 750

engine built in late 1972, you may well have a real rarity.

Along with the capacity increase came a number of other improvements. The number of fastenings holding down the cylinder head went up again, to ten, and the power output, remarkably, went down, resulting in less vibration and lower levels of stress generally. Primary drive was now handled by a triplex chain to cope with the extra torque of the bigger engine.

The BSA collapse, the Meriden sit-in and the final emergence of Triumph as a workers' co-operative hindered the pace of development for the next couple of years, and the big news for the 1976 models was the transfer of the gear change lever to the left of the engine, to meet American legislation.

A new head, complete with new carbs, arrived for 1979 (the T140E – for 'Environment', apparently), along with Lucas electronic ignition. The latter was definitely a good thing, as the previous contact breaker assembly was notoriously difficult to time accurately. And for 1980, finally, came the option of an

electric start. And, unlike some, this was generally a reliable enough device. Also introduced was a new oil pump, with four instead of two valves to offer greater reliability.

Strangely, one of the most likeable 750 twins was actually one that had been reduced back to 650cc! The TR65 Thunderbird was an economy model and was simply a single-carb engine with the stroke shortened. It was very sweet . . .

And finally, the 750 gained its last major modification for 1982 when the TSS model, which featured an eight-valve cylinder head, was introduced. Sadly, although the opportunity was taken to redesign the rockerboxes, the pushrods that operated the eight valves still ran inside the same old pushrod tubes.

Production ended at Meriden at the end of 1982, and although further 750s were built (in Devon, by L. F. Harris Ltd, under licence from the new owners of Triumph), engine development had ceased. The quality of these last engines can be suspect, despite their being hand-built in batches, rather than

Below, left: A 650cc afterthought. The TR65 Thunderbird revived an ancient name and offered a short-stroke version of the revered twin engine. Happily, the motor was a treasure in road use.

Right: In their last attempt to increase the performance of their ageing twin, Triumph fitted their venerable engine with an eight-valve cylinder head. The new model, the TSS, can be problematic but is surprisingly fast when running well.

on an automated line. There are good ones . . . and there are bad ones.

The bicycle

When the new 650 twins appeared, the bicycle was as instantly recognisable as a Triumph as was the engine unit. Gone was the earlier 650s' duplex cradle, however; the new twins came in a single-downtube frame, with utterly conventional rear swinging arm suspension and front forks, brakes and styling all quite familiar.

The new twin was available in three versions for the home market. These were the touring Thunderbird (6T), the sporting Trophy (TR6) and the roadburning Bonneville (T120), and their tinware reflected their intended roles. The Thunderbird retained the nacelle-mounted headlamp, while the others matched the increasingly stripped-down stance of the smaller twins.

New improved front forks appeared for 1964, while the frame's geometry was altered for 1966 in a bid to make the handling match the engine's performance. Riders were still, plainly, building Tritons. The front brake was also improved for '66, although it remained an 8-inch sls device, waiting another two years to gain that extra leading shoe.

Yet another new front fork joined the new 2ls front stopper for 1968, and the big twins were now at what many consider to be their peak, with the small improvements made prior to the 1971 new look serving to hone a very well-developed motorcycle.

And of course, 1971 brought a complete revision of the twins' bicycle, when the BSA Triumph Group introduced their oil-bearing frame, complete with new forks, wheels and ancillaries, and which is described in the BSA chapter.

This bicycle was to last the Triumph twin throughout the final 12 years of production, varying in detail to suit alterations to the wheels, brakes and tinware as the years progressed. A disc front brake arrived for 1973 (by which time production of BSA twins had ended), and it was joined by a second disc at the rear for 1976, when the gear shift moved from right to left.

The Triumph was available in several variants through its last decade, but the mainstays were actually two main models. These were the UK version, which carried a four-gallon petrol tank, and the export model, which boasted a rather smaller – but much more shapely – tank. Apart from higher handlebars, to give a laid-back riding position, the UK and US versions were much the same.

As the line drew to an end, Triumph trimmed their venerable twin in some very neat styles, and a couple of these are such pleasant motorcycles that they are worthy of a special mention. The eight-valve TSS model, when well set-up and running well, is – in my view – the only real competition

By 1961 the sporting Triumph rider had a choice of machines at his disposal: the fast dual-purpose off-roader, the Trophy, or the most iconic of them all, the T120R . . . the Bonneville.

Still 1961: this TR6 is plainly from the jukebox era . . .

for Norton's Commando in the 'Britain's Best Twin' stakes, while the sadly rare TR65 Thunderbird, the single-carb 650cc economy model, is – again in my view – one of the best Triumph twins of all.

Finally, the very last Triumphs of the old school were the models built by L. F. Harris Ltd in Devon, after the collapse of the Meriden co-op and prior to the emergence of the new Triumphs from their new home in Hinckley.

These last Tigers and Bonnies differed from their immediate predecessors in several ways, as the small concern struggled with the twin realities of a small production run and a lot of worn-out machinery. The front forks were changed from Triumph's own (those introduced in 1971!) to a set from the Italian Paioli concern, and these brought with them a pair of twin front disc brakes from Brembo. Rear suspension came from the same source. Likewise, silencers were sourced in Italy while the switchgear came from Magura.

Model designations

The unit 650s began with the Thunderbird (6T), Trophy (TR6) and Bonneville (T120) models in 1963. The Thunderbird passed on in 1966, but the other models, with their overseas variants, carried on until the whole range was revamped for 1971. From this point, the designations can become a bit confusing, but I shall try to cover the major variants. The new range began with the Tiger (TR6R) and Bonneville (T120RV); the 'V' in the model number indicated the presence of a fifth ratio in the gearbox. Thus, for 1972 the Tiger gained an extra gear and became the TR6RV, and the TR6R was also available until

The Triumph 750 twin, nestling inside its 1971-on oil-bearing frame. This one has been fitted with a single SU carb.

all the 650 twins petered out in 1974. Because of the confused state of the industry at this time, it was not unusual for bikes to be sold well after they were built, so the only true guide to their actual model year can be gained by checking their engine/frame numbers with an expert.

The 750 Bonneville (T140V) arrived with its single-carb Tiger (TR7RV) for 1974, and became the T140E when it gained Mk 2 Amal Concentric carbs for 1979. Confusingly, the 'E' in T140E, which originally stood for 'Environment', can also stand for 'Executive', a well-accessoried version that was available from 1980, and for 'Electric', as in the electric-start T140ES Bonneville (or Tiger) Electro. The Bonneville Special (T140D) was a version with different styling, cast wheels and a single-sided exhaust system for 1979–80, while other special models included the 1977 Jubilee Bonneville and the 1981 Royal Bonneville, both available in home and export versions. The year 1981 saw the introduction of the new 650 Thunderbird (TR65) and the Tiger Trail, available as both 750 (TR7T) or 650 (TR6T). The latter is a particularly pleasant motorcycle, although it is very rare indeed. The eight-valve TSS and strangely custom-styled TSX arrived for 1982 and both lasted until the range folded late that year. The Devon-built twins were available as both twin-carb Bonneville and single-carb Tiger models.

Top: *The end of the line. The final twins were built in Devon and featured many Italian components to complement the trad Brit twin.*

Middle: *1969's T120R Bonneville was a well-developed and well-rounded (if a little vibratory) motorcycle.*

Bottom: *When production of Triumphs was reduced to just a single model, the 750cc T140, several special editions were released. This is a 'Silver Jubilee' Bonneville, which waved the flag for British patriots everywhere.*

THE NEW TRIUMPH RANGE '79.

BECAUSE NOT EVEN LEGENDS CAN REST ON THEIR LAURELS.

RIDE A LIVING LEGEND
TRIUMPH

On the road

All of these Triumphs are pleasant enough on the road, and all of them make good working bikes for today's roads. The earliest 650s are the least fun, largely because although the engines are peppy enough, the bicycle side of things rather lets the plot down a little. The steady improvements meant that by 1968 Triumph were building a very fine, quick and well-handling model, although it was becoming a little taut and vibratory in its Bonneville tune.

The four-valve 750s were never as fast as the 650s they replaced, and although the oil-bearing chassis is a fine handler it lacks the precision of the last of the 650s and has sadly restricted ground clearance if scratching is your game. However, the disc brakes are well up to modern traffic, and the popularity of the bikes ensures that the spares side of things is very well catered for. My own favourites among the wide range of Triumph twins are the very late TR65 Thunderbirds, which are only marginally slower than the 750 Bonnie but are a lot more pleasant to ride, and the 1968–70 650 Trophies, for the same reasons. If I was to buy one . . . it would be a TSS eight-valver, because when they go well they are electrifying, and they go wrong so often that many cheerful hours can be wasted fixing them!

Top: *Another special edition, the Bonneville Special, offered the West Coast look to UK riders.*

Middle: *A slightly unlikely off-roader, the TR7T Trophy Trail harked back to the days when Triumph twins ruled off the tarmac as well as on it.*

Bottom: *The very handsome Bonneville Royal, seen here in its UK livery, painted the electric-start twin engine black and housed it in a set of silver cycle parts.*

The Trident, one of the most charismatic of classic British motorcycles. This 1969 T150 shows off its early 'slab' styling.

The Trident

(See also the BSA Rocket 3 section in Chapter 7.)

The Triumph Trident (T150) and its BSA equivalent, the Rocket 3, were the ailing BSA Group's answer to the increasingly evident threat from Japan. They argued, quite correctly, that motorcyclists of the 1970s were going to want bikes of rather greater performance, presence and stamina than those available via the traditional British parallel twin route. Norton's answer was the Commando – an up-rated and modernised version of their ancient twin – and the BSA Group's was the pair of three-cylinder models. Neither was up to the task in hand, and today's world rides its roads largely aboard descendants of the machines that won that contest.

But the Trident is a fine, charismatic and absorbing motorcycle, for all its failings when viewed against its more successful contemporaries. And although it is easy enough to belittle the machine when comparing it with those produced by the might of industrial Japan, in fact the achievement of those involved in designing, building and marketing it is considerable.

The BSA Group made a serious effort to distance their new bikes' styling from those of their well-known twins, and although it is popular to deride the 1960s Space Age looks of the early threes, BSA and Triumph deserve credit for trying to advance their marketing. The early Trident was more recognisably derived from the Triumph twins than was the BSA from the products of Small Heath,

The last of the triples was the electric-start T160 for 1975. This one has been much improved and features twin discs and less restrictive breathing arrangements.

but like the BSA it boasted the famous 'ray gun' silencers and strangely slab-sided styling. The Americans – the most important market for Triumph – hated it.

As a result of this, the T150 Trident was rapidly offered a styling kit, to disguise it as a three-cylinder Bonneville, and by the time the final electric-start T160 Trident appeared it was a very cleanly styled and handsome machine indeed.

But it was, of course, too late by then. The battle for the marketplace had been fought and lost.

The three-cylinder engine

The common introduction at this point is to describe the three-cylinder Triumph engine as being merely a unit twin with an extra cylinder tacked on to it. This would be inaccurate and gives little credit to the designers involved, who worked engineering miracles with risible resources. Indeed, having ridden thousands of miles on both the British triples and their oriental rivals, it is plain that those designers and engineers deserve praise indeed for developing an engine that would compete with the best Japanese 750s for several years, and for mounting it in a bicycle that also out-performed those rivals.

Having said that, the engine was

easily recognisable as a development of the existing twin and, sadly, inherited several of the failings and compromises of that 30-year-old design. It followed the traditional Triumph approach of having two camshafts mounted on either side of the cylinders, and followed the time-worn Triumph twin route of pushrod valve operation – including the separate pushrod tubes and rockers mounted in boxes bolted to the head rather than integral with it.

The gearbox was also basically the four-speed unit fitted to the unit twins, carburation was provided by three Amal Concentric units, and Lucas supplied the 12-volt alternator electrics. The vertically split crankcase, long the bane of anyone attempting to combine hard use with oiltightness, remained, although there were three of them.

Happily, the triple departed from established twin practice in several ways. The three-throw crank carried no flywheel, and ran in four main bearings, the centre two plain shell bearings, with a ball race on the drive side and a roller on the timing side. The primary drive was by triplex chain, but there convention ended, as the multi-plate clutch was operated by a diaphragm spring, rather than by a collection of traditional small coil springs. It worked well, too, running dry in its own compartment between the gearbox and the primary chaincase. Meanwhile, the 12-volt alternator had departed from the chaincase and reappeared mounted in the timing chest, directly below the *three* sets of contact breakers that timed the spark.

The cylinder block was cast in aluminium, with handsome close-set cooling fins, and the plunger oil pump was binned in favour of a gear device driven from the crank. Oil temperatures were controlled by an oil radiator, mounted under the nose of the fuel tank, and there was even provision of effective filtration for

the oil, with a renewable filter mounted in the centre crankcase as well as the more usual one in the oil tank.

The resulting engine was nothing like the trad twins in operation, offering high performance and vivid acceleration combined with relative smoothness in operation. Compared with a four-cylinder engine, the triple is rather gruff in operation, but when compared to a Bonneville it feels almost sophisticated! The triples also feature a most distinctive sound, especially when under hard acceleration, and although they don't rev as freely as do the twins, they are rather less tiring to ride far, fast. The best performers are the earlier versions, as increasing intake and exhaust silencing requirements blunted things as the years rolled by. Happily, liberating the engine's true performance is not too difficult, and the bikes are served by a handful of proficient specialists.

The Trident's engine development was hindered more than a little by the collapse of the parent company and by the ensuing chaos, although a fifth gear arrived in 1972 and there were the customary year-on-year detail changes to improve oil consumption and leakage.

The triple engines can be profligate in their use of both fuel and oil, and many are the hints, tips and alchemy offered as solutions. By the twins' standard, oil consumption at around 200 mpp and fuel consumption well below 40mpg is pretty dreadful, but such is the strange appeal that many owners – myself included – overlook it for the pleasures of riding these strange Triumphs.

The final version of the Trident, the T160, arrived for 1975. This was much improved over the earlier machine – at least it was improved in the sense that it boasted an electric starter that was at least generally reliable, and a more modern-looking engine, with the cylinder block canted forward to

accommodate the starter. The starter motor drives the clutch, and is a neat installation. Sadly, the changes forced upon induction and exhaust silencing by increasing legislation blunted the performance, and the T160 is slower than the T150V that preceded it. The T160 also shifted its gears with a pedal mounted on the left, and lost its triplex primary chain, replacing it with a duplex alternative.

The T160 also acquired a new exhaust arrangement, with the three-into-two manifold that had been with the bike since its launch being replaced with a three-into-four-into-two system. This gave the centre cylinder a pair of small-bore exhaust pipes of its own, and at a brief glance made the bike appear to have four cylinders . . .

The bicycle

In the same way that the Trident's engine was immediately recognisable as a Triumph, so was its bicycle. This shared its single-downtube mainframe and bolted-on rear subframe design with the twins of the time, along with its forks, brakes and many ancillaries. The Trident gained a neat housing for the speedo, tacho and ammeter, as well as the characteristic slab-sided fuel tank, slatted side panels and unmistakeable 'ray gun' silencers.

Development followed that of the twins until the great re-launch of 1971, when although the Trident gained the forks, wheels and clocks from the revised range, it did not get the oil-bearing frame. Opinion is divided over whether the conical front brake was an improvement over its predecessor, but the loss of the distinctive silencers was mourned by many – in retrospect at least.

A disc front brake joined the list of desirable features for 1973, and the revamped T160 for 1975 also had a rear disc, operated by a right foot pedal. The T160 frame itself was a lowered development of the

Although the engine and the bicycle of this bike were BSA components, the X75 Hurricane was badged as a Triumph – a striking Triumph too, it has to be said.

earlier one and handled at least as well as that. Sadly, it was rather heavier, thirstier and indeed slower than the T150, and like that bike was available with a choice of petrol tanks, 4.8 gallons for the home market and 3.7 for overseas. Both were handsome, and both were comfortable for the rider.

And there are two footnotes to this relatively short-lived but famous motorcycle. There was an export police version that was re-imported in some numbers after production ended and was sold off in the UK as the Cardinal, complete with single seat, panniers, front windscreen and white paint. And there was the Triumph X75 Hurricane, which wasn't a Triumph at all, really.

The Hurricane was one of the very first of the factory customs, vying with Norton's Commando Hi-Rider for that dubious honour. Unlike the Norton, the Hurricane is generally held to be a thing of beauty, even though it sold slowly when it was available new.

The bike was a styling job done on the BSA Rocket 3, and used that bike's engine and bicycle, but fitted with a swoopy orange tank and seat unit that looks striking to this day. It also boasted extended front forks, its own cylinder head, with wider finning, and a set of three silencers, all arranged on the right-hand side of the bike to provide a truly impressive view – from the right, at least. With the irony customary in these cases, although it was not a great seller when new, the Hurricane is the most sought-after triple today, and fakes are not too uncommon.

By 1974 the T150V Trident had gained five speeds, a disc front brake and was built by the old BSA factory.

Model designations

The first Triumph 750cc (67 x 70mm = 740cc) was the T150, launched in 1968, and replaced by the T150V for 1972. In turn, the T150V was replaced by the T160 in 1975.

On the road

Once, when I was compiling a price guide for a magazine, I remarked that 'everyone should own a Trident – once', and have had that quoted back at me many times over the years. But it is true. In some ways the Trident was the ultimate development of the old British industry, even though it was outlived by its twin

brother by over a decade. The Trident was certainly the last, best hope of the old industry, and when its production ceased in 1975 we knew that all was effectively over.

A quarter of a century later, the Trident is still a fine machine to ride. Its steering, stop and stomp departments are still perfectly adequate for today's traffic, and with its striking looks and unusual sound, it still turns heads. The supply of spares is probably better than it was all those years ago, and many of the wearing spares have been developed and improved over that time. The bike benefits enormously from a dedicated and excellent owners' club, and is little

The modern Triumph concern recognised their heritage when they introduced this Thunderbird.

more expensive to buy than the twins.

However, it can be an expensive model to run, with high fuel consumption and high oil consumption to match. And many owners could feel intimidated by the complex and slightly unfamiliar design, preferring to run a twin as a result. Do not be put off, however. Although there are pitfalls for the unwary, as with most of the more interesting British classic bikes, owning and riding a

Trident is a rewarding occupation, and providing its maintenance is by the book, you can have many happy miles together. But beware of buying one that smokes, rattles or is not fitted with a healthily reading oil pressure gauge. And join the Trident & Rocket 3 OC first, anyway.

New Triumphs for the '90s

The Triumph story cannot be

allowed to end with the demise of the Bonneville and Tiger 750s, of course. The early years of the 1990s witnessed that most rare of events when a new British motorcycle factory commenced production of new British motorcycles. That, of course, was the Triumph factory at Hinckley, and although their bikes have little in common with the Meriden models apart from their names, they are inevitably going to become described as classics when their production has reached an end. Indeed, one of the favourite questions of *Classic Bike Guide* readers is which of the new Triumphs will be the classics of the future. Which indeed?

There are already several defunct models, and of these the short-stroke Daytona 1000 is being hailed by some as the first Hinckley classic. However, you should bear in mind that Triumph are a commercially successful operation, and the early demise of certain models was entirely because they sold badly, not because they were particularly wonderful. If forced to offer an opinion of my own, I would venture the thought that the 900 Sprint is likely to be looked back upon as being a most effective model in terms of riding pleasure, style and longevity. On the other hand, the Speed Triple (in black, please, none of your obnoxious orange!) is possibly the best-looking of all the first generation – in the way that the 1997 T509 is not.

As I write this Triumph are riding the crest of a successful wave, therefore providing a happy note on which to end this chapter. Hurrah!

Chapter 10

The Best of the Rest

Many are those who will fail to understand why I have not included large chapters on Royal Enfield, say, or Sunbeam, Velocette or even Vincent. My reasons are simple. The five marques covered in greater detail are those marques whose machines continue to appear in decent numbers in the 'bikes for sale' ads today. True, a lot more Triumphs are advertised than Ariels, and there are always at least a few Sunbeams for sale every month, but I had to draw a line somewhere. And as any author will tell you, the problem is not what to include, but what to leave out. So I chose to include a full chapter on Ariel, because of their market popularity . . . and because of their BSA connection, which brings with it a certain spares availability, but to exclude Royal Enfield, despite the wide range of models they offered and despite the fact that they survived both Ariel and AMC, albeit as part of Norton-Villiers. Blame a shortage of time and space. Laziness, or even a personal preference for mainstream motorcycles, it was not.

Enthusiasts of the less common marques are often even more dedicated to their machines than those of the big few. It is, for example, hard to imagine more devoted riders than those doughty folk who inhabit the worthy ranks of the Panther Owners' Club, one of the truly excellent and most colourful of marque clubs. And I would never belittle the effort required to keep a Scott up to scratch and on the road – both being merely examples.

From a buyer's perspective, while it is easy enough to decide to ride an old, aka 'classic', machine, simply because of the rewards and pleasures offered both by the bikes themselves and by the socialising that goes with them, it is a wise buyer who understands that the challenges offered by ownership of a less-well-known machine are different. In other words, it is easy enough for the rider of today to own, run, maintain and restore a Triumph Bonneville, but it is less easy should the bike of your dreams be a Panther 100.

For that reason, and that reason alone, I would recommend that anyone new to the world of classic motorcycling should choose to buy one of the more common classics. Spares are generally more easily available and the fund of lore that is so invaluable to anyone running an out-of-production motorcycle is much larger.

The other side of the coin is that ownership of a more obscure model can offer rewards of its own. I have met no Scott owner, for example, who was less than a minor authority on both the marque itself and upon his own model. And the same applies to more unusual models from the mainstream manufacturers; there is a truly excellent club dedicated entirely to the three-cylinder models produced by BSA and Triumph in their dying days. The club produces a magazine that is second to none, and is more active than several of the more massive marque clubs. Speaking personally, I am a fan of the rotary Nortons (for which there is also a single-model club), and find keeping one on the road as everyday transport much more involving and rewarding than running a new BMW, for instance.

All of this is a long-winded justification for offering little detail of the bikes produced by the smaller manufacturers. Should you decide that a Sunbeam S7, for example, is the bike for you, join the club, meet other owners, read the books, absorb The Knowledge and buy with advice and guidance from someone who is familiar with the pitfalls.

And yes, I do understand from personal experience that the activities of the Cosmic Motorcycle Supply Company will one day result in your being confronted with a sudden bargain about which you have absolutely no knowledge, but which you suddenly really need to own. The love of old motorcycles is never logical – buy it anyway . . .

A question often asked in the

Although they were rarely considered glamorous, Royal Enfield singles have an unmistakable style.

columns of magazines and in clubrooms everywhere is why did all of the smaller manufacturers disappear when their bikes maintained a dedicated following? The answers are simple: their bikes were too expensive to build, and they could not afford to develop new ones. So long as there was room in the marketplace to allow a meaningful demand for a small number of individual, characterful models, then the likes of Velocette, Scott and Panther could remain in production. But without the economies of scale available to the bigger manufacturers, and without new models to compete with the mainstream, their bikes appeared

to be increasingly unrealistic purchase propositions as they aged.

At the end of the day, the great majority of purchase dilemmas are decided by price, rather than loyalty or a desire to be different, and when the 'alternative' machine can claim only character and heritage to offset its higher cost and lower performance, its day, is, truthfully, done. Which makes some of the heroic efforts made by the smaller manufacturers to stay afloat and in contention all the more laudable.

Royal Enfield

In the 'classic' post-war period,

Royal Enfield offered a fine range of single, twin and even two-stroke models. Although they were never really top-flight sellers in the BSA and Triumph manner, their four-strokes were always worthy and often interesting.

Unusually, but not uniquely, Royal Enfield motorcycles were sold in the US badged as something else, in this case 'Indians', with a range of minor trim and ancillary differences from the UK originals that can make life very interesting for anyone attempting an accurate restoration. These Indians also bore some truly remarkable model names. How about 'Tomahawk 500' for a 500 twin, or 'Hounds Fire Arrow' for a worthy (but dull) 350 off-roader? They make 'Clipper' and even 'Bullet' sound a bit limp.

The singles

Royal Enfield, despite being one of the smaller manufacturers, also had several identifying features that they presumably considered to be superior to the conventional way of doing things in Britain at the time. Thus their Bullet singles and all of the twins combined what some would claim to be the best features of unit construction with those of the non-unit method. The gearboxes, which were Albion rather then RE's own, were bolted rigidly to the back of the crankcases, with adjustment of the primary chain by means of a slipper tensioner. This arrangement, which was also used by BSA for their first twins, allowed for compact construction and a civilised method of chain

The 1948 500cc model J2 is a good example of an early post-war working single.

adjustment, while avoiding the expensive casting complexities of the early unit engines.

The later, Crusader, singles were of proper unit construction, and were unconventional in other ways.

The engines also featured a unique type of oil pump. This was in effect two pumps; one supplied oil to the big ends, while the other sent lubricant straight upstairs to the rockers. Enfield engines stored their lube differently, too. Instead of an oil tank mounted on the frame, as was the norm for these things, RE cast an additional compartment with their crankcases, and the oil lived there. Like Panther, which employed a similar system, this was not a true wet-sump design, but at least it did away with external oil piping. Only their final model, the excellent Mk 2 Interceptor twin, was of true wet-sump design.

However, whatever the merits or otherwise of their slightly unusual engine design, the performance offered by Royal Enfield's Bullet singles was not greater than that offered by, say, AMC or BSA equivalents.

The non-unit single-cylinder design was joined by a new generation of unit-construction engines, starting with a 250 single, announced in late 1956. Once again, the design was interesting,

Top: *With a rigid frame, a sprung saddle and their own brand of telescopic forks at the front, Royal Enfield were generally up to date, as this 1949 350 model G shows – sound, workaday, unpretentious.*

Middle: *Neat rear suspension became an RE characteristic, as were a primary chaincase fastened by a single bolt, a casquette to tidy up the headlamp area and a leading-axle front fork.*

Bottom: *The trials version of the Bullet was as neat and cobby as its contemporaries. However, the sump, visible here between engine and gearbox, always looked vulnerable with Enfield's open-frame design.*

and Royal Enfield had done well to advance into the unit-construction era so early (especially when you consider that the AMC giant never managed it for AJS and Matchless).

The new engine demonstrated some original thinking on the part of its designer, too. Although it was of conventional pushrod valve operation, the camshaft was driven by a duplex chain from the left-hand end of the crank, outboard of the primary drive, which was by simplex chain to a conventional multi-plate clutch. More oddities abounded: the alternator lived in a housing on the right side of the engine, with the points housing next to it. The points in turn were operated by a slim shaft that was driven by the camshaft – on the other side of the engine!

Oddities aside, this was a neat, effective and relatively advanced engine for its day, and later in its life it gained the distinction of being the only British lightweight to boast five speeds in its (sometimes fragile) gearbox. Sadly, it didn't perform much better than its rivals from BSA, Norton and AMC, and developed something of a reputation for being unable to retain its oil and for knocking out its shell big-end bearing due to poor lube supply.

The bicycle was a more conventional RE job, with the engine taking the place of the bottom frame rails, and acting as a stressed member. Styling was neat enough, and the bike's 17-inch wheels made it easy for smaller (and younger – remember the 250cc learner limit) riders to handle.

Top: *In common with many other manufacturers, RE scaled down their bigger bangers to produce 250s like this 1954 Clipper.*

Bottom: *By 1960, although the old single engine was getting long in the tooth, the bike's appearance had been kept largely up to date.*

The new machine underwent the customary process of tuning, styling and nomenclature changes, following the trend away from commuter bikes to flash, brash and sporty bikes for the young. It even gained a radical front end for a while, when the Super-5 appeared wearing a leading-link design. It was unpopular . . .

The stroke of the 250 engine was stretched to provide a 350, the New Bullet, but this too was unpopular, and because many of them were converted back to 250s they are very rare today. RE were truly forward-thinking, and offered their bikes with a range of fairing styles to suit them, most remarkably the 'Airflow', which was truly vast and came complete with the world's most massive front mudguard to match it. Riding a big twin fitted with one of these is a fair touring experience; the 250 single suffered from being suddenly under-powered and from grounding the fairing on every corner.

But the unit singles went out on a high note, with the rather splendid Continental GT model, which was the definitive learner rocket of its day. It looked good, sounded good and sometimes even held together long enough for its learner rider to pass his test.

We cannot leave a section on RE

Top: *In its later 'big head' Bullet form, the Enfield single made a reasonable sidecar tug.*

Middle: *Royal Enfield's unit-construction single, seen here in a 1962 250cc Crusader, showed a lot of innovative and thoughtful design.*

Bottom: *Royal Enfield were not conservative thinkers, and although constrained by the financial limitations of a relatively small company, they came up with many advanced ideas. This is the prototype of the Airflow Crusader. The unusual rear end failed to make it to production, but the fairing did. Airflow Enfields are rare today, but they still occasionally appear.*

singles without mentioning the Madras-built Indian Enfield Bullets. The best advice I can offer is that if you wish to own an Enfield, make it a real Royal Enfield. Although the 'modern' Bullet offers much in the way of period charm, all too often my mail at the *Classic Bike Guide* has contained sad letters from disillusioned Bullet owners. If you must buy one, buy it cheap.

Non-unit single model designations

The Bullet singles kicked off with the 350 (70 x 90mm = 346cc) G2, which ran from 1949. It was joined by the 500 (84 x 90mm = 499cc) JS in 1953, and both types ran until 1962. Along the way, they were joined by the 350 Clipper (1958–59), which was replaced by the Clipper de Luxe (1960–62). The new 250 (70 x 64.5mm = 248cc) Crusader joined the range in 1956 and was joined by the Clipper Series II for 1958, the Crusader Sports for 1959 and the Crusader Super 5 for 1962. That only lasted one season; the Crusader passed over in 1962, the 250 Clipper in 1965 and the Crusader Sports in 1966. The Continental joined up in 1963 and was replaced by the Continental GT from 1965 to '66.

Royal Enfield also sold a two-stroke twin, the Turbo Twin, with a Villiers engine. This arrived in 1964, along with the Turbo Twin Sports, which lasted until 1966; these are

Top: *Royal Enfield extended their Airflow concept to a sports version, but the author has never actually laid eyes on one of these.*

Middle: *The forward thinking extended to a leading-link design of front end for 1962, but this was unsuccessful.*

Bottom: *The hottest of the mid-'60s sports 250s? Every cafe racer's dream – in 1966 – was the Continental GT, complete with speedflow fairing.*

The twin, when it finally arrived, showed RE thinking with originality as usual.

perfectly fine if you like Villiers-engined motorcycles.

The twins

Royal Enfield were also purveyors of a flawed, but individualist and charismatic twin. Like the AMC device, this engine used two separate cylinder castings and two cylinder head castings, but didn't bother with the AMC centre bearing. It also followed the general RE principle of carrying its oil in a 4-pint container cast integrally with the crankcases, with the result that the oil got very hot very quickly and had a pronounced tendency to leak from several of the joints.

It used the same bicycle and Albion gearbox as the 350 Bullet, which at least helped to keep the weight down.

For some reason the RE twins were never wildly successful, and even though the capacity increased from 500 to 700cc for 1953, thus leapfrogging the BSAs and Triumphs of this world – except in sales. Changes continued the traditional British development path, and the RE twins are all handsome, in a beefy kind of way, sharing the majority of their cycle parts with the singles. Even a capacity boost to 750cc for 1963 to match Norton's Atlas failed to lift the big twins into the sports league . . . and they were actually pretty fast.

Their main problem is that they do leak a lot when poorly maintained. Not for nothing did they gain the classic nickname of 'Royal Oilfield'. They are also vibratory when worked hard, and although they steer competently they feel dated when compared

The 500cc sports twin was compact and unusual. Sadly, it wasn't very fast and had no great reputation.

with similar products of the day, and their unusual twin front brakes are not entirely exciting, given the performance and weight of the bikes.

Having said that, Interceptors are impressive machines, with more go (on paper at least) than comparable BSAs, Triumphs and Nortons, and since the re-importing of large numbers of bikes from the US to the UK they are more common than they were,

most new machines having been sold for export. But spares availability is not good, certainly when compared to more mainstream machines.

The final big twin (introduced after the failure of the original company and its acquisition by Norton-Villiers) was the 1968 Interceptor Mk 2, which was a surprisingly thorough redesign of the earlier engine. The Mk 2 also benefited from the attachment of

Onward and upward – the twin steadily gained capacity.

Norton's 'Roadholder' front fork, and the 8-inch brake that went with it, and oddly enough the combination of Norton front end and trad RE main frame works well enough.

These final twins are exciting machines to ride, although they could never have succeeded commercially in a home marketplace dominated by the first superbikes from BSA/Triumph and Norton, or in the US, where Honda's 750 four was leading the field. It also suffers from the retention of the ancient Albion four-speed gearbox, which mars the riding a lot. Every time I have had the pleasure of riding one of these impressive (looking, sounding and riding) bikes, I have hated the gearbox's slow change and mis-matched ratios.

Production ended in 1970, and 137 remaining power units were built into Rickman rolling chassis, giving rise to the semi-legendary Rickman Interceptor. Rarity breeds reputation, and although these are interesting and slightly brutal machines with fine steering, as you would expect, they are always over-priced.

If you contemplate the purchase of a Royal Enfield, the best advice to offer – once again – is that you join the owners' club and seek their guidance first. Not after.

By 1968 RE's big twins, the 750 Interceptors, were being produced underground. Here a clump of them pose for the camera with their factory riders looking happy enough.

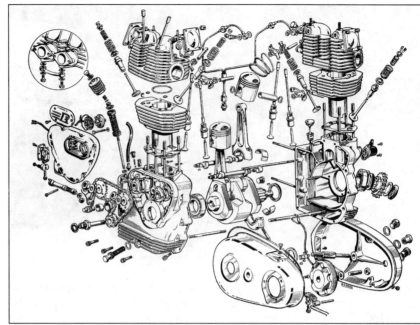

Above, left: *The final big twin, the Mk 2 Interceptor, featured true wet-sump lubrication and brutal performance. Sadly, it was rendered obsolete by the Trident and Commando and wasn't helped by a chasm between third and fourth gear ratios.*

Above, right: *The Mk 2 Interceptor engine.*

Spares availability for some models is less than perfect, and OC folk are the ones to help with advice and knowledge.

Twin model designations

The 500 Twin (64 x 77mm = 495cc) appeared in 1949 and ran on until 1958. It was joined by the 700 Meteor (70 x 90mm = 692cc) in 1953, which was replaced by the Super Meteor for 1955, and that lasted until 1962. In 1958 the range was expanded by the addition of the 700 Constellation and 500 Meteor Minor, both of which ran on until 1963, when the 750 Interceptor became the sole RE twin on offer. It was superseded by the Interceptor Mk 2 in 1968, and it all ended two years later.

Sunbeam

Post-war Sunbeams comprised one basic model in two guises, and although they are unusual, many are still in use today. The Sunbeam's charms lie in its radical

difference from the British parallel twin norm, and although no Sunbeam twin was ever going to exactly blister the tarmac with its performance, riding one remains a unique – and very pleasant – experience.

During the Second World War BSA acquired the rights to the Sunbeam name from AMC, who

GO Interceptor

ENFIELD MOTOR CYCLES, BRADFORD - ON - AVON, ENGLAND.

The first post-war Sunbeam looked every inch a gentleman's conveyance.

had bought it to provide a higher 'quality' brand to sit alongside their AJS and Matchless marques. BSA's idea was plainly the same, and when the war was over the two weekly motorcycling titles had carried so many scoops and tasters about the forthcoming machine that no one could have been surprised when the new model was announced for sale in 1947.

It has been fashionable to criticise the Sunbeam twin, and in particular its designer, one Erling Poppe, has come in for quite a lot of stick over the years. In fact, given that his brief was to design a thoroughly luxurious motorcycle around the bicycle of a wartime

BMW, his achievement is considerable, especially considering that his work was undertaken during the war.

The bike is a tourer, BSA having decided that this was where the post-war market would lie for their new marque. And what a tourer! The engine is a parallel twin like so many of the new Brit generation, but unlike all of them the Sunbeam bore its cylinders in line with the direction of travel, rather than at 90 degrees to it. The engine was of all-aluminium construction and boasted a chain-driven overhead cam to drive its valves – this in an age when the volume sellers were cast-iron single-cylinder models. Following

car practice – and this should have been no surprise to anyone, as Mr Poppe had something of an automobile background – the camshaft drove the distributor at the rear, and the carb and exhausts lived together on the right side of the engine, with the spark plugs sitting under a stylish alloy casting opposite.

Drive was taken through a car-type clutch direct to the four-speed gearbox and thence by shaft to the rear wheel. Once again we have a well-reasoned departure from the norm; shaft drive was seen by many of motorcycling's dreamers as being the answer to chains, with their noise, mess and need for frequent adjustment. Sadly, the choice of final drive was the wrong one (an underslung worm, rather than conventional crown wheel and pinion), and its fragility dogged the bike throughout its production life.

The bicycle was also pretty unconventional for a British machine, which is hardly a matter of great wonder, given that it was copied from a wartime BMW. It consisted of a substantial duplex cradle that located the engine via rubber mounts, running back to a pair of plunger rear suspension units. Front suspension was handled by a set of telescopic forks, but even these were unusual in their early form. Instead of each fork leg containing its springs and valves to control the damping, they were simply sliders, with the springing and damping handled by a single central unit that ran from the top yoke to the front mudguard's bridge. In principle, and with a nice twist of irony, it is

Although not entirely standard, this 1952 S7 shows off to great effect the balloon tyres, curvaceous styling and progressive engineering.

not a million miles from the current BMW Telelever set-up, if you ignore the latter's use of a wishbone instead of a conventional bottom yoke.

The lack of convention extended even to the choice of wheels and the seating arrangement. The S7 fitted its single saddle with a cantilever springing arrangement, and decided that both wheels should be interchangeable – thus the front wheel shared the rear's unusual 4.75 x 16 tyres.

Sadly for Sunbeam, sales were slow, and what development there was seemed to be dedicated to reducing the model's individuality, rather than solving its engineering failings.

So it was that a 'sporting' version of the S7, the S8, appeared for 1949. This boasted a BSA front fork and 19-inch wheel to match the 4.00 x 18-inch rear, and an altogether lighter appearance. Oddly, the S8 gained its own unusual cast aluminium silencer, rather than the more conventional chromed 'Goldie'-pattern item used on the S7.

Production chugged along until 1956, when it faded quietly away. Today, Sunbeams occasionally come to the market, and they are often in very standard, un-messed-about-with condition. This isn't a complete mystery because there were – and are – very few ways of upping the

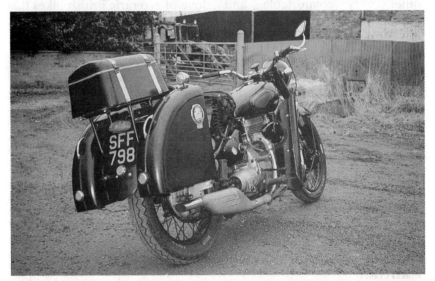

Top: *The S8 was an attempt to popularise the rather frumpy twin by fitting it with more conventional wheels and forks. This 1951 example shows off the changes to advantage.*

Middle: *The Sunbeam's specification made it ideal as a touring mount and many riders used them for serious travelling. This 1953 S8 is wearing steel legshields to match its Rodark pannier set.*

Bottom: *Although badged as a Sunbeam, this BSA scooter had nothing to do with the noble marque.*

performance of the bike, and although I have seen one cafe racer, it was plainly horrid – and slow.

The spares situation is dependant upon one specialist concern and, as you might expect for such an individual machine, there is plenty of lore available. Both the fat-tyred S7 and the S8 are very pleasant to ride, and they represent one of the great blind alleys (the other was Velocette's LE) down which the otherwise very conservative British manufacturers took a step or two. If you do not need to own a classic that is fast, or flashy, or brash in any way, but which is instead quiet, very comfortable, and reliable within its limits, as well as attracting a lot of attention wherever classic fans gather, I would recommend that you consider trying a Sunbeam twin. You should take a long test ride too, because they take a while to grow on you.

Model designations

The 500 (70 x 63.5mm = 487cc) S7 was launched for 1947, and was replaced by the S7 De Luxe in 1949, the same year as the S8 was launched. Both models ran on until 1956.

Panther

The Cleckheaton in Yorkshire-built Panther is another of those marques whose reputation far exceeds their success – at least so far as the post-war period is concerned. Several British marques can accurately be described as being legendary, and Panther is up there with the most legendary of them all. Relatively few riders chose to buy Panthers, and fewer still ride them today, but I've yet to meet a classic enthusiast who doesn't know all about them. All about the legend, that is – the reality is rather more elusive.

Whenever the subject of Panthers comes up in classic conversation, thoughts and talk inevitably turn to the slopers, the epic 600 and 650cc big pussies of myth and tall tales. But Panthers also sold separate ranges of smaller machines, both four-stroke singles and two-stroke singles and twins. These bikes rarely command the veneration afforded to the slopers, but they certainly have a charm – and most certainly a character – of their very own. Once again, I find myself admitting to a terrible bias here. I started my riding career on a Panther, a 197cc two-stroke Model 10/4, and although it was a machine of spectacular dreadfulness it confirmed in me a love of eccentric British bikes that has endured to this day.

The middleweights

The reason behind the mighty name of Panther becoming associated with the slightly less revered name of Villiers was simple; the four-stroke range was selling in numbers that were too small to balance the books. Enter the lightweights.

Panther's strokers were, of course, eccentric. Not content with cladding them in some of the least attractive tin enclosures seen on a British motorcycle, they also benefited from great weight and low power, and, combined with an unusual design of leading-link front forks that gave them a certain unruliness of steering, these factors might suggest that someone was having a small chuckle somewhere. This combination of unique selling points proved to be too much of a good thing for the Great British buying public, and two-stroke Panthers are very rare today.

Having said that, they do of course have a certain charm and an undoubted rarity value. And, to be fair, the later 'sports' 350 twins are no worse than most of the other Villiers-powered utilities of their day. The later, bigger strokers also used the forks and brakes from the big bangers, so they did at least steer and stop, if a little ponderously.

And, unusually for the time, the Villiers twins were also available fitted with a Siba Dynastart unit, which was an early form of electric foot originally intended for invalid carriages. In fact, these are quite pleasant, and an electric-start Panther two-stroke should certainly attract attention at events from the knowledgable. But they are rare today, with only around 200 being built.

My own Model 10/4 200cc single (which was donated to a bemused but unsurprised dustman by a friend's mother) boasted only three of its alleged four gear ratios, could never start without a run-and-bump, and broke its frame just above the swinging arm pivot. As the friend who loaned it to me to start my riding career said at the time, 'If you can learn to ride this, then you'll be able to ride anything.' How right he was.

As well as the strokers, Panther also sold a range of light(er) four-stroke singles. The design of these was in principle very close to that of the big slopers, including several of their features. Like the bigger models, the Models 65 and 75 (250 and 350cc respectively) carried their oil in a compartment cast as one with the crankcases. They used Burman gearboxes, and they operated their overhead valves via a pair of pushrods that ran up through a chromed steel pushrod tube, itself a distinctive feature of the slopers.

Early versions came mounted in a rigid frame that might accurately be described as being robust, and a swinging arm version appeared for 1953. They were unusual at the sharp end too, with suspension up front being provided by a set of the once-infamous Dowty Oleomatic air-sprung forks. And you thought that the Japanese invented air suspension!

These forks, which were apparently developed from

aircraft landing gear, gave a smooth, well-damped ride when in good condition, but when wear set in, especially if that wear included the seals drying out (for example if the bikes were left standing for any length of time) then leaking, proud owner had problems. Spares availability for these forks is not good, and membership of the Mighty Panther Owners' Club is essential should fate find you owning a machine fitted with them.

Styling of these models was unremarkable, with the possible exception of the rare Stroud trials version. These are very rare indeed – in fact, I have never seen one. A genuine one, that is – I have ridden two 'replicas', or fakes, as we might uncharitably call them, although both were being offered for sale as the real thing.

Little development work was carried out on these machines, with the bulk of the company's limited resources being directed to their assault upon the scooter market. As this is a book about motorcycles, I should mention the Panther scooters, and so I have. They were unsuccessful. And French.

Model designations

The 250 (60 x 88mm = 248cc) Model 65 standard and de-luxe and the 350

Top: *As well as producing the legendary slopers, Panther also attempted to crack the lightweight market. Unhappily, despite the supposed charms of bikes like this Model 65, they failed.*

Middle: *The range of Villiers two-stroke-powered lightweights helped cashflow through the 1960s, but in this shot of a Model 35 twin, it is sadly evident that the admiring gazes are being directed elsewhere.*

Bottom: *Right at the end P&M attempted to stave off the inevitable by converting their venerable sloper to alternator/coil electrics and fitted an AMC gearbox. Just the one was built.*

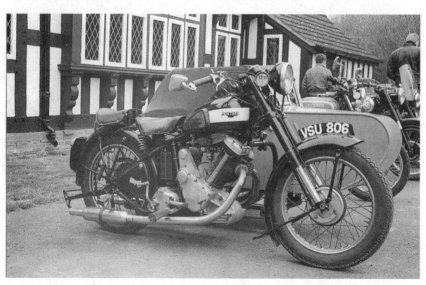

(71 x 88mm = 348cc) were launched for 1949, and were joined by the Models 65S and 75S (for 'Sprung', not 'Sports') for 1953, the rigid versions dying out a year or so later. The sprung models ran on until 1960 (Model 65) and '61 (Model 75).

In 1956 the Model 10 two-stroke single was introduced, available as Model 10/3 – with three gears – and Model 10/4. No prizes. The 10/3 used the Villiers 8E engine, and the 10/4 the 9E, and confusion for future restorers was increased for 1957 when the Model 10/3A appeared, bearing a three-speed 9E engine unit. The 10/3 left the range in 1960, and the other singles ended their runs two years later.

The 250 (50 x 63.5mm = 249cc) Model 35 was the first two-stroke twin to appear in 1957, and it was joined a year later by the Model 35 Sports. The 350 (57 x 63.5mm = 324cc) Model 45 Sports joined the fleet in 1959, as did the Model 50 Grand Sports. The 35S, 45S and 50GS all went in 1962, and the surviving 35 was joined by the Model 35ES in 1964, before fading out in 1965. The Model 35ES survived until 1968, and was the last of all the Villiers-engined utility twins.

The heavyweights

Generally, when enthusiasts discuss Panthers, the bikes they are referring to are the big pussies, the redoubtable big 600 and 650cc

Top: *The classic Panther. This rather quaint rendering of a 1947 600cc Model 100 shows it all: aggressively sloping engine, forward-thrusting cylinder, oil-carrying crankcases, air-sprung forks, twin pipes and rigid back end. Truly a classic in its own dimension.*

MIddle: *By 1953 little had changed. The old thunderer continued to thunder.*

Bottom: *Now, as then, most Panthers seen on the roads haul sidecars. The more eccentric the better, it seems.*

singles, Models 100 and 120 respectively.

The big Panther is a machine that had no right to survive the last war, really, and as the British motorcycling scene moved increasingly towards the more revvy and exciting world of the parallel twin, the big single was viewed increasingly as the preserve of either the pure sportster – or as the preferred choice of Sidecar Man. The Cleckheaton Clunker dives squarely into the latter category. Not that there was anything wrong with that, of course, so long as there was a thriving market for sidecars and thus the bikes to haul them.

Way back in the mists of British motorcycling history, the founders of the company that built Panthers (Phelon and Moore – the Panther name itself started out in 1922) decided to dispense with the conventional push-bike-based frame design's front downtube and bottom rails, replacing them with the engine. This was a fine piece of forward thinking, and indeed the use of the engine as a stressed frame member is not uncommon today.

Panther modestly advertised themselves as 'the perfected motorcycle', and by the dawn of the classic age that was not too wild a claim, given that their staple engine design had been in production for decades. And a remarkable piece of design it was, especially viewed in the context of the British post-war motorcycling scene.

Big singles were not common in the 1950s, but they were around, with 600s being available from Norton and BSA. But the Panther engine was still a unique beast.

The big engine was unconventional in many ways. For a start, the barrel and cylinder head were clamped to the crankcases, not by bolts or studs in the usual way, but by a pair of lengthy U-bolts. These looped around the main bearing housings on each side of the engine and passed up to the top of the cylinder head, where nuts tightened everything up. An odd, but effective method, which was dispensed with for the M120, as the extra performance dictated a redesign of the main bearing housings. The other most remarkable feature, in a bike that is wholly remarkable, was the stone-age lubrication system.

Like Royal Enfields, Panther singles used a cast-in extension of the crankcases as an oil tank. Unlike the rather more sophisticated Enfield, Panther relied upon a slightly arcane (or ancient, if you prefer) method of returning the oil to the tank after its lubing and cooling duties around the engine. Quite simply, the hot oil was thrown over the weir that separated the crankcase proper from the oil store by the crankshaft's flywheels as they rotated. Does this sound a tad hit 'n' miss? It was, and must go a long way towards explaining the engine's high oil consumption. But think positive: high oil consumption should at least ensure that the quality of oil in the sump remains high. Maybe . . .

The rest of the engine was mainly conventional, although there were a couple of nice touches. Like the little lever at the front of the timing cover that operates a 'half compression' device to ease kicking the long stroker over. Like the neat facility to remove the magneto (and later the magdyno) without disturbing the timing or the timing case's oiltightness. Like the option of ordering the bike with either a single or a twin port head. The story goes that the twin piper, with its pair of silencers, was quieter, but I think that P&M fitted them because they looked good. In any case, the bike was also available fitted with just the one.

Power was transmitted via a simplex primary chain and a conventional multi-plate clutch to a Burman gearbox, similar to those used by several manufacturers after the war. But be warned, the Panther/Burman box carries its primary chain adjusters underneath, using the top gearbox mounting bolt as the pivot. Spares for these boxes are not as common as they are for the more common bottom-pivoting devices, so bear that in mind when buying.

When it re-entered production after the war, the Panther continued with its rigid frame and girder forks, but a set of the Dowty Oleomatic air-sprung forks arrived for 1947, and the frame

1954 saw a great pounce forward – the arrival of Panther's own front fork.

developed a suitably rugged swinging arm for 1954, when Panther's own similarly rugged forks replaced the Oleomatics.

A much improved interchangeable 8-inch hub and brake arrived for 1956, and that was effectively that as far as development went, apart from the introduction of the 650 Model 120S for 1958. Engineering changes for the transition from 600 to 650 were really too many to be justified by sales, as they included major changes to the engine's bottom end. The famous, and long-lived, U-bolts mentioned above proved to be incapable of handling the increased loads, and were replaced by a more conventional method of assembly. The crankcases had to be redesigned to suit, as well as strengthened, and the flywheels were also redesigned, all of which must have put something of a burden upon the company's resources. The illustrious old concern had insufficient capital to develop a new heavyweight model, and demand for the sloper was fading fast, despite its capacity boost.

Panther slopers are odd. That is perhaps the best word to describe them. They are also charismatic, anachronistic, quaint, charming, stylish and raucous, and they remain, to my knowledge, the only motorcycle ever described as an aspidistra. Riding them is the same.

Solo, they are a little harsh of suspension, long of stride and low on sophistication. But they have a rhythm all their own, and they attract a breed of rider all their own, too. In harness the true strength of the beast shines through. They are capable of lugging quite extraordinary loads with equally extraordinary stamina – even if they do have a tendency to knock out their clutch centres while doing so.

But the bikes are an acquired taste. They are undeniably primitive, even by the standards of the day, with rugged construction rather than up-to-the-minute styling being valued more by their builders.

I once wrote that the best reason for owning a Panther was the obligatory membership of the Panther Owners' Club – and I was only half joking. The bikes have no vices that are not already well known to that doughty band, and it is gratifying that such an individualistic motorcycle has gathered to itself a similarly characterful band of devotees. Long may it continue.

Model designations

The 600 (87 x 100mm = 598cc) Panther Model 100R entered production in 1946, was joined by the swinging arm Model 100S for 1954 and lasted until 1957. The Model 100S was joined by the Model 100S de-luxe, and lasted until 1963. The 650 (88 x 106mm = 645cc) was introduced for 1959, and survived – if only just – until 1967. At least in theory . . .

Velocette

Velocette, along with Vincent, is a marque that is so festooned with reputation and hype that I was undecided about whether it should be included in this book at all. With both of the 'V' marques, it is essential that you take expert advice before parting with your money. This is advice that I have repeatedly offered, and it is sound. I have probably seen more horror stories involving Velocette singles than any other British bike. The reasons for this? Well . . .

Velocettes built two distinct ranges of motorcycle. They built their classic – nay, legendary – single-cylinder machines, and they built a range of lightweight twins based around the utility LE model. I have never yet seen an LE disguised as anything that it isn't (that would be quite hard!), but I have seen a lot of fake sports singles.

As is the case with top-of-the-range sportsters from the bigger manufacturers (BSA Rocket Gold Stars, Triumph Thruxton Bonnevilles, Norton Internationals, for example) it is quite easy to style a cooking Velocette roadster as one of their rare Venom Thruxton models. And although it is usually easy enough for a marque specialist to spot the fakes, there isn't room in a book like this to tell you what to look for. A very short time ago, as I write this, I was invited to road test a

The Venom, for many the greatest of all the classic British singles.

Although modified year by year to keep its performance on a par with the opposition, by 1967 the Thruxton's way of going was undeniably outdated.

'Thruxton Venom' for the *Classic Bike Guide*, and when I arrived I was presented with a very tidy and impressive machine indeed. But I was suspicious.

Aren't all Venoms 500s? Proud Owner agreed at once, adding, 'But it's got all the right bits. . .'

The bike was in fact mostly a Viper, a worthy enough machine in its own right, but not worth anything like the elevated figures asked for genuine Thruxtons. And there is nothing at all wrong with an owner customising his or her own machine to make it resemble the bike he would really like but which he cannot afford. And there is nothing at all wrong with selling such a replica when the need arises. The dishonesty lies in pretending that the bike is something it is not; that dishonesty is called fraud. You would do well to both be aware of it and to avoid it.

In another case of my close acquaintance, a rider bought his 'Thruxton', discovered that it was a fake (or 'replica', perhaps) and returned in search of redress. Only to be told by the vendor that he had never claimed that the bike was a Thruxton – and there were no witnesses. Even the ad said merely 'Sports Velocette for sale'. This unfortunate had paid out Thruxton money (about £7,500, at the time) for a tarted-up MSS (worth about £2,200 at the time). And the reason he'd not taken a marque specialist? He wanted to keep the news of the bargain to himself . . .

The Singles

The Velocette singles' designers plainly had a fixation with the width of their power units. Indeed, this is the most compact of all the British engines of its type,

and a comparison with a Panther sloper is a worthy study in different approaches!

Although the engine design principles are much as other pushrod singles of the era, with their robust crank, single gear-driven cam, external pushrod tube and gear oil pump, Velocette crankcases are very narrow indeed, and they offered a unique approach to transmission configuration, which found the final drive sprocket situated outside of the primary chain and outside of the clutch, too. This unusual layout has given rise to the Velo's reputation for having a terrible clutch.

I have been assured by several enthusiasts of these idiosyncratic singles that clutch adjustment is easy when you know how, but it is undeniably different from anything else. From a modern-day buyer's viewpoint, it makes the extended test ride doubly essential (assuming, of course, that you are not already a Velo expert; I would suggest that your tame expert takes the test ride). If the clutch is slipping, dragging, or both, you are in for a spell of concentrated learning or expense. Or both.

The engine of the original 350 MAC model was redesigned to provide both a 350 and a 500 sharing a common stroke, and the company produced the inevitable

year-on-year developmental changes, offering a bewildering array of components and specifications, which is one reason why the modern buyer should tread with care. So many of the touring MSS models have been converted into Venoms, and so many Venoms into Specials, Thruxtons and Clubmans, that originality is increasingly valuable. And increasingly rare.

The bicycle started out as being rigid-framed, conventional and pretty old-fashioned, with the original girder forks being replaced by Dowty Oleomatics (see the Panther section) for 1948. They didn't last long, however, and Velocette introduced their own conventionally sprung front fork for 1951, with rear suspension arriving a couple of years later.

Velocette's rear suspension is worthy of a mention, too. Unlike all the other UK manufacturers, Velocette decided to offer an adjustment system at the rear, which allowed each suspension unit's top mount to be slid along a curved slot, thus altering the geometry and the available damping. Other than that, the frame's construction remained obstinately conventional, and although it was altered reasonably continuously, nothing really changed until the end of the line.

It was a little surprising that so

traditional a concern as this should find itself affected by market fashions, but Velocette acknowledged the late-1950s enclosure craze by offering their own. However, unlike anyone else, they opted to enclose the bottom end of the power train with some fairly style-free fibreglass panels, leaving the cylinder poking skyward like a ship's funnel. Very odd, and quite rare today, as many owners ditched the panels, preferring to gaze instead upon their engine's handsome castings. In any case, the panels' styling never did match that of the trad fuel tank, and left the oil tank and tool box enclosed on the right side, while covering up the battery on the left.

Velocette singles also featured their own unique silencer, a fishtail design throwback to distant pre-war days, without which – or so The Velo Lore tells us – the engines will not run properly. They certainly sound good, look distinctive and cost a lot of money to replace.

As the years rolled by, more of the company's efforts went into developing their dreams of successfully marketing a Motorcycle For Everyman, and the singles languished, retaining their leaky tin primary cases, ancient frame and post-vintage styling until their demise in 1971, by which time they were certainly offering an unusual alternative to Honda's CB750 and Norton's Commando!

But Velocettes inspire devotion and marque loyalty because they are very fine riders' machines. If they were not rewarding to own and ride they would not be as

Top: *Although its performance is beyond doubt, Velocette's engine requires a certain dedication from its owner.*

Bottom: *This view of the single's drive side shows its unusual layout. The primary chain and clutch live inboard of the final drive sprocket and chain.*

Velocette joined the trend towards enclosure but, as ever, they did it their own way. Thus they enclosed the most beautiful part of their motorcycle, the engine, in a tub of unattractive fibreglass, here modelled by a 1960 Venom Veeline.

revered as they are today, and they would be surrounded by no more mystique than that which accompanies BSA B44s or Norton ES2s.

For a start (if you can indeed start them – Velocette starting rituals are of course the stuff of legendary difficulty) the sporting engines punch out their power in a very satisfying, hard-edged manner, a manner that is matched exactly by the very fine steering of the single-downtube bicycle. The later the bike, the better its braking and the less unreliable its electrics, but the essential character of the machine is the combination of a good engine and a taut chassis. Riding a well-set-up Venom is one of Brit biking's great experiences.

The downside involves the sensitivity of the engine to bad maintenance and non-enthusiast ownership. This brings with it monstrous oil leaks, poor transmission performance and early component failure. The knowledgeable examine with care the condition of the drive-side crankcase around the main bearing housing, for example, for hard-worked and poorly maintained machines can crack badly around here.

The touring models are more robust, but are equally sensitive to poor adjustment and maintenance. Having said that, were I in the market for a Velo single, I would look first for an MSS, which combines most of the go with most of the style, usually at a lower price than anything claiming to be a Venom.

If you really do fancy owning one of these most quirky of singles, persuade an owner to loan you his machine, decide whether

you can live with it, then take him with you when you go to view. Join the owners' club and buy through their ads.

Model designations

The 350 (68 x 96mm = 349cc) MAC re-entered production in 1946 and was available until 1959, although its replacement, the 350 (72 x 86mm = 349cc) Viper had joined the range in 1956. The Viper Sports arrived for 1959, the Viper Clubman for 1960, Viper Special for 1963, and the Viper Clubman Mk 2 for 1967. Apart from the Viper Clubman, which left the nest in 1966, the remaining 350s ended their run in 1968.

The 500 (86 x 86mm = 499cc) MSS entered the range for 1954, and was joined by the more sporting Venom for 1956, by the Venom Sports for 1959, the Venom Clubman for 1960, the Venom Special for 1963, the Venom Thruxton for 1965 and the Venom Clubman Mk 2 for 1967. There were also some scrambles versions . . . Apart from the Venom Clubman, which ceased production in 1966, and the Thruxton and Clubman Mk 2, which survived notionally until 1970, all the 500s wound up in 1968.

Twins: the LE

After the war Velocette became obsessed with building that elusive motorcycle for Everyman.

That way, they thought, lay great sales and great reward. It is hard to argue with the reasoning – just ask Honda how many step-thrus they've sold. Velocette, however, wanted to do it their way.

Their answer to the riddle that asks what sort of bike Everyman would buy was a little unlikely. They decided that he would want to ride an almost silent, almost performance-free and completely style-less device that bore little resemblance to anything else. So, with their vast experience of racing ohc single design, they decided to construct a 149cc side-valve flat twin, with the added complications of water-cooling and a shaft final drive. The audacity of this is still breathtaking, especially considering the small size of the company.

As well as the features listed above, early versions of the LE (for 'Little Engine', so tradition has it) also featured a hand starter and a hand gear-change. Velocette's band of loyal sporting singles riders must have gazed upon this small grey offering with some bemusement.

Nothing about the LE was British conventional. Even the frame was made out of ugly swathes of pressed tin, and the engineering effort alone still makes the mind boggle a little.

Sadly Everyman preferred the

Velocette's attempt at a motorcycle for Everyman was the bizarre LE. The cost of tooling for this strange device ultimately brought about the demise of the company.

more conventional ride-to-work delights offered by the likes of BSA's Bantam and the Villiers-powered brigade. So he failed to buy LEs by the tens of thousands, as the fellows at Velo's had confidently predicted. In fact, the bulk of sales went to various police forces, who liked the quiet, unassuming little machine for suburban patrol duties, and discovered that with effective maintenance routines the little bike could cover impressive mileages.

A capacity hike to 192cc for 1951, and four speeds, a conventional gear-change and a kick-starter all appeared for 1957. Thereafter there were the customary incremental changes until the line expired in 1970.

Although the above may read like a catalogue of disaster, mixed well with commercial stupidity, the Velocette LE is highly prized by a band of devotees to this day. Good examples command relatively high prices, and there are still loads of them around. And I have to admit to having enjoyed every ride I have had on an LE, despite the lamentable lack of performance. They really are marginal in today's main-road traffic, though, and when I have tested them I have kept to lanes and backstreets, where they are most comfortable.

Hill-climbing is a relaxed process, and the bike's silence and smoothness make for a gentle progression towards any destination that is unequalled in British bike terms. You would have to be made of stern stuff to attempt too many distant destinations, but many riders over the years have covered impressive trips aboard them.

Braking and handling are fine, but the bikes were let down by a host of mechanical and electrical maladies that a decent production volume would have solved (because they sold slowly, they failed to generate sufficient profits to devote to further r&d). A quirky machine, with an owners' club all its own. Even the final development, the fibreglass-panelled Vogue, which at least looked less like a scrapyard refugee, failed to save the day, and the LE must rank as one of the UK industry's most heroic failures.

Twins: the Valiant and Viceroy

Incredibly, not content with the lack of commercial success that had greeted the introduction of the LE, Velocette compounded their mistake by producing a sports version, which had its own engine, frame and tinware, and a scooter, which utilised the flat-twin concept, but was a two-stroke!

The sporting version of the Velocette flat twin range was the 1957 Valiant, which used the basic bottom-end design of the side-valve LE, but with a pair of ohv top ends. It also dispensed with

A late attempt at introducing some style to the LE – the Vogue – failed to raise sales.

the water-cooling, and gained a neat, strong and fine-handling duplex tubular frame. Sensibly, the engine's unlovely crankcases and gearbox were enclosed by fibreglass covers.

Throw in a conventional fuel tank and dual seat, add a pair of neat chromed silencers and you had . . . an expensive 200cc bike of gentle performance. Exactly who was supposed to buy it remains something of a mystery, as 250-restricted learners would buy the more sporting models from BSA, Triumph and so forth, while commuters would surely opt for the Villiers brigade. But never mind . . .

In common with the sporting singles, the Valiant was also offered with a full fairing, as the Veeline Valiant, which slowed it a little more. Depressingly, for us fans of unusual motorcycles, sales were poor, and production ended in 1964.

If the decision to invest time and money into building the Valiant was questionable, then building a two-stroke scooter along the basic LE principles seems verging on the insane. Especially when you consider that the scooter boom was effectively over by the time Velocette launched the Viceroy, their epic scooter.

Once again, they had undertaken considerable research and development to produce a machine that almost no one wanted, which is heroic in the extreme. For that alone the Viceroy is worth a mention. The two-stroke air-cooled 250 flat twin was placed in front of the rider's feet, below the scooter footboards, and drove the gearbox/swinging arm assembly via a drive shaft. Wonderful complexity . . . You are unlikely to find one today, as only about 300 were built, but if you fancy Something Really Different, they don't come much more different than this.

Both Valiant and Viceroy are . . . interesting to ride, but spares are not exactly common, and they are slow by modern A-road standards.

Vincent

At the start of the section on Velocettes I talked about my initial reluctance to include that marque in this book. That reservation applies equally to Vincent. In fact, given that the Stevenage factory built only a tiny number of motorcycles by the standards of the mass-producers (a post-war total figure of around 11,000 is quoted), my reluctance to attempt to offer general thoughts and comment on such a specialist subject plagues me as I write this.

Essentially, Vincents built just two types of motorcycle – a single and a twin. And although the legends that surround the marque could lead you to think otherwise, only the twin is truly special. The single, in either its Meteor or Comet incarnations, is always an interesting and unusual machine to ride, but it is rather less than half the motorcycle its twin brother is. I have been taken to task in the pages of the *Classic Bike Guide* and elsewhere before for saying this, but it remains my opinion. And I have ridden several Vincents, both single and twin.

The heart of a Vincent is that its engine and its bicycle so perfectly compliment each other. This is true of depressingly few British motorcycles, the majority of which featured a steadily evolving bicycle that was expected to handle a variety of power plants. Thus, for example, the excellent Norton featherbed was available with engines ranging from a 350 single of lukewarm performance to a 750 twin capable of some serious hooliganism. Other motorcycles designed as one? Velocette's LE, Sunbeam's S7, Norton's early rotaries and the Hesketh spring to mind, and there are sadly few others. But the Vincent twin was designed as a whole, and it is remarkable for that as well as for much else.

Like the post-war Sunbeam, the Vincent was intended to appeal to the 'gentleman motorcyclist'. Unlike the Sunbeam, which offered all of the design sophistication that our hypothetical gentleman might want but lacked the vital performance ingredient, the Vincent twin boasted fine individual design, a justifiable claim of engineering excellence, an outstanding appearance, and performance that was second to none. It inspired loyalty, dedication and legend completely out of proportion to the number of bikes actually built, and whereas the mass-market leaders were inevitably and increasingly built to a price, the Vincent twin was built to a standard. Does this read like a eulogy? It shouldn't – although I have ridden many of the snarling beasts, I have never owned a Vincent, and neither would I particularly want to. The reason? Maybe I would prefer to believe the legends . . .

There is no room here for me to describe in any depth the wealth of original thought and painstaking design that went into Vincent's twin. For a start, it was a V-twin, making it unique in the British post-war marketplace. Indeed, after its demise at the end of 1955, there were to be no British V-twins before the Hesketh.

At the heart of the big engine – and it was indeed massive in every sense – was a substantial crankshaft that carried the two big-end bearings side by side on the same crankpin. The two cylinders ran 50 degrees apart, and each cylinder had its own camshaft, driven by a large idler gear from the crank itself. Although pushrod operation of the valves was conventional enough for the time, the method of actuating the valves was pretty unusual. The rockers, prodded as usual by the pushrods, did not push down on the end of the valve stem. Instead, they worked against a collar placed about halfway

The snarling beast – a glorious
celebration of performance made
metal.

down it, necessitating not one guide per valve but two.

Oil was pushed through the engine by a 'Pilgrim' rotary plunger pump driven by the crank, and although pressures were low, the engine's many ball and roller bearings were capable of surviving for many fast miles. Many tales have been told about Vincent oiling, and perhaps I should mention that these engines are reputed to wear prematurely if used mainly for short runs.

The primary drive was by a triplex chain to a most unconventional clutch. This remarkable device was in fact not one but two clutches, having a

unique 'self-servo' action involving a second clutch that appears to work more like a drum brake than a conventional sliding disc clutch. In practice, the clutch can feel a little odd, with the engagement point managing to vary unpredictably. More predictable is that Vincent lore insists that the thing can be made wonderful. Oddly, at least two of the Vincent twins I have had the pleasure of riding were fitted with dull conventional Norton clutches.

The gearbox itself was a four-speed device of relatively conventional design, but built on an appropriately herculean scale for the task of handling the big

engine's legendary output. Unlike other British gearboxes of the period, it was a cross-over box, in which the drive from the engine is applied at the left side, and drive to the back wheel is taken from the opposite, right, side.

The bicycle was, if anything, less conventional than its power train. For a start, there was almost no main frame, with much of the loading being taken by the massive unit construction engine and gearbox assembly. The frame itself, such as it was, comprised a steel box to which was fixed the steering head and the engine's cylinder heads. The box also contained the engine's oil supply.

Front suspension started the post-war period as a set of girder forks, but in 1949 Vincent (of course) introduced their own unique set of front forks – the Girdraulics of legend. Unlike just about everyone else, Vincent chose not to use forks working around the telescoping-tubes principle. Instead, they developed the girder design a stage further, using forged blades to replace the girders, with a single central damper and a pair of long spring boxes next to each blade. Naturally, these new forks were adjustable to provide either solo or sidecar trail settings.

Rear suspension was also unique for the post-war British scene. The whole of the triangulated rear subframe, which carried the wheel spindle at its rear, pivoted at the bottom, the vertical movement being controlled by two springs and a damper operating against the rear of the oil tank/main frame. It sounds complicated, but was an inspired piece of design and was in fact years ahead of its time. It had the slightly odd side effect that the seat rose and fell with the rear wheel, affording the motorcycle an unusual 'cantering' sensation to a rider used to more conventional machines.

Predictably, although front and rear braking was provided by drums, the Vincent was unusual in using a pair of 7-inch examples, working back-to-back on each wheel. They worked very well indeed, too, especially by the standards of the time.

The final version of the beast, the 1955 Series D, brought with it a redesigned frame, with different rear suspension arrangements, a sprung subframe for the seat, a separate oil tank, and voluminous enclosures. The rider was protected from the elements by a full fairing, while the mechanicals were hidden away beneath a set of rear skirts, remarkable for both size and deep blackness.

The list of other extraordinary Vincent features would fill (and has filled) a book on its own, so I shall stop there.

The single was based around the front cylinder of the twin, but with a Burman gearbox and clutch. Although it boasts the same bicycle as the twin, the engine's performance is more on a par with that of other more conventional – and considerably less expensive – 500 singles of the day, and although a worthy enough machine in its own right, big brother is still the headline-grabber.

On the road Vincents are unusual to ride, as you would hope, given the price differentials that have existed between them and more mainstream machines from the time when they were current up to the present day. Only you can decide whether you want one enough to pay out the elevated prices still being asked for the big twins. My main piece of advice remains the same – join the

Top: *Black power.*

Bottom: *Many of us can only dream of a find like this . . .*

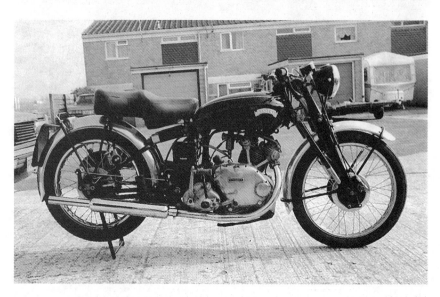

wholly excellent Vincent Owners' Club (you will need to do so should you buy one anyway, as this is the best way to obtain those inevitable spares), meet owners, pick their brains, and if possible buy your Vin from someone in the club who has decided to struggle no more.

Be particularly careful should you decide to purchase any Vin with pretensions to a sporting pedigree, and *always* take an independent expert along with you before you buy.

All of the unique features of the bike can give rise to their own unique problems. Owning and running a big Vin is not like running a big BSA, for example, and you should be aware of this before you part with a lot of money. A good friend of mine once remarked, as he was totting up the cost of his own Comet, which he had originally bought for the proverbial but elusive song, 'There are no cheap Vincents. None . . .'.

P. C. Vincent was an idealist, a man who wanted to solve all the shortcomings of the other motorcycles around in his time. He and his team designed a machine to the highest of standards, a machine that answered questions other manufacturers had not even asked. His was a machine built by an idealist to realise his own ideal, and it is almost unique in that. As such, it could never make money because it is almost impossible to sell such a machine and make a profit while doing so, because the mass-producers will produce a motorcycle that performs almost as well at a far lower price. This is,

Top: *The Shadow – a full litre of well-engineered, well-developed performance.*

Middle: *This overhead view of the Shadow shows how slender a 1000cc sporting twin can be.*

Bottom: *The 500cc Comet, although a pleasant machine to ride, lacks much of the appeal of its big brother.*

has been, and always will be the case. But there was no harm in trying . . .

Model designations

The 1000 (84 x 90mm = 998cc) Series B Rapide entered production in 1946, and was joined by the Series B Black Shadow in 1948. They were joined by the Series C Rapide and Black Shadow in 1949, and the Series Bs ended a year later. The Series Bs ran until 1954, and were replaced by the Series D, in Black Prince, Black Knight, Black Shadow and Rapide versions for 1955. Production ended at the end of that year.

The 500 (84 x 90mm = 499cc) Meteor was introduced for 1948, and was replaced by the Comet (with Girdraulic forks) later that year. The Series changes for the single mirrored those of the twins.

Part 3: Classic British Bike Clubs and Price Guide

AJS (Matchless in brackets)
Club Contact: Northants Classic Bike Centre, Victoria St, Irthlingborough, Northants

Model 14 (G2)
248cc ohv single. 340lb, 75mph. 1958–66.
Prices: low £500, high £950.

Model 8 (G5)
348cc ohv single. 350lb, 70mpg, 80mph. 1960–62.
Prices: low £500, high £1000.

Model 16 (G3)
348cc ohv single. 400lb, 80mpg, 75mph. 1945–66.
Prices: low £850, high £1800 (comp models a lot more).

Model 18 (G80)
498cc ohv single. 400lb, 55mpg, 80mph. 1945–66.
Prices: low £1400, high £2200 (comp models a lot more).

Model 20 (G9)
498cc ohv twin. 410lb, 60mpg, 90mph. 1948–61.
Prices: low £1400, high £2000.

Model 30 (G11)
593cc ohv twin. 410lb, 60mpg, 90mph. 1956–58.
Prices: low £1400, high £2000.

Model 31 (G12)
646cc ohv twin. 430lb, 55mpg, 100mph. 1959–66.
Prices: low £1400, high £2400.

Matchless G15/45   (Matchless only)
749cc ohv twin. 430lb, 50mpg, 105mph. 1963.
Prices: High (if you find one)

Model 33 (G15)
745cc ohv twin. 420lb, 45mpg, 110mph. 1964–69.
Prices: low £1800, high £3000.

ARIEL
Club Contact: Andy Hemingway, 80 Pasture Lane, Clayton, Bradford, West Yorks BD14 6LN

Colt
197cc ohv single. 270lb, 80mpg, 65mph. 1954–60.
Prices: low £350, high £850.

Leader
247cc 2-stroke twin. 330lb, 55mpg, 70mph. 1958–65.
Prices: low £800, high £1800.

Arrow
247cc 2-stroke twin. 305lb, 55mpg, 75mph. 1960–65.
Prices: low £800, high £1800.

NH (Red Hunter)
347cc ohv single. 365lb, 70mpg, 75mph. 1945–58.
Prices: low £1200, high £1800.

VH (Red Hunter)
497cc ohv single. 375lb, 55mpg, 85mph. 1945–58.
Prices: low £1400, high £2200.

VB
598cc sv single. 370lb, 50mpg, 60mph. 1945–58.
Prices: low £950, high £1800.

KH (Fieldmaster)
498cc ohv twin. 390lb, 65mpg, 90mph. 1948–58.
Prices: low £1400, high £2000.

FH (Huntmaster)
648cc ohv twin. 400lb, 55mpg, 100mph. 1954–58.
Prices: low £1600, high £2400.

Square Four
997cc ohv four. 480lb, 45mpg, 100mph.
Prices: low £2400, high £3500.

BSA
Club Contact: BSAOC, Irene Seabrook, PO Box 4, Hythe, Southampton SO45 5ZB

Bantam
174cc 2-stroke single. 230lb, 85mpg, 65mph. 1948–71.
Prices: low £450, high £900.

C10
249cc sv single. 310lb, 75mpg, 55mph. 1945–57
Prices: low £400, high £800.

C11
249cc ohv single, 320lb, 80mpg, 60mph, 1945–55.
Prices: low £400. high £800.

C12
249cc ohv single, 320lb, 75mpg, 67mph, 1956–58.
Prices: low £400, high £800.

C15 Star
249cc ohv single. 280lb, 70mpg, 75mph. 1959–67.
Prices: low £500, high £1000.

C25 Barracuda
249cc ohv single. 330lb, 60mpg, 75mph. 1966–70.
Prices: low £500, high £1200.

B25SS
249cc ohv single. 290lb, 55mpg, 80mph. 1971–72.
Prices: low £500, high £1250.

B31
348cc ohv single. 365lb, 80mpg, 75mph. 1945–59.
Prices: low £1000, high £1700.

B32 Gold Star
348cc ohv single. 360lb, 65mpg, 85mph. 1949–57.
Prices: low £2500, high £4500.

B40
343cc ohv single. 305lb, 80mpg, 75mph. 1960–65.
Prices: low £500, high £1000.

B44 Victor
441cc ohv single. 335lb, 65mpg, 85mph. 1966–70.
Prices: low £800, high £1650.

B33
499cc ohv single. 420lb, 70mpg, 80mph. 1947–59.
Prices: low £1400, high £2000.

M33
499cc ohv single. 370lb, 70mpg, 70mph. 1947–57.
Prices: low £1400, high £2000.

B34 /DB34 /DBD34 Gold Star
499cc ohv single. 410lb, 55mpg, 110mph. 1950–62.
Prices: low £4500, high £7000.

B50SS
499cc ohv single. 340lb, 60mpg, 85mph. 1971–72.
Prices: low £1600, high £2000.

M20
496cc sv single. 425lb, 55mpg, 65mph. 1945–55.
Prices: low £950, high £1800.

A7
497cc ohv twin. 420lb, 55mpg, 90mph. 1946–61.
Prices: low £1800, high £2200.

A50 Royal Star
499cc ohv twin. 420lb, 60mpg, 90mph. 1962–66.
Prices: low £1450, high £2200.

A10
646cc ohv twin. 440lb, 55mpg, 105mph. 1951–63.
Prices: low £1600, high £2400. RGS low £4000, high £6500.

A65
654cc ohv twin. 425lb, 55mpg, 120mph. 1962–73.
Prices: low £1650, high £2200.

A70 Lightning
751cc ohv twin. 425lb, 50mpg, 120mph. 1971.
Prices: High – if you find one.

A75R Rocket 3
740cc ohv triple. 520lb, 35mpg, 125mph. 1968–72.
Prices: low £2500, high £3500.

DOUGLAS
Club Contact: Reg Holmes, 48 Standish Avenue, Stoke Lodge, Patchway, Bristol, Avon

Mark IV and V
348cc ohv flat twin. 340lb, 65mpg, 75mph.
Prices: low £1500, high £2200.

Dragonfly
348cc ohv flat twin. 395lb, 55mpg, 75mph. 1954–57.
Prices: low £1450, high £2250.

FRANCIS-BARNETT
Models to look out for include the amazingly styled Fulmar, which has a small AMC engine to propel its spine frame, leading link front forks and swoopy bodywork slowly along, and the Cruiser twins (89 & 91), which have some sort of performance. Prices for the whole range are similar. And low. Owners Clubs (Their own, as well as the British Two-Stroke); scarce spares, apart from Villiers engines.
Club Contact: Neil Buckle, 54 Kennedy Drive, Pangbourne, Berks RG8 7LB
Prices: low £400, high £800.

GREEVES
Built in Thundersley, Essex, the Greeves range of lightweight, competition-based machines were always a bit different from the mundane commuter bikes with which they shared the use of Villiers engines. The most striking features are the alloy beam-based frame and leading-link forks which used rubber in torsion as the spring medium. Any bike which could be described as 'off-road' will command a higher price, but the roadster models, using Villiers singles and twins, can provide superb steering, some style and a little performance. Silverstone road-racers are coveted by both collectors and riders.
Club Contact: Dave McGregor, 4 Longshaw Close, North Wingfield, Chesterfield, Derbyshire S42 5QR
Prices: low £600, high £1400.

HESKETH

Launched at an amazed world as yet another Great British world-beater, Lord Hesketh's monster V-twin was an expensive flop, largely because the splendid-looking power unit was inadequately developed and lacked the sophistication required by those spending around £6000 on a motorcycle. It was also panned by the press. Production of a sort dribbles on to this day, but there are a few low mileage examples about which could make better sense, especially if they have been up-dated with the EN10 kit of improved engine parts.

Spares supply excellent.

Club Contact: Peter White, 1 Northfield Road, Soham, Cambs CB7 5UE

V1000
992cc dohc V-twin. 560lb, 35mpg, 120mph. 1982–1990.
Prices: low £4500, high £5500.

JAMES

The other AMC 2-stroke builder, probably most well-known for their Cadet and Captain commuters, which were very dull indeed. Once again, the better buys are those which are powered by Villiers rather than Piatti-designed AMC engines, and the very late (1966) Superswift twin is probably the one to find. Some were built with the Villiers 4T unit, which is a little less slow. The scooter (which was sold as the Matchless Papoose in the US!) is the one to avoid – unless you are a collector of lost causes. However, a lot of low-cost riding can be had from any of the James range, and they can't depreciate much. Like most British 2-strokers, they have a dedicated band of expert fans.

Prices: low £350, high £750.

MATCHLESS

The once-famous marque was offered a new lease of life from a new home in Newton Abbot in Devon. Only one model was offered; a 500cc single, either with or without electric start. They suffered from over-pricing, sadly, and didn't do well.

G80
499cc ohc single. 390lb, 55mpg, 95mph. 1987–90.
Early starting and finish problems would appear to have been overcome on the later bikes, and the G80 makes a pleasant, practical 'classic' styled bike for everyday use. If you have a choice, opt for the electric start and twin front discs.
Prices: low £1200, high £1700.

NORTON

Club Contact: Shirley Fenner, Beeches, Durley Brook Road, Durley, Southampton SO3 2AR

Jubilee
249cc ohv twin. 350lb, 75mpg, 65mph. 1958–66.
Prices: low £600, high £1000.

Navigator
349cc ohv twin. 350lb, 65mpg, 75mph. 1960–65.
Prices: low £600, high £1450.

Electra
394cc ohv twin. 360lb, 55mpg, 75mph. 1963–65.
Prices: low £1000, high £1900.

Model 50
348cc ohc single. 400lb, 75mpg, 75mph. 1956–63.
Prices: low £1500, high £2000.

Model 40 (International)
349c ohc single. 340lb, 65mpg, 85mph. 1946–58.
Prices: low £4000, high £5000.

16H
490cc sv single. 365lb, 55mpg, 65mph. 1945–55.
Prices: low £1250, high £2000.

ES2
490cc ohv single. 380lb, 60mpg, 75mph. 1947–62.
Prices: low £1800, high £2400.

88
497cc ohv twin. 420lb, 60mpg, 90mph. 1951–66.
Prices: low £1800, high £2650.

Model 30 (International)
490cc ohc single. 360lb, 60mpg, 95mph. 1946–58.
Prices: low £4500, high £6000.

Model 19
596cc ohv single. 385lb, 60mpg, 70mph. 1955–57.
Prices: low £1600, high £2200.

Big 4
596cc sv single. 400lb, 50mpg, 65mph. 1947–54.
Prices: low £1500, high £2000.

99
596cc ohv twin. 420lb, 55mpg, 100mph. 1956–62.
Prices: low £2000, high £3000.

650SS
646cc ohv twin. 420lb, 50mpg, 110mph. 1960–69.
Prices: low £2200, high £3500.

Atlas
745cc ohv twin. 420lb, 50mpg, 110mph. 1963–68.
Prices: low £2000, high £3000.

N15
745cc ohv twin. 420lb, 45mpg, 110mph. 1964–68.
Prices : low £2000, high £3500.

P11/P11A/ Ranger 750
745cc ohv twin. 400lb, 45mpg, 110mph. 1965–69.
Prices: low £2200, high £3500.

Commando
745cc ohv twin. 450lb, 55mpg, 125mph. 1968–73.
828cc ohv twin. 450lb, 50mpg, 120mph. 1973–77.
Prices: low £2200, high £3500.

Classic
588cc twin rotary. 498lb, 40mpg, 130mph. 1988–89.
Prices: low £5500, high £6500.

PANTHER
Club Contact: Graham Dibbins, Oakdene, 22 Oak St., Netherton, West Midlands DY2 9LJ

Models 65/75
248/348cc ohv singles. 340/350lb, 75/65mpg, 63/72mph. 1947–62.
Prices: low £800, high £1200.

Model 100
598cc ohv single. 440lb, 60mpg, 75mph. 1946–63.
Prices: low £1500, high £2200.

Model 120
646cc ohv single. 440lb, 55mpg, 80mph. 1959–65.
Prices: low £1500, high £2200.

ROYAL ENFIELD
Club Contact: John Cherry, Meadow Lodge Fm, Henfield, Coalpit Heath, Bristol BS17 2UX

Clipper
248cc ohv single. 350lb, 85mpg, 60mph. 1953–57.
Prices: low £750, high £1000.

Crusader
248cc ohv single. 330lb, 75mpg, 75mph. 1956–66.
Prices: low £750, high £1000.

Continental
248cc ohv single. 320lb, 65mpg, 80mph. 1962–67.
Prices: low £1000, high, £1500.

Bullet
346cc ohv single. 400lb, 70mpg, 70mph. 1949–63.
Prices: low £1100, high £1800.

Meteor Minor
496cc ohv twin. 420lb, 60mpg, 85mph. 1959–63.
Prices: low £1500, high £2000.

Super Meteor
692cc ohv twin. 430lb, 55mpg, 100mph. 1952–60.
Prices: low £1500, high £2200.

Constellation/Interceptor Mk 1
692/736cc ohv twin. 435lb, 110mph, 1959–71.
Prices: low £1500, high £2400.

Interceptor Mk2/Rickman Interceptor
736cc ohv twin. 442lb, 112mph, 1971–72.
Prices: low £1800, high £3000.

SCOTT
Made in Birmingham by the Aerco Jig Company after moving production from the Shipley factory and compromised the long-established specification with sophistication that just seemed to add weight. An intriguing mix of old and almost modern with sweet manners if you're not in a great hurry.
Club Contact: Brian Marshall, Walnut Cottage, Abbey Lane, Aslockton, Nottingham NG13 9AE

Squirrel
596cc 2-str. twin. 400lb, 50mpg, 80mph. 1947–mid 60s.
Prices: low £2000, high £3500.

SUNBEAM
Club Contact: Stewart Engineering, Church Terrace, Harbury, Leamington Spa, CV33 9HL

S7/S8
490cc ohc in-line twin. 490lb, 55mpg, 80mph. 1946–57.
Prices: low £1800, high £2500.

TRIUMPH
Club Contact: Mrs M. Mellish, 4 Douglas Avenue, Harold Wood, Romford, Essex

Tiger Cub
199cc ohv single. 230lb, 85mpg, 65mph.
Prices: low £750, high £1200.

Blazer SS
249cc ohv single. 320lb, 55mpg, 80mph. 1971–2.
Prices: low £850, high £1250.

3TA
348cc ohv twin. 360lb, 70mpg, 80mph. 1957–69.
Prices: low £850, high £1400.

5T Speed Twin
498cc ohv twin. 375lb, 65mpg, 90mph. 1946–57.
Prices: low £1800, high £2200.

Tiger 100
498cc ohv twin. 370lb, 60mpg, 100mph. 1946–57.
Prices: low £1800, high £2800.

5TA
498cc ohv twin. 385lb, 50mpg, 85mph. 1958–66.
Prices: low £1600, high £2200.

TR5T Adventurer
498cc ohv twin. 330lb, 50mpg, 80mph. 1973–74.
Prices: low £2200, high £3000.

TRW
498cc sv twin. 375lb, 65mpg, 70mph. 1948–65.
Prices: low £1000, high £1800.

Thunderbird
649cc ohv twin. 400lb, 60mpg, 95mph. 1950–61.
Prices: low £2200, high £2800.

TR6
649cc ohv twin. 400lb, 55mpg, 105mph. 1954–73.
Prices: low £2300, high £3000.

Bonneville (T120)
649cc ohv twin. 400lb, 50mpg, 110mph. 1959–62.
Prices: low £4500, high £6500.

Bonneville (T120)
649cc ohv twin. 410lb, 50mpg, 115mph. 1963–74.
Prices: low £2800, high £4000.

Trident
740cc ohv triple. 503lb, 37mpg, 120mph. 1968–75.
TR3OC. Club Contact: Martin Pink, 13 Eastbrook
Close, Woking, Surrey GU21 5DQ
Prices: low £2200, high £4200.

Bonneville 750 (T140V)
744cc ohv twin. 440lb, 50mpg, 110mph. 1973–88.
Prices: low £2200, high £4000.

Tiger 750 (TR7RV)
Prices: low £2200, high £3200.

TSS
744cc ohv twin. 420lb, 45mpg, 120mph. 1982–83.
Prices: low £2400, high £3200.

VELOCETTE
Club Contact: Mike Spink, 32 Westport Crescent,
Wednesfield, Wolverhampton WV11 3JP

LE
192cc sv l/c flat twin. 250lb, 100+mpg, 55mph.
1949–71.
LE Club Contact: P. Walker, Grantley House,
Warwicks Bench, Guildford, Surrey GU1 3SZ
Prices: low £600, high £950.

Vogue
192cc sv l/c flat twin. 330lb, 95mpg, 55mph. 1963–68.
Prices: low £850, high £1200.

MAC
349cc ohv single. 370lb, 70mpg, 75mph. 1952–60.
Prices: low £1800, high £2400.

Viper
349cc ohv single. 390lb, 60mpg, 85mph. 1956–69.
Prices: low £1900, high £2500.

MSS
499cc ohv single. 400lb, 60mpg, 80mph. 1953–68.
Prices: low £1900, high £2800.

Venom
499cc ohv single. 400lb, 55mpg, 95mph. 1956–68.
Prices: low £2400, high £3600.

Thruxton
499cc ohv single. 390lb, 50mpg, 105mph. 1964–71.
Prices: low £3500, high £7000.

VINCENT
Club Contact: c/o Little Wildings, Fairhazel,
Piltdown, Uckfield, East Sussex TN22 3XB

Comet
499cc ohv single. 400lb, 60mpg, 85mph. 1948–54.
Prices: low £2500, high £3500.

1000
998cc ohv V-twin. 460lb, 50mpg, 120mph. 1950–55.
Prices: low £8000, high £14000.

Index

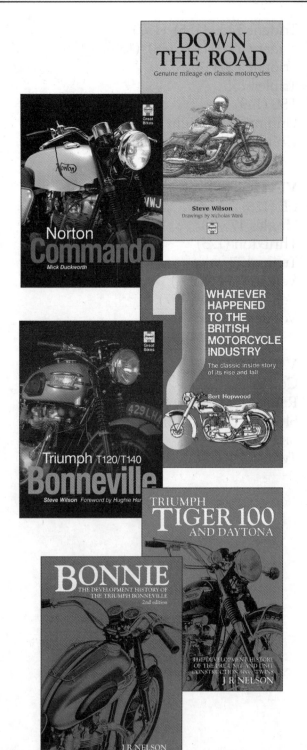

DOWN THE ROAD
Steve Wilson
Illustrations by Nicholas Ward
ISBN 1 85960 651 2

HAYNES GREAT BIKES SERIES: NORTON COMMANDO
Mick Duckworth
ISBN 1 84425 021 0

WHATEVER HAPPENED TO THE BRITISH MOTORCYCLE INDUSTRY?
The classic inside story of its rise and fall
Bert Hopwood ISBN 1 85960 427 7

HAYNES GREAT BIKES SERIES: TRIUMPH T120/T140 BONNEVILLE:
Steve Wilson
Foreword by Hughie Hancox
ISBN 1 85960 679 2

TRIUMPH TIGER 100 AND DAYTONA (Re-issue)
The development history of the pre-unit and unit construction 500cc twins
J.R. Nelson ISBN 1 85960 428 5

BONNIE (2nd Edition)
The development history of the Triumph Bonneville
J. R. Nelson ISBN 0 85429 957 2

For more information please contact: Customer Services Department, Haynes Publishing, Sparkford, Yeovil, Somerset BA22 7JJ, UK
Tel. 01963 442030 Fax: 01963 440001
Int. tel: +44 1963 442030 Fax: +44 1963 440001
E-mail: sales@haynes.co.uk Web site: www.haynes.co.uk